A COOK

— ON THE —

WILD SIDE

A COOK
— ON THE —
WILD SIDE

Hugh Fearnley-Whittingstall

BOXTREE

First published in 1997 by Boxtree, an imprint of
Macmillan Publishers Ltd, 25 Eccleston Place, London, SW1W 9NF and Basingstoke

Associated companies throughout the world

ISBN 0 7522 1115 3

Inside text designed by Robert Updegraff

Cover designed by Roger Hammond

1 3 5 7 9 8 6 4 2

A CIP catalogue record for this book is available from the British Library

Printed by Bath Press Colour Books, Glasgow

Front cover photographs by Andrew Palmer;
back cover photographs by Andrew Palmer (top), Stuart Sadd/Channel 4 (bottom).

CONTENTS

For Marie, the *bain* of my life

And a big thank you to British Waterways for keeping us afloat

ACKNOWLEDGEMENTS

It has always struck me that thank yous are not enough said in the business of television. Salaries are often a poor substitute for gratitude (as are 'salamis', which is the word I wrote before spell-checking this paragraph) and I would like to begin by thanking everyone whose hard work helped to make both series of *A Cook on the Wild Side* a success, an adventure, and a pleasure - especially Holly North, Dot Prior, Gina Hobson, Emma Reeves, Katie Ferguson, David Allen, Tim Watts and Richard Hill. Thanks also to Malcolm Brain and Andy Plant for work on the *Bain Marie* and especially to Gavin Lowery for a song, a spanner and a smile. At Channel 4, thanks to Sylvia Hines and Karen Brown, for their support and encouragement with the whole *COTWS* venture. And a special thanks to Eleanor Stephens and all at Stephens Kerr.

I would also like to thank everyone at Boxtree who has worked hard, and against the clock, to make this book happen. Special thanks to Susanna Wadeson, my editor, who has shown enthusiasm and flexibility throughout this project, and to Emma Mann, who took over with no less commitment; to Robert Updegraff for finding some elegant solutions to some tricky design problems; and to Annie Lee, for her eagle-eyed copy-editing. And thanks, as always, to my ever-supportive agent Carol Heaton, for her good counsel.

Both this book and the series were further aided and abetted, directly or indirectly, by many friends.

Thanks particularly to Zammy Baring, for editing well beyond the call of duty; to the Raven family, for the generous presence of Ardtornish both in the Scottish episode and in this book (call 01967 421288 to book a holiday in this magical place); especially to Jane Raven, for hospitality at Drumnadrochit, and to Sarah Raven, for the loan of Innibeg, and for sharing enthusiasm for cockling and 'shrooming'; to Martin Thomas, for non-punitive legal advice with jokes at no extra cost; to fellow enthusiasts of fish, fur, feathers and fungi – especially Ivan and Pots Samarine (the latter also for comments on the text) and Charlie Taylor (for sharing many hours of fishing, a few actual fish, and the odd duck); to Aurea Carpenter, for rich pickings (in the brain department) and unselfishly sharing her husband; and, of course, to Mum, Dad and Soph, for always making home the best place to work, rest or play.

But the two biggest 'without whoms', for both the series and the book, are due to Hattie Ellis, for her unremitting help and restorative culinary enthusiasm. Cheers, Hattie. And to Andrew Palmer, the other half of KEO films, for shouldering, among many other burdens, the not unimportant question of what it all looks like. The wonderful food pictures in this book are the product of his talents with a camera (and a little bit of luck with the weather). He also directed both television series. Thanks, mate.

FOREWORD

As a food writer, I've always upheld the principle that you should insist on being able to taste before you buy – when you have to pay for your food, that is. The wild food forager, of course, can always enjoy the privilege of a pretaste, and pick, or not pick, hunt, or not hunt, accordingly. (Admittedly it's hard to let a rabbit go if you don't like the taste of his back legs – but you can always spare his cousins.) But this book, I'm sorry to say, is not a giveaway. So it seems that the very least I can do before exposing you to 90,000-odd words of my prose is to offer a few hundred on what you might and might not reasonably expect from this book if you hand over the cash and take it away. (And if, with a rush of blood to the head, you have already done that, you can at least get some inkling of whether it might occasionally be a good idea to bring it down off the shelf.)

Whilst the two television series of *A Cook on the Wild Side* both contain a fair amount of practical information on wild food and wilderness living (however obliquely communicated), the ten programmes are primarily intended as entertainment, adventure and, to a certain extent, social documentary. What you see on the screen (if you watch the series) is there because we feel it makes good television – informative and entertaining, we hope, but always bound by the competitive visual demands and ephemeral restrictions of the medium. It did not seem wise to spend 24 minutes 15 seconds (the duration of each show) demonstrating how to make a pigeon pie – even though a good one would take you rather longer than that – when there were so many people to meet, thoughts to provoke, roads (and waterways) to travel, and landscapes to enjoy.

This book, by contrast, is essentially a practical volume. It was of little interest to me to write the kind of 'TV tie-in' that merely trotted out a few recipes from the series, prefaced by anecdotes of the hilarious things that happened off-camera and behind the scenes (in my experience such attempts at confessional professional intimacy are best summed up by the phrase, 'You had to be there'). So while you will find a fair few references to characters and incidents from the series, they are there largely to show what can be learned from alternative perspectives on country life, food and the wilderness environment. By far the larger part of this book consists of practical information about gathering and cooking wild food that there simply wasn't space for in the series. In fact, this is pretty much the book I would like to have written about wild food, even if there had not been a television series.

But there is no good practice without sound underlying theory, and before providing what I hope is useful information on the 'how to' side of wild food cookery, I would like briefly to address the cynic's question, 'Why bother with it?' If there's one thing we don't have in this country, it's a food shortage – which is not to say that nobody goes hungry. But if I pretended that the main purpose of either our series, or this book, was to help those on the breadline eke out a subsistence from wild ingredients, I would be rightly accused of hypocrisy. *A Cook on the Wild Side* was never meant to be a serious exercise in survivalism, and this book is not a survival manual. Although the information that follows might certainly be handy for all those looking to glean a free meal, I have no doubt that anyone who made a serious long-term commitment to wilderness living would soon have much more to teach me than I have to teach them.

So the shortages for which our series, and this book, are intended as a partial remedy are not the urgent ones of nutrition and shelter. Rather I am hoping to address, in a small way, the far more widespread modern social famines in quality of life, closeness to the natural environment, and understanding of the origins of what we eat.

This latter factor may perhaps seem obscure to many people — and that is precisely the problem. Where once we selected our food directly from the land around us, now we are divorced from the process of food production by several removes. The result is that most of us know little or nothing about it. We don't know how the vegetables we eat are fertilized, or genetically altered. We don't know what chemicals are sprayed on our cereal crops, or even our breakfast cereals. And until the deaths of thousands of cattle, and several humans, brought the appalling information to light, how many of us knew that we were feeding dead sheep to our cows, and dead chickens to their own children?

Remember that every single plant and animal that is used for food is descended from a wild ancestor — and many of those wild ancestors are alive and well in our fields, forests and hedgerows. An understanding of wild food is therefore, in part at least, an education about food history, and food safety. Best of all, it is not a force-fed education, but one that both taps and nourishes inquisitiveness, a delight in the natural world, and a sense of adventure.

One thing, however, that you will definitely need to reap the benefits of this book, and of the wild food harvest, is time. And perhaps it is the time famine that is the greatest blight of our age. But as we head towards the end of the millennium, many of us are growing discontented with the questions that sustained us through the decade of greed: 'How long have I got?' 'How much can I have?' and 'How fast can I get it?' Some of us are beginning to ask new questions — about how our quality of life might be improved by a more fulfilling relationship with the natural environment. Gentle answers to these questions, or hints at them, can occasionally be found, I feel, while gathering our own food in wild places. For this is an activity that not only demands a little time, it gives a little back: time spent in pursuit of wild food — walking, picking, diving, fishing, hunting — is *your* time.

Yet more answers seem forthcoming back in the kitchen, when we prepare a meal, a free meal, with the fruits of our foraging. Here there is time to be creative, to make something special out of something commonplace, that cost you nothing. And with any luck there is also time to spread the enjoyment to others. I have always found sharing food with friends to be among the highest of pleasures. Sharing wild food is particularly satisfying: I see everyone who partakes in it sharing an unsung communion, ingesting a little of the wilderness spirit into themselves. And it reminds me that wild food is more than just something for nothing. It's something for everyone.

Hugh Fearnley-Whittingstall
November 1996

INTRODUCTION
RESPONSIBILITIES, RIGHTS AND RISKS

My foreword, I hope, makes it clear that I believe wild food has a great deal to offer to anyone who enjoys the countryside, and is interested in food. But alongside the question of what we can get out of the land around us is the equally vital one of what we can put back into it. No natural resource can be justly seen as offering anything to man if it is not sustainable. So the theme of this brief introductory chapter might reasonably be summarized as: 'Ask not only what wild food can do for you — ask what you can do for your wilderness environment.'

Responsibilities

In the field guides in the chapters that follow, I have specific comments and advice on foraging with care and respect for the natural history both of individual species of plant and animal, and of generic aspects of our environment: the beach, the riverside, the forest floor, etc. But there is one part of the environment which is of particular importance to the free food forager, perhaps his or her happiest hunting ground, and it seems worthy of special mention at the outset.

Many of the edible plants, herbs, fruits, nuts, mushrooms — and even some of the animals — listed in this book are to be found in what is loosely referred to as 'the hedgerow'. Technically speaking the term defines that enormous web of shrubs, trees and herbs that create the physical borders of our fields, tracks and roads. It is, for the most part, man-made — at least in the sense that man allows it to grow where it does — but it is not, or is only minimally, man-managed. That is to say, we don't plant the things that grow there, or water them, or kill them. And this is what makes the hedgerow an invaluable part of our ecology and pastoral culture: it is natural — not pristine wilderness, maybe, but throughout most of this heavily cultivated land of ours, the nearest thing to it.

There is no doubt in my mind that using it as a food source is one of the best ways to enjoy and understand this natural resource, and there is every reason to believe that enthusiastic foraging fosters a sense of environmental responsibility. Even so, the hedgerow is by no means immune to the pressures of wild food gatherers. You might think it would take a very large army of us to put any species at risk, but one of our loveliest wild flowers, the cowslip, has already proved that these things can happen. It has been brought to the brink of extinction, the victim of a bygone passion for a country wine flavoured with its pretty yellow flowers. The plant is now protected by law, and rightly so. As someone who is, through this book and the medium of television, actively encouraging people to go out and gather wild food, I urge you to do so responsibly.

In the Gastrowagon kitchen with eels and elderflowers

Remember that it is almost always possible to gather the edible leaves of a plant without killing it – by removing only a few leaves from each plant. If you do so, you may be rewarded with a second crop – even within a matter of days. Some wild food plants – nettles, chickweed and wild chervil, for example – are often found in super-abundance. Others, like sea kale and bistort, are scarcer. In these latter cases, don't pick more than you need, and if the scarcity of a plant in a particular place means you will end up with less than you want, then at least ensure you have the comfort of hoping there may be a better crop next year: leave it, and find something else for supper.

At least as important is to be aware of other, inedible, 'innocent' plants that may stand between you and your lunch. Take care where you tread; if you are gathering from a footpath or road, try to stay on it.

If your first responsibility as a wild food gatherer is to the environment, your second is certainly to other human users of this resource. Gathering wild food is only one of many ways of enjoying our countryside and coastline. Riders, ramblers and dog-walkers, sun-seekers, sailors and surfers, and many others, all have a right to pursue their passions, and are due the same respect from you that you would no doubt like to receive from them. The unwritten rules that follow from this hardly need spelling out: simple courtesies like closing gates, not frightening animals, respecting rights of way on land and water, and not dropping litter should be second nature to anyone seeking to enjoy our natural resources. (On the latter point I would add only one simple thought: it is psychologically harder to leave litter in a clean place than in one which is already dirty. For that reason removing other people's litter, unpleasant though it may be, is doing an environmental service of lasting impact.)

Besides the question of interaction with other land users, there is the (often thornier) issue of interaction with landowners. On many a foraging expedition you will inevitably find yourself on, or bordering on, land belonging to private citizens, and especially to the professional food-growing community: our farmers. For both their peace of mind and yours, you should be aware of the second of the three Rs of wild food gathering.

Rights

As long as you stick to the public rights of way, i.e. country lanes and designated footpaths, you are entitled to gather leaves, flowers, fruits, nuts and fungi provided that you do not uproot, remove or destroy any plant. If you do wish to dig up and remove a plant, even from right on the footpath, you must have the landowner's permission. Similarly, if you want to stray from the right of way, for example to pick mushrooms in a field, or even crop a patch of nettles, technically you should seek permission first. Bear in mind that there is much to be gained from a good relationship with a friendly farmer: if you do take the trouble to ask, the worst you risk is a couple of rural expletives, but you could gain privileged access to rich pickings.

Be aware, also, that many communally or nationally owned areas of land have their own rules and guidelines about foraging. In the New Forest, for example, a limit has been imposed on the weight of mushrooms that any individual can remove, to deter commercial pickers. I don't necessarily agree with this policy (see Chapter 7), but the intentions behind it are decent enough, and it seems reasonable to go along with those entrusted with responsibility for sustaining this particular resource.

The time you spend in the country may lead you to decide, as has my friend the environmentalist George Monbiot, who came and foraged with me in the Norfolk episode of the first series, that the land laws in this country are unjust. George is a self-styled 'conscientious objector' to the legally imposed limits on our rights of way, and his favoured method of demonstration is wilful trespass. If you choose to follow his example, you should be aware that the law is *not* on your side, although it is not entirely weighted on the side of the landowner either. While damage to property, theft and poaching are all criminal offences, the simple act of trespass is not: you can be prosecuted for it only by civil action. And few landowners would go to such extreme lengths to discourage a few blackberry gatherers or mushroom pickers.

The trespasser's lot is a risky one, especially in areas where conscientious gamekeepers are ever on the lookout for poachers. If you are apprehended by an angry farmer, please don't say I sent you! But if you would like more information about the struggle to improve our access to the countryside, contact The Land is Ours, Box E, 111 Magdalen Road, Oxford OX4 1RQ, (telephone 01865 722016).

Risks

Gathering wild food is hardly a perilous activity, but it is not entirely risk-free either. There are of course some poisonous plants and mushrooms to look out for – and I will say more about these in the chapters that follow. But natural poisons are not the only ones to worry about. Pesticides and other agricultural chemicals are sprayed on fields, most especially on arable land, and any hedgerows or wood edges that border on sprayed fields are liable to be contaminated. Signs that wild plants in such places might be affected by agricultural weedkillers are intermittent patches of dead greenery, and unnatural yellowing patches on the leaves of plants. Any plants affected should not be picked for eating.

Plants sprayed with insecticides are harder to identify, since the plants themselves may not be adversely affected. But any danger from such chemicals is restricted to the period immediately after spraying, and thorough washing will usually remove any serious risk from any plant that is itself clearly healthy. As a general rule, it is worth bearing in mind that lanes and footpaths bordering on woods and grazing pasture are less likely to be contaminated by agricultural chemicals than those adjacent to crop fields.

Those are my three Rs – not, I hope you will agree, a discouraging collection. Now, on with the wild food adventure...

RECIPES ILLUSTRATED

SPRING GREENS

My passion for wild food goes back to a country childhood tacked on to the end of a metropolitan infancy. When we moved from London to Gloucestershire in 1971 I was six years old, and perfectly poised to explore this unbounded adventure playground which my parents referred to as 'the country'. We arrived in the late summer, and I was quickly initiated by my new friends in the village into the harvest of wayside freebies. But while I have clear and happy memories of guzzling blackberries, picking mushrooms, scrumping apples and checking the snares with the local gamekeeper, my boyish enthusiasm did not at that time extend to hedgerow greens – I guess I was still struggling with the cultivated kind. And if you couldn't sell me a plate of spinach, you were hardly going to sell me an almost identical pile of wilted greenery under the unappetizing name of chickweed – with or without a knob of butter.

In fact my conversion to the leafier forms of the wild harvest came only a few years ago, when a friend of mine served me a superb creamy nettle soup. And the process of further self-education really took off when it looked as if *A Cook on the Wild Side* might be on the cards. In the spring and summer of 1994 I ate my way fairly rapidly through the British hedgerow, and encouraged friends and family, who were sometimes more than a little sceptical, to join me in my feasting. We made some fine and surprising discoveries, and every spring since has been made all the more exciting by the promise of a fresh harvest.

But I should emphasize that I have tried by no means every plant deemed edible by folklore or science. Nor have I liked everything that I have tried: goosegrass, apparently popular in Elizabethan times, is so disgusting it's hard to believe it's not poisonous – I'll stick to the goose, thanks. So what appears below is not an exhaustive botanical index of the edible, but simply, I hope, a useful list, with pictures to aid identification, of the thirty-odd wild plants and herbs that I have found really worthwhile in the kitchen.

TIPS FOR FORAGERS

Remember that the hedgerow is not the only place to look for edible shoots, leaves and flowers. Wild plants will grow wherever birds, insects or the wind gives them a chance. If conditions are right where the seed falls, and the ground remains undisturbed, the plant will grow. Foragers should always be ready to look in 'unlikely' places, and expect the unexpected.

The best place to start foraging is, literally, your own back yard. I imagine there is hardly a garden in the country so immaculately kept that there is not some edible weed lurking in a neglected corner: and there are certainly millions of gardens where the uninvited greens hold sway! Once you find what you can do with them, you may decide to adopt the kitchen scissors as your preferred means of control, in place of nasty chemicals.

Converts to foraging with the right combination of laziness and enthusiasm should consider setting aside an area of the garden as an 'edible weed patch'. Better still, several areas: one light, one shady, one damp, one dry. Let them go and see what grows. Many plants, such as chickweed, sorrel and sow thistles, will grow back fast, and can be treated as a cut-and-come-again provider throughout their season.

FAVOURITE HEDGEROW GREENS
(see pages 22-23 for illustrations)

By 'greens' I mean to refer to the leaves, shoots and stems of edible wild plants which can be used as principal ingredients in recipes or which, when simply cooked, give you a more or less substantial 'portion' of a vegetable that can be an accompaniment to another dish. Some of the more strongly flavoured plants, whose leaves or other parts are used in small quantities as flavourings rather than as vegetables, are listed in the next section as 'hedgerow herbs'.

ALEXANDERS (*Smyrnium olusatrum*)
Alexanders, a biennial, is one of the best wild vegetables of spring, especially since the part of prime interest to the wild foodie is not the leaf, but the fleshy and succulent stem – so good, it's worth serving on its own, like asparagus.

Despite being named after a Greek hero, the plant was introduced by the Romans, who ate it themselves and grew it in profusion to feed the dark green leaves to their horses. Monks of the Middle Ages take credit for its further distribution, as it was a popular item in the monastery vegetable garden. It seems to thrive on a sea breeze, and is particularly widespread in coastal regions in the south of England. In Norfolk, Dorset, Devon and South Wales, you will often find great swathes of Alexanders growing on the road verge, almost to the exclusion of other plants.

Picking and preparation
The stems can be picked from February in a good year, and are at their best as the first flower-buds begin to appear in late March and April. Cut the stems close to the ground and strip away any leaves or side shoots. Cut into 10-12cm/4-5 inch lengths and peel away the outer membrane (easily done with a sharp knife).

The stems can then be steamed or boiled. Tossed in butter and seasoned with freshly ground black pepper, they are worth serving on their own (with brown bread) as a starter – or as an accompanying vegetable (particularly with fish).

The leaves and flowers are also quite edible, both having a mild aniseed flavour with a slightly bitter note. Choose younger, smaller leaves to add to salads.

The flowers, which change from greeny yellow to cream as they develop, can be picked from April to early June. Briefly blanched, they can be served as a pretty garnish for the stems. Or they can be eaten raw in salads, or deep-fried in batter (a good treatment, as they are relatively 'meaty' flowers, with a strong flavour – see page 32 for recipe).

To make a 'Lenten potage': Add to a sautéed chopped onion in a large pan 2 good handfuls each of Alexanders leaves, nettles and watercress. Cover with chicken or vegetable stock, and simmer until all the greens are tender. Purée in a blender with a little cooked potato, rice or pot barley as a thickener. Reheat and serve.

BISTORT OR EASTER LEDGE (*Persicaria bistorta*)
Bistort is a perennial plant most common in west and north-west England, where it forms the basis of a traditional dish known variously as Easter-ledge pudding or dock pudding – some villages still hold annual competitions to hail the best pudding-maker in the region. In the final programme of the second series I had great fun preparing a version of dock pudding under the scrutiny of the good ladies of the Calder Valley, near Hebden Bridge, Yorkshire. I thought mine was pretty good, but they were merciless in their judgement and pronounced it somewhat inauthentic. The recipe on page 29 has been slightly adapted to take account of their harsh criticism!

Bistort is rich in tannin and has always been used as a tonic herb – in some quarters it is credited with aphrodisiac qualities. Some of the ladies I spoke to freeze their dock pudding in vast quantities for use throughout the year. I wonder why.

'Dock' is a local misnomer for bistort, but the broad leaves look a bit similar to dock leaves – they are a fresher green, though, with less pronounced veins and no trace of the red sometimes seen in dock leaves. Bistort prefers damp soil and often forms large patches on roadsides, grassy river banks and meadows. It is easy to spot in the summer with its pretty spikes of soft pink flower-heads.

Picking and preparation

Pick the leaves selectively, a few from each clump, and the plants will continue to thrive and flower. Leaves should be stripped of the tough middle stem, and skilled pickers will do this as they pick to save time later. Like spinach, bistort leaves shrink to nothing when cooked — you will need a good carrier-bagful to make a decent pudding.

Bistort is a little too tannic and astringent to enjoy on its own as a vegetable, but a handful of leaves will add body and flavour to green soups — especially of herbs, nettles, watercress, lettuce or spinach.

The bistort dish is of course dock pudding: see page 29 for the full recipe.

CHICKWEED (*Stellaria media*)

This tough creeping annual is common throughout Britain on waste ground, likes damp and shade, and often appears uninvited in gardens. Don't kill it: control it and eat it.

Picking and preparation

Chickweed is often abundant throughout the year, from early spring until the first frosts. It is at its best in spring and autumn, when the leaves are fresh and succulent. In a dry summer the plant can become straggly and is not worthwhile.

In salads: Leaves trimmed of tougher stalks are delicious enough to stand solo in a salad — dress with lemon and good olive oil. The little white flowers that appear from spring onwards are also edible, and make a very pretty garnish to any salad.

To serve as a green vegetable: Pick out and discard only the coarser stems, then wash and either wilt in a pan with just the water that is clinging to it, or cook in a steamer for 4-5 minutes. Drain well, pressing out excess liquid with the back of a spoon, then season with salt and pepper, perhaps a pinch of nutmeg, and toss in a little butter.

Chickweed soup: As for nettle soup (see page 34). Serve hot or chilled, with a garnish of chopped chives.

COMMON MALLOW (*Malva sylvestris*)

This common perennial is frequent in southern England, becoming less so further north. It is found on wasteland and roadsides — especially the wide verges of A roads and dual carriageways — and is easily identifiable in summer from its beautiful pink flowers.

Picking and preparation

The leaves are best picked in the summer months, when the plant is in flower. They contain a resin which makes them stretch like clingfilm, and gives body and richness to the excellent Arabic soup, *mouloukhia*, that is made from them. Choose large leaves, but not ones that are dry around the edges. Strip off the stalks, and wash well before cooking. Being slightly furry, the leaves are not particularly pleasant raw.

The leaves of the pretty white garden flower, musk mallow, can also be used for *mouloukhia*. See page 40 for the full recipe.

DANDELION (*Taraxacum officinale*)

Like nettles, dandelions are perennial plants, extremely common and easily identified — so the leaves are one of the wild greens that everyone can find and enjoy. The romantic name of this perennial herb means, literally, lion's teeth (*dents de lion*) — which presumably refers to the jagged edge of its leaves. The plant is a rich source of folklore and gossip, but is best known perhaps for its diuretic effect, as expressed by traditional names in both French and English: *piss-en-lit* and pissabed.

The bitter flavour of dandelion leaves will not be to everybody's taste, but if you like chicory and endive (to both of which the dandelion is closely related) you will find dandelion leaves an excellent alternative.

Picking and preparation

The outside dark green leaves are likely to be unpalatably bitter, even to enthusiasts, so pick leaves from close to the centre. The whiter, lower parts of the leaves will be sweeter, and the greener parts can be broken off.

There are two ways to counteract the bitterness. Leaves that you have cut can be stood in fresh, cold water overnight. Alternatively, if you have time to invest in your crop, blanch the plants as they grow, by cutting away all the outer leaves and covering the whole plants with flower-pots or black plastic bags: the new leaves, shaded from sunlight as they grow, will be pale and sweet. By pinching off flower heads as they appear, strong prolific dandelion plants can be used as a cut-and-come-again source of salad into the winter months.

I only really use dandelion leaves as a salad, but they can be cooked, and are sometimes added, with nettles, to a dock pudding (see page 29).

The dried, ground roots of dandelion are used as a coffee substitute, and the flowers to make beer and wine (see Chapter 6).

FAT HEN (Chenopodium album)

For a plant with such a derogatory set of local names – 'dirty dick' and 'pig-weed' among them – this extremely common perennial herb is remarkably classy eating. It's found on wasteland and field edges all over Britain, quite often next to paths or growing against walls. It's often one of the first plants to colonize newly broken ground, on building sites and around road works. It was once a staple food, and its seeds were identified in the celebrated stomach contents of 'Tolland man', a 1,500-year-old corpse recovered entire from a bog in Denmark in the 1950s.

Picking and preparation

Like so many leafy greens, this shrivels to nothing, so pick several times more than you think will be enough! In early spring, young shoots of about 15cm/6 inches high can be cut just above the ground and cooked and served like asparagus, as a starter or side vegetable. Later in the year, choose the tender leaves and flower-heads from the top of the plant, and pick over to discard any tougher stalks before cooking. Always wash thoroughly.

As a green vegetable: Wash the picked-over leaves and put in a pan with just the water that is clinging to them. Cook as for spinach: wilt down, turning frequently, and simmer until tender. Then drain well in a colander or sieve, pressing excess water out with the back of a spoon.

Young fat hen with anchovy sauce: Boil or steam young fat hen shoots for 6-8 minutes until tender and drain well. Finely chop a small tin of anchovies with a small bunch of wild chervil (or parsley) and maybe a few capers. Stir in just enough olive oil to make a thick dressing. Trickle over the fat hen and serve.

Fat hen soup: As for nettle soup, see page 34.

HOGWEED (Heracleum sphodylium)

One of the first hedgerow greens I ever tried, and still a firm favourite, hogweed is an extremely common biennial herb widely distributed throughout Britain, and is easily found in hedgerows, on towpaths, at road verges and along the edges of woods. It has a most unusual, slightly camphorous taste which I predict will grow on you even if you don't take to it at once.

Picking and preparation

The young shoots appear first in a kind of envelope, actually a closely furled leaf, on the side of the main stem. They can be picked at this stage, or a little later when they have uncurled, but choose always the young, fresh shoots that point upwards, rather than stems with open leaves lolling on their side. Most plants will be overgrown by the end of June, but where road verges have been mown down later in the summer you can expect to find a vigorous second crop.

To serve as a first course: Whole shoots with their leafy ends do not need peeling or trimming, and can be steamed or boiled for 5-6 minutes, until tender but still a bit crunchy. Serve them with a ramekin of warm melted butter flavoured with lemon zest and black pepper.

Smaller shoots and the curled shoots inside the 'envelopes' are delicious deep-fried in batter – see page 32 for recipe.

HOP SHOOTS (Humulus lupulus)

This perennial climber is not really a wild plant but a marauding escapee. It can be found in hedgerows, thickets and at wood edges – and sometimes climbing up telegraph poles – wherever hops have been or are being grown for the brewing industry. But the hop was a food plant long before it became the principal flavouring of our national drink. The Romans brought it here, perhaps never realizing just how grateful we would be.

Picking and preparation

The best culinary morsels are the shoots (or hop tops) of young spring growth – which usually means picking before the middle of May at the latest.

Hop leaves have a slightly sticky residue and accumulate dust and dirt easily, especially by roadsides: they therefore need a thorough washing in several changes of cold water – though I have not found the soaking in cold salted water that some recipes suggest to be necessary.

I like hop tops as a spinach-style side vegetable: i.e. wilted in a pan with just a little water, squeezed almost dry and then heated through with a little butter, salt and pepper. A sprinkling of Parmesan doesn't go amiss. Cooked like this, it also makes a nice filling for a pancake or omelette.

LIME LEAVES *(Tilia cordata)*

The lime is a fast-growing, hardy deciduous tree, not a native in Britain, but quite common owing to its popularity among landscape gardeners of the last two centuries. It is frequently encountered in country parks, village greens and tree-lined streets.

Picking and preparation

The young leaves, pale and soft, taste fresh and pleasant, and are best eaten raw in a salad. They should be picked before late May/early June, from which time on they are liable to start exuding a sticky residue — actually the product of an aphid that lives on the leaves. Those who have parked their cars under lime trees for a few days and come back to find them covered in a thin layer of glue will know just how sticky and tenacious this substance is — only hot soapy water will remove it. It is not poisonous, but makes the leaves less pleasant to eat, and is almost impossible to wash off without damaging the leaves.

By way of compensation, the tree offers up its superb flowers a few weeks later: see page 152 for how to make lime flower tisane.

Lime leaf and cucumber sandwiches: Wash a handful of young lime leaves. Peel and finely slice ½ a cucumber. Spread thinly sliced white or brown bread sparingly with butter and/or cream cheese. Arrange a layer of cucumber and a layer of lime leaves. Season with salt and freshly ground black pepper. Complete the sandwich with a second slice of buttered bread and cut into triangles. Serve with a well-made pot of tea.

MALLOW, see COMMON MALLOW (page 13)

MARSH SAMPHIRE or GLASSWORT *(Salicornia europaea)*

This succulent plant of the tidal zone looks almost like a miniature cactus. It is one of the most distinctive and worthwhile of all wild vegetables, with its excellent *al dente* crunch and distinctive sea-fresh salty flavour.

It has been harvested and used as a vegetable for centuries, and with its seashore origins it has long been a popular accompaniment to fish. Until recently there was a tradition in many fishmongers of giving away a couple of handfuls of samphire to customers while the plant was in season, but I haven't reaped this benefit for a good few years now. The vegetable has become trendy, and sells for fairly silly prices in up-market grocers.

Picking and preparation

The answer is to gather your own: samphire is local, but prolific, on salt marshes and tidal mudflats all around the coast — most famously in Norfolk and south-west Wales. It can be picked at low tide, traditionally from the longest day (21 June) until the end of August when, after flowering, it tends to become fibrous and tough.

Picking samphire is both messy and tough on the back — bending over, shin-deep in mud, to pull the little shoots up by the roots (to cut samphire is a misguided conservation measure, as a plant thus damaged will die anyway). The way to enjoy it is to put on old clothes and make a party of it. If it descends into childish mud-slinging then so be it: both you and the samphire are sure to need a thorough washing when you get home.

Very young and tender samphire can be nibbled raw, but in most cases it will need cooking.

Samphire asparagus style: After rinsing thoroughly in fresh cold water, the samphire sprigs can be cooked, roots and all, in a steamer, or in simmering unsalted water, for 6-8 minutes until tender but still just crunchy. Drain, and serve on warmed plates with warmed ramekins of melted butter. Each little bunch can then be picked up by the slightly woody roots, dipped in the butter, and stripped of the tender green flesh with the teeth (practice makes perfect).

Samphire as a side vegetable: If you want to serve samphire as a side vegetable (e.g. with fish) so that all that appears on the plate is edible, then it needs a thorough picking over: after an initial rinsing, remove and discard the slightly woody roots and any stems that are not fresh, crisp and green. What's left can then be steamed or boiled as above, tossed with a knob of butter, and served.

Pickled samphire: The fleshy samphire has a perfect texture for pickling, retains its sea-fresh taste even in its vinegar bath, and keeps for months. Choosing the freshest, greenest parts, trim your crop of samphire to short, unbranched lengths of about 2.5cm/1 inch. Blanch in unsalted boiling water for just 2 minutes, then refresh in cold water. Shake dry in a cotton cloth. Pack into jars, and cover with a spiced pickling vinegar made in the following way: put 1 litre/2 pints white wine (or malt) vinegar in a pan with 1 tablespoon of cloves, 1 tablespoon of allspice berries, 1 tablespoon each of black and white peppercorns, 2 sticks of cinnamon, 5 bay leaves and a 5cm/2 inch piece of root ginger, sliced (optional). Heat very gently for 1-2 hours, to infuse the spices, but do not allow to boil or the vinegar will start to evaporate. Leave to cool, then strain out the spices. (This adaptable spiced vinegar can be used for pickling all kinds of things, from elder buds to broom flowers – see respective entries.)

The pickle is ready after 2 weeks, and will keep for 6 months. Serve with bread and cheese, cold meats and smoked fish. Also, use to flavour the wild tartare sauce on page 41.

NETTLES, see STINGING NETTLES (page 18)

ROCK SAMPHIRE (Crithmum maritimum)

This is the rather lovely plant that I risked my neck for in the first series, abseiling down a cliff in imitation of the sixteenth-century samphire gatherers alluded to by Edgar in King Lear:

> The crows and choughs that wing the midway air
> Show scarce so gross as beetles; halfway down
> Hangs one that gathers samphire, dreadful trade!
> Methinks he seems no bigger than his head.

This plant, which occasionally grows in shingle, and on the cracked concrete of old sea defences, as well as on cliffs, is unrelated to the marsh samphire but has similarly fleshy leaves, which can be prepared in much the same way. Its main use, however, when harvested in the past, was as a restorative condiment, pickled in barrels of salt, then mixed with other pickles (i.e. cucumber and capers) and served with meat – both as a flavouring and an aid to digestion.

Rock samphire makes an interesting, if rather medicinal tasting pickle, if you follow the procedure as for marsh samphire (see above, on page 15). In the series I pickled it in some neat elderberry wine with an unusually high alcohol content: when it came to sampling this rather experimental condiment, I found I rather preferred drinking the samphire-flavoured wine to eating the pickle. I'm sure a sixteenth-century quack would have approved.

SEA BEET or SEA SPINACH (Beta vulgaris maritima)

This is the genetic ancestor of our cultivated forms of beet, from Swiss chard to beetroot: the mother of all spinach, if you like. The thick, leathery leaves are even more succulent than those of cultivated spinach varieties, and although in the raw state they taste a little soapy and tannic, they really come into their own when cooked. This annual or perennial herb is common on seashores, often growing around cliffs and sea walls, and by the coastal paths, all around the British coastline, though less frequently in Scotland.

Picking and preparation

The leaves can be picked from late March until the first frosts, but good sized, succulent leaves are harder to find in high summer, when the plant is flowering and can become straggly.

In early spring the stalks may be tender enough to cook with the leaves, but generally they should be stripped off and discarded. As with all spinach, always wash the leaves well, in at least 2 changes of fresh water, or the dishes you prepare from them may be gritty.

Substitute for spinach in any recipe.

Creamed sea spinach: In the second series I picked abundant sea beet from the Norfolk coast to accompany my razor clams. Wilted, drained and finely chopped, I stirred it into a thick creamy béchamel, to produce a particularly fine version of that all-time great comforter, creamed spinach. Good on the side with any shellfish, it's also delicious on its own, with a bit of grated Cheddar or Parmesan added, if you have any handy.

Sea beet, fennel and salmon tart: See page 36 .

SEA KALE (Crambe maritima)

This cabbage-like native perennial grows close to the sea in shingle or shingle-and-sand. It used to be relatively common all around our coasts from southern Scotland downwards, especially on the big shingle beaches of the south coast. But commercial demand for it as a fashionable vegetable in the early nineteenth century seriously depleted numbers. It seems to be on the increase again but should not be over-picked: just take a few stems from each plant and let it grow to seed.

Picking and preparation

Early spring is the best time for picking: the young leaves, stalks and broccoli-like flower-heads are all edible, but become tough and bitter later in the year. It is worth scrabbling into the shingle with your fingers and cutting the stems as low as possible: the pale shoots growing under the stones are naturally blanched and have the best flavour.

A real labour of love, but a rewarding one, is to blanch sea kale plants yourself. This is traditionally done before the end of March, by pushing shingle and sand up around the growing stems. Or you can cover a whole plant with a bucket or large flower-pot – practical only if your plants have relative privacy and your blanching covers are not likely to be mistaken for beach litter. Revisit the plant after 2 or 3 weeks to harvest.

As a vegetable: Treat sea kale pretty much as for broccoli. Wash well and cut away any too tough stalks. Steam, or boil in salted water, for 8-15 minutes until tender (as with broccoli, the cooked vegetable should retain a little bite and not be allowed to become mushy). Toss in butter and season with freshly ground black pepper and a sprinkling of good sea salt.

Sea kale with pasta: A simple and delicious supper dish is made by tossing the cooked sea kale with penne or other short pasta shapes, a few chopped anchovies, and a little melted butter. Or serve cold as a salad, tossed in an olive oil dressing instead of butter.

SORREL *(Rumex acetosa)*

This perenial herb is common throughout the British Isles and, along with nettles and fat hen, must rank in my top three wild leafy greens. Far from being just another spinach substitute, it has an inimitable gooseberry-lemon tang that can be enjoyed raw in salads or cooked in soups and sauces. A few leaves plucked straight from the hedgerow are a refreshing and restorative snack on a hot summer walk.

Picking and preparation

Sorrel can be found in the hedgerow and in open meadows and pastures throughout the year, but is at its best in early spring (as early as February after a mild winter), when the thick and succulent shield-shaped leaves are just coming up. Later in the summer when the plant is flowering the leaves are thinner, drier and tougher, but younger leaves at the bottom of the plant will still be worthwhile.

Before using sorrel either raw or cooked, pick over the leaves, discarding the stalks, and wash thoroughly.

Try to avoid using steel or iron pans and utensils when cooking sorrel, as the acid chemicals react with iron and this can affect the flavour. Sorrel always turns a dirty green when cooked.

Sorrel sauce: Shred about 500g/1lb of washed and trimmed sorrel and put in a pan in which you have melted 55g/2oz butter. Cook the sorrel to a purée and cook out most of the water. Stir in 3 or 4 tablespoons of béchamel sauce and 1 tablespoon of thick double cream. Season well. This simple sorrel sauce is excellent with pork and veal (hot or cold) and fish.

Sorrel salad: Sorrel is often added to sophisticated green salads along with all kinds of aromatic herbs and salad leaves, and though that can be nice I think the best way to enjoy raw sorrel leaves in a salad is in a simple mix with 2 or 3 times as much good sweet lettuce (cos or little gems) and a plain dressing of olive oil, sea salt and black pepper. A few rocket leaves make up a good trio.

Warm potato and sorrel salad: Cook small new potatoes, and immediately after draining transfer to a salad bowl and toss with a few handfuls of shredded sorrel leaves and either a good olive oil dressing or plain butter. The heat of the potatoes will wilt the sorrel to delicious effect. Eat while still warm.

Sorrel soup: See page 37 for the full recipe

SOW THISTLE *(Sonchus oleraceus)*

This annual or over-wintering plant takes its name from the observed habit of lactating sows to eat the plant, whose beneficial vitamins and minerals may well help them with milk production. It looks like a cross between a dandelion (its yellow flowers are similar but smaller) and a thistle. Common all over Britain, except in the Scottish highlands, this is another delicious and versatile green and, like fat hen or chickweed, is good eating either raw or cooked, especially in spring when its young leaves are most succulent and tender. There is sometimes a second growth in autumn.

Picking and preparation

All leaves can be used, provided they are green and fresh-looking, but for salads the younger leaves are best as the spiky edges will still be soft enough to eat. If you take the trouble to trim off the edges with a pair of scissors, the larger leaves can also be eaten raw.

As a vegetable: Steam or wilt the leaves as for spinach. Drain well, pressing out excess liquid, return to the pan with a knob of butter, and serve. Sow thistle leaves can be cooked like this in a traditional mix with nettle tops and dandelion leaves.

As a salad: Wash and dry the leaves and serve either alone or mixed with lettuce, tossed with a garlic and olive oil vinaigrette.

Sow thistle soup: As for nettle soup, page 34.

STINGING NETTLES *(Urtica dioica)*

This perennial herb is abundant throughout the British Isles and hardly needs describing: every young child is taught to identify it so that they can avoid its vicious sting. We should all be taught to cook with it as well, because it really is one of the most worthwhile of all the free greens. It's full of good things too: iron, formic acid and natural histamine. Nettles are therefore an excellent tonic, particularly good for improving blood circulation and purifying the system.

Picking and preparing

The best thing about nettles is that they are so easy to find. I said in the series, while I was making nettle soup for the East Anglia willow coppicers, that no one is ever more than ten minutes' walk from a bunch of nettles, and a few days later my claim was put to the test. I promised to cook nettle soup for a sceptical friend, and had picked a good bagful of nettle tops at the bottom of my parents' garden in Gloucestershire before returning to London on a Sunday afternoon. Back in my Euston flat, I'd already defrosted some chicken stock and was sweating my onion when I realized I'd left my bag of nettles on the train (a strange find for some unsuspecting guard – I hope he didn't get stung). I was loath to abandon my cooking, so I dashed out into the street in search of urban nettles. I'd barely turned two corners before I found them: lush, green and vigorous in a poorly maintained flower-bed outside an office block. I hardly need add that my sceptical friend was dead impressed with the soup.

A stout rubber glove or gardening glove is the best way to put an impenetrable barrier between your picking hand and the nettles' sting. (I don't advise attempting to 'grasp the nettle' bare-fisted in line with the old proverb: it may work once, but by the time you have enough leaves for a soup your hand will be as red as a raspberry and throbbing like hell.)

The best nettles for cooking are the young shoots of early spring (March, usually), no more than a few inches high. They can be cut from just above the ground and used stalk and all. As the plants get bigger, choose only the crown of new small leaves at the top.

By the time the nettles are in flower (May/June) they are usually too tough and straggly for cooking, but wherever they have been cut back you will find new young shoots coming through, especially after rain. If you have a nettle bed in your garden, instead of weed-killing it why not strim it every few weeks and reap the benefits of a regular crop throughout the summer.

As a vegetable: Unless you have very small shoots only, pick over the nettles and discard any tough stalks. Wash well (and carefully – they can still sting for some time after picking), and wilt in a pan with just the water that is clinging to them, and a sprinkle of salt. Keep turning for a few minutes until they are wilted and tender, then drain off excess water, add a good knob of butter, and season with freshly ground pepper and a pinch of nutmeg

Nettle bahji: Prepare as above until cooked, then squeeze as dry as possible in a colander. Sweat a chopped onion in a little oil until soft and golden, add a teaspoon of mild curry powder or curry paste, and cook with the onion for a few more minutes. Roughly chop the cooked nettles, add to the onions in the pan with a good knob of butter, and heat through. Garnish with chopped roasted chestnuts or cashew nuts (optional).

Fresh nettle tisane: See page 152

Nettle soup: See full recipe on page 34.

NOTE: The tops and young leaves of the **white dead nettle** *(Lamium album)* can also be prepared in the same ways.

WATERCRESS *(Rorippa nasturtium aquaticum)*

Watercress, a fairly common lowland plant, is found everywhere in Britain except the highlands of Scotland and central and northern Wales. It grows only in moving water, usually shallow streams and ditches, and is often found in the summer months in great profusion. It is now so familiar as a cultivated salad leaf found in almost every grocer and supermarket that few take the trouble to gather it. But in terms of freshness, satisfaction and flavour, the wild stuff can't be beat.

Picking and preparation

When picking wild watercress there is a very real danger from liver fluke, a nasty parasite spread by cattle and sheep. If there is any grazing upstream of where you are picking, the watercress is certainly not safe to eat raw.

Your best bet is to enquire locally, and any watercress that you do pick should not be eaten until it has been thoroughly washed in fresh clean water (not from the stream). Don't take any chances with raw watercress: the safest option is to cook it, which will kill the parasite.

Soup: Watercress makes one of the best soups of any wild vegetable. Follow the recipe for nettle soup on page 34.

WOOD SORREL (*Oxalis acetosella*)

This little perennial herb is found in woods and hedgerows, especially in the damp shade of tree trunks. Its small clover-shaped leaves have the same sharp taste as sorrel but are more delicate and tender. Collecting enough to make a soup with would be a major undertaking, but a sprinkling of leaves in a salad, or as a garnish on simply grilled fish, adds a delicious lemony tang. In the first series, I sprinkled a handful on my Scottish breakfast of sautéd cockles with larch boletus mushrooms, and the combination was quite outstanding. I have since often used wood sorrel to garnish simple mushroom dishes (see page 180).

YELLOW FLOWERING ROCKET OR WINTERCRESS
(*Barbarea vulgaris*)

In the past ten years, cultivated rocket has emerged from total obscurity to become one of the best known 'alternative' salad leaves on the restaurant scene, enjoyable for its crisp texture and hot peppery taste.

The wild version is a common biennial or perennial herb which grows all over Britain (though rather less in the north), in hedgerows and wasteland, and particularly along footpaths near the sea (it seems to like the sea air). It is one of the first edible leafy plants to appear, and in a mild winter can be found as early as late January or February.

Picking and preparation

The first fresh green leaves of rocket are particularly good for salads. If the flower-heads are pinched off as the plant grows, it can be regularly cropped throughout the spring.

The plant flowers from June to September and the little yellow flowers are also peppery hot and delicious — either raw in salads, or thrown in at the end of a stir-fry of greens. The leaves on the flowering plant will be thin and coarse, but they still have a good flavour, and can be picked provided they are clean and fresh.

From mid September, small seed-pods will show after the flowers. These can be collected when almost dry, and rubbed gently in the hands to release the little round seeds. These have the same heat and flavour as mustard seeds, and can be used in the same way. Collect enough of them and you could even crush them to make your own delicious fresh wild mustard.

FAVOURITE HEDGEROW HERBS

(see pages 22-23 for illustrations)

The following wild plants are also worthwhile, though used more as flavouring herbs than as vegetables.

CHIVES (*Allium schoenoprasum*)

This tough little herb is reliably one of the first to show, often pushing its spiky shoots through February snow. Though found throughout Britain, wild chives tend to be common only locally, although they are becoming more frequent, perhaps as escapees from cultivated herb gardens. In some country lanes, in the first warm days of spring, you can smell their oniony savour a long way off.

Uses

One of the most versatile of all herbs, chives can be added to soups, sauces and salads whenever that green oniony bite is called for.

Chive sour cream: Chopped chives mixed with sour cream, crème fraîche or thick yoghurt can be added as a garnish to many soups, especially chilled summer soups (e.g. the nettle soup on page 34). The same mixture makes a lovely filling for a baked potato.

COW PARSLEY OR WILD CHERVIL (*Anthriscus sylvestris*)

An extremely abundant biennial herb, wild chervil is the plant that defines the British roadside verge in summer: its white flowering stems, growing up to 1.2 metres/4 feet high, can be seen for mile after mile on country roads and motorway verges throughout the British Isles: it is infrequent only in the northernmost highlands of Scotland.

It is to cultivated chervil, and not parsley, that this herb is most closely related, and it has a similar spicy, grassy flavour. The leaves are tenderest and have the most delicate flavour when the plant is still only a few inches tall in early spring (March), but it remains worthwhile until the stem has become woody and hollow and the leaves tough and hairy (usually May/June). Being biennial, tiny new young plants will appear in the autumn, but they remain hard to find and identify until the following spring.

WARNING: Wild chervil can be confused with several poisonous plants, notably fool's parsley and hemlock water dropwort. I encountered a particularly fine specimen of hemlock in the series while foraging near the Severn with expert hedgerow gleaner Roger Worsley: growing, as it always does, with its feet in water, it looked like a very succulent cross between celery and parsley. A scary thought, because it is absolutely deadly and a few leaves of it would, as Roger put it, 'have you at the undertakers by the end of the afternoon'.

The distinction from hemlock is relatively easy: wild chervil has fine hairs, becoming thicker as the plant gets older, on its ridged stem. The stem of hemlock is smooth, and blotched with purple spots. Fool's parsley is a flimsier plant than wild chervil, has darker, cream coloured flowers (as opposed to white) that grow in closer clusters than chervil, and has small drooping green bracts beneath the flower-heads.

Uses

Young chervil leaves are an excellent all-round herb for salads and garnishes, and make a good companion to chives: snip either or both over potato salad, throw into an omelette, use as a garnish for soups, and add to other wild greens recipes for extra flavour.

FENNEL, see **WILD FENNEL** (page 21)

GARLIC, see **HEDGE GARLIC, WILD GARLIC** (below, and page 21).

HAIRY BITTERCRESS (*Cardamine hirsuta*)

This common native annual herb is found growing on bare rocks, on paths and at the bottom of walls, as well as on bare ground in the hedgerow and on wasteland. It is one of the earliest-flowering of the wild spring herbs, and when young, can be eaten whole – flower, leaf and stem.

Uses

Pick leaves and flowers from the middle of the plant upwards, and wash well. Bittercress has an excellent spicy flavour, somewhere between mustard and cress, and is excellent raw in sandwiches, as well as being a fine addition to any salad.

HEDGE GARLIC, GARLIC MUSTARD, JACK-BY-THE-HEDGE (*Alliaria petiolata*)

Another mildly garlic-flavoured leaf, this biennial herb is found in the hedgerow and at the shady edges of woods, commonly in England and Wales, less so in northern Scotland and Ireland. The thin pale green leaves can sometimes be seen as early as February, if the winter has been mild. From then until it flowers (usually April/May) the leaves are at their mild oniony best.

Later in the summer it develops a bitter, cabbagey taste, making it rather less palatable – even worse when cooked. But there is often a second crop of new shoots and seedlings in September or October.

Uses

A few chopped leaves will add a mild oniony flavour to soups or salads. I put garlic mustard, along with nettle beer, in my bunny à la runny honey (see page 65) – climactic dish of the first ever episode of *A Cook on the Wild Side*. The soggy leaves weren't very pretty by the end of cooking, and were discarded, but the flavour they imparted to the stew was excellent.

Garlic mustard sauce for early spring lamb: (A recipe from our series consultant, Richard Mabey, author of *Food for Free*). In late March or April, pick garlic mustard leaves and a handful of hawthorn buds. Chop both finely, mix well with wine vinegar and a little sugar, and serve with lamb.

HORSERADISH (*Armoracia rusticana*)

Horseradish is found throughout Britain (though infrequently in Devon and Cornwall), usually on cultivated or broken ground. This perennial herb is easily recognized by its large thick leaves, pointing skywards like giant asses' ears. But it is the thick root beneath them that is of interest to those who like a little heat in the kitchen.

Uses

The root can be dug up as soon as the plant can be identified by the leaves (usually April). It should be washed, peeled, grated and used sparingly. It is the combination of horseradish with vinegar (or acetic acid) that makes the commercial sauces so inferior. All you need to do to make a wonderful horseradish sauce is to stir I tablespoon of the freshly grated root into 2 tablespoons of very thick cream or crème fraîche, and add a little salt to taste.

Fresh horseradish has a clean, aromatic heat that complements many foods. Its famous partnership is, of course, with roast beef, although I happen to think it makes a rather more exciting marriage with smoked fish, especially eel. After netting and smoking some eels with farmer Robert Gaze in the Norfolk programme, I was delighted to see the giveaway greenery in abundance in his overgrown vegetable patch. Its nearest neighbours, however, were abundant nettlebeds, and in my over-vigorous attempt to uproot the radish, I tumbled backwards into the nettles. I was stung so visciously that the skin on my back came up like a red and white mountain range. When sheer agony had subsided into a persistent hot throbbing I tucked into a hot smoked eel and grated horseradish sandwich. And a great comforter it proved to be.

MEADOWSWEET (*Filipendula ulmaria*)

This common plant needs permanent moisture, and is consequently found prolifically in bogs, marshes, at the edges of ponds, streams, rivers and canals and in wet ditches that tend not to dry up in the summer. It appears all over Britain, and has long been part of the traditional hedgerow herbal medicine cabinet – not surprisingly, as it was recently discovered to contain aspirin.

Uses

Not really a culinary herb (although you could use the leaves in a salad or to garnish a chilled soup), I include meadowsweet because the leaves have a pleasant cucumbery flavour and are nice to chew – I used to keep a regular supply on the *Bain Marie*, which was easily replenished as meadowsweet is prolific on many stretches of canal. Meadowsweet leaves also make an excellent tisane: steep a few sprigs of fresh or dried leaves (flowers too, if available) in boiling water, either on their own or with a couple of nettle tops for extra body and flavour, and leave for 5 minutes. Add a little honey to sweeten, if you wish.

When in flower (June to September), meadowsweet was once used in vast quantities as a 'strewing' herb, scattered over the bare wood floors of country houses to make a sweet-smelling carpet. The flowers and leaves are still used as a flavouring in country wine-making: see page 157.

WILD FENNEL (*Foeniculum vulgare*)

For me, this highly successful garden escapee is one of the most exciting plants to find growing wild. From the first pungently aromatic aniseed-flavoured shoots of early spring, to the tall vigorous stems of high summer, the plant is a joy to behold, to smell and to use. I rarely pass a specimen without, at the very least, plucking off a few green fronds to chew. Happily fennel is increasingly common and is now widespread in the coastal zone of middle and southern England, often appearing on the coastal path, on cliff tops and on road verges and waste ground near the coast. The perimeters of seaside car parks seem to be a particularly happy hunting-ground.

Uses

As a flavouring herb for fish, fennel is hard to beat. When baking fish in foil, stuff it with fennel fronds and/or seeds, and use more chopped fennel to finish a sauce made from the juices and a little cream. Add to mixed herb salads. Remember that the fine fronds of wild fennel can always be used as an alternative to dill. Crème fraîche mixed with chopped fennel is a nice thing to serve with blinis and smoked fish.

Dried Fennel. Come the late summer, when the plant is overgrown (sometimes to 2 metres/6 feet or more) and has seeded, cut down whole plants 30cm/12 inches or so above the ground (don't worry, they will grow back next year) and take them home for drying. Hang them in bunches upside down in a warm airy place until quite dry. The stalks of fennel dried in this way can be used on next year's barbecue for cooking fish, particularly seas bass, sea bream (dorade) and red mullet, which will be infused with a smoky, aniseedy flavour. Dried fennel can also be used when cooking inside on a cast-iron grill pan – the kind with the raised ridges. Heat the grill on the hob and lay on a few stalks of dried fennel, as well as plenty of twiggy bits and dried flower-heads, crushed up. When the fennel is charred and smoking, lay the fish on top and grill until cooked. Fish cooked over charred fennel in this way ranks among the best things I have ever eaten. Ever. You can also collect the seeds from the flower-heads of the dried fennel, and use them to flavour soups and stocks, especially when cooking fish.
NOTE: It would be a mistake to attempt to eat the roots of wild fennel in the belief that they will bear any resemblance to the fennel bulbs you buy in the shops. You will find them tough, stringy and unpleasant.

Alexanders

Bistort

Chickweed

Common Sorrel

Common Mallow

Corn Salad or Lamb's Lettuce

Dandelion

Fat Hen

Fennel

Hairy Bittercress

Hedge Garlic

Hogweed

Horseradish

Lime Leaves

Marsh Samphire or Glasswort

Meadowsweet

Rock Samphire

Sea Beet or Sea Spinach

Sea Kale

Sow Thistle

Wall Pennywort/Navelwort

Watercress

Wild Chervil or Cow Parsley

Wild Garlic

Wintercress or Yellow Flowering Rocket

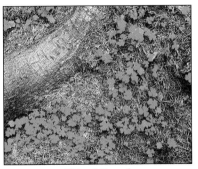

Wood Sorrel

WILD GARLIC (*Allium ursinum*)
Very common throughout England and Wales, less so in Scotland and Ireland, this native bulb is found in damp woods and shady lanes; you will often smell the plant before you see it. Folklore credits wild garlic with all kinds of beneficial properties, chiefly warding off vampires and evil spirits. Ros Foskett, the Welsh white witch who showed me how to make oak-leaf wine and nettle beer, made me a lovely garland of willow and wild garlic flowers to bring me good luck. I kept it in the cab of the Gastrowagon for a day or two, but the smell got too much and it was banished to the kitchen in the back. Eventually the smell penetrated the taste of my breakfast tea, and I reluctantly discarded it: after a while, reeking of garlic seems a high price to pay for safety from vampires.

The young green leaves, picked before the flowers have died (usually early May), have a strong garlicky smell but are pleasantly mild in flavour and can be used raw in salads and sandwiches. They are also good for cooking, and can be added finely chopped as a flavouring for soups, as a mild alternative to cloves of cultivated garlic.

I made a fine wild garlic and goose egg omelette with Roger Worsley in the second series — my first piece of on-camera cooking on my charcoal-fuelled, pedal-fanned gastrobike cooker. It worked out pretty well, except that Roger said he didn't like his omelette runny ('biscuity' was his preferred consistency).

A delicious hedgerow version of garlic bread can be made by beating soft butter with finely chopped wild garlic, chives, and wild chervil. Spread the butter into cuts made at intervals in a baguette or other stick loaf, wrap in foil, and bake in a hot oven for 20 minutes.

FAVOURITE EDIBLE FLOWERS
(see page 26 for illustrations)

The shoots and leaves are not the only edible parts of the hedgerow vegetation. Flowers are not just a novelty garnish: they have flavours ranging from sweet and aromatic to hot and spicy, and are always fun to cook with.

See also Chapter 6, page 151, for tisanes, cordials and wines made from flowers.

ACACIA, see **FALSE ACACIA** (page 25).

BROOM (*Sarothamnus scoparius*)
This native shrub is common throughout Britain, on heaths, wasteland and by the side of the road, particularly on sandy soils. In an early spring, the first butter-yellow flower-buds appear in March, and can be picked sometimes until early June.

The flowers should be picked when still in bud, when they have a wonderful leguminous flavour, reminiscent of runner beans. I love to throw a handful into a salad, but also into a stir-fry of green vegetables (leeks, beansprouts and pak choy) for just the last 30 seconds.

The freshest, tightest broom buds can be pickled in spiced vinegar and used like capers. Lightly rinse the buds and pat them dry with kitchen paper, then pack into jars. Prepare a spiced vinegar (as for marsh samphire, on page 15). Leave it to cool, and pour over the buds. Use after 2 weeks, and for up to a year. Pickled

broom buds make an excellent addition to my wild tartare sauce (see page 41).

Broom flowers make one of the best country wines (see page 157).

CLOVER, see **RED CLOVER** (page 27)

CRAB-APPLE (*Malus sylvestris*)
The delicate pink and white blossom of the crab-apple tree is seen in the hedgerow in April or May. It is pleasantly scented, and makes a particularly good flower fritter (see page 32). See also page 134 for the entry on the fruit of this tree.

ELDER (*Sambucus nigra*)
This deciduous tree-shrub is found abundantly everywhere in Britain, except northern Scotland and the Scottish isles, in woods, roadsides and wasteland. It seems like a generous gift from nature that such a common hedgerow plant can have so many, and such delectable, culinary uses.

Elderbuds: The first crop, seasonally speaking, is the little round flower-buds, which can be taken from the spray in late April or May before they flower, and pickled. Cover them in a brine made from 175g/6oz of salt to 1 litre/2 pints of water, and leave for a week. Drain, then cover in spiced vinegar (as for marsh samphire, page 15) in a pan, bring slowly to just short of boiling point, leave to cool and repeat heating, then put in jars and cover with the vinegar. Serve chopped and mixed with herbs (e.g. wild chervil and chives) as a sauce for lamb or pork.

Elderflowers: The creamy-coloured sprays of highly scented flowers are without doubt the elder's greatest gift to the kitchen. You don't need many, and whatever liquid, syrup or batter you dip them in will be infused with their intense and delightful muscaty taste.

They can be used in many ways, imparting their flavour to sorbets, ice creams, cordials, jellies and jams. The affinity with gooseberries is particularly well known (see page 145). The transfer of flavour is easily achieved: pick the flowers, if possible, on a dry sunny day, and choose those that are well opened, but still fresh — the sprays should be full, not yet losing any flowers. Flowers can simply be dipped into syrups, ice mixtures and the like to infuse for a few minutes, then strained out. For jams, jellies and ices that are not going to be strained, 3 or 4 flower-heads can be wrapped in muslin or a square of cotton, dipped into the pan of jam, jelly or syrup while it is hot and bubbling, and removed after a few minutes.

In this way, you can experiment with the flavour of elderflowers in many ways. But there are four elderflower recipes worth having down pat: fritters (see page 32), cordial (see page 164), wine (see page 160) and, my own favourite...

Elderflower sorbet: Dissolve 225g/8oz caster sugar in 600ml/1 pint water, bring to the boil, and boil hard for 7 minutes to get a light syrup. Off the heat, add 4 elderflower sprays and the juice and thinly grated rind of 4 lemons. Leave to infuse until cool, then strain and pour into an ice cream machine. Or part-freeze, remove to whisk, part freeze, and whisk again, in the traditional fashion (an egg white can be folded into the half-frozen slush before the final freeze).

For uses of the fruit, see page 134.

FALSE ACACIA *(Robinia pseudoacacia)*
Originally introduced to Europe from the USA, the false acacia is not a common tree in the hedgerow in this country, although it has been planted often enough in gardens and parks, and as a municipal tree, so that escapees are not unheard of. It likes a mild climate and is unlikely to be found in situations that are liable to hard frost.

This deciduous tree, with its thorny twigs and pretty pinnate leaves comprising up to eleven pairs of leaflets, can grow up to 24 metres/70 feet high, and is quite stunning when in blossom in April or May. It is the highly scented blossom bell-cluster (raceme), shaped like a bunch of grapes, that is the delicacy. If you wish to try it, you should closely monitor the progress of any local false acacia, as the flowering period lasts only a week or two.

In the Loire valley, and other regions of France where the false acacia flourishes in the wild, the brief season is eagerly awaited every spring. The whole raceme of flowers is dipped into batter, deep-fried, and served as a dessert, sprinkled with sugar. It makes perhaps the best of all flower fritters, better even than elderflowers, and when I have some I serve them unaccompanied by other flowers. The batter described for the other flower fritters on page 32 is ideal.

There are many ornamental subspecies of *Robinia pseudacacia*. The leaf shape and colour of the blossom may vary, but the flowers of all are edible.

HAWTHORN *(Crataegus monogyna)*
The hawthorn is one of the single most frequently occurring wild trees, and in May and early June you can see mile upon mile of hedgerow frosted a brilliant white by its pretty little flowers. These can be eaten, and are particularly good when just coming out of bud. The fresh young leaves of hawthorn are also edible. West Country schoolchildren would traditionally pick and eat both leaves and flowers on the way to school, and called the combination 'bread and cheese'. A salad of beetroot, garnished with both leaves and flowers of hawthorn, is particularly nice. The flowers are really too small to make fritters, though a scattering of fresh hawthorn flowers is a nice way to decorate a plate of fritters made from other flowers.

Both flowers and berries can be used for making wine (see page 154).

LESSER CELANDINE *(Ranunculus ficaria)*
The little yellow flower on this very common perennial herb is one of the first to show in the spring: in the south of England it appears consistently in the last week of February, hence one of its local names, spring messenger.

Broom

Crab-Apple

Dog Rose or Wild Rose

Elder

False Acacia

Hawthorn

Lesser Celandine

Lime Flowers

Primrose

Red Clover

Sweet Violet

The plant is also known as 'pile wort' and, as hedgerow historian Roger Worsley pointed out to me, it is a fine example of the application of the so-called 'doctrine of signatures', whereby the medicinal uses of plants were believed to be indicated by signs from God. In the case of celandine the reasoning was simple: the nobbly tumerous roots of the plant look uncannily like piles. Therefore an ointment made from the crushed roots must be God's intended cure for piles.

Of more culinary interest than the roots are the flowers and leaves. Both are edible and pleasant raw in salads, though neither is worth more elaborate preparation.

PRIMROSE *(Primula vulgaris)*

The lovely primrose, which is a common perennial growing in shady lowland woods, on chalk banks and often in railway cuttings, gets its name from the Latin *prima rosa*: the first flower of spring. Though it may appear as early as late March, it is more often found in April and early May.

Like the cowslip, primroses were traditionally used to make a country wine. But given the fate of the cowslip (which is now so rare in the wild it has become a protected species), it is hard to justify picking primroses in the kind of quantities that are needed for wine-making.

The flowers are pleasant-tasting, and have a little pool of nectar inside which makes them a refreshing mouthful on a walk. They can be used to decorate a salad (in which the young leaves can also be included), or used in flower fritters (see page 32).

Primroses, like violets, can also be crystallized in sugar and used for decorating cakes and mousses, though this is not a practice in which I indulge.

RED CLOVER *(Trifolium pratense)*

This perennial herb is found all over Britain in meadows, road verges and other grassy patches. Its little green leaves go largely unnoticed, until suddenly in June the purple-crimson flowers explode all over the grass.

In fact the leaves, an important fodder crop for cattle in this country, were widely eaten by the American Indians. They are quite palatable if collected in any quantity and cooked like spinach. But more interesting, as much for their shape and colour as for their mildly scented grassy flavour, are the aforementioned bauble-shaped flowers. They can be picked throughout the summer, from May to September, and used as an (edible) garnish for salads. They look wonderful mixed with the similarly-shaped flowers of chives and scattered on top of a potato salad.

They are also good for including in a batch of flower fritters (page 32) because they hold the batter well, making neat little crispy balls.

Red clover flowers make a good dry wine (see page 157).

SWEET VIOLET *(Violata odorata)*

The sweetly scented violet was obviously one of Shakespeare's favourite-smelling flowers, as he uses it often for comparative purposes to pay his female characters olfactory compliments. It is a native perennial herb, reasonably common in shady hedgerows and scrub, less so in the north and in Ireland. Do not confuse odorata with the larger flower of the dog violet, which has practically no smell at all.

In the kitchen, it is best known as a flavouring for confectionery, particularly the soft sugar sweets known as Parma violets, or when crystallized. I have to say that the 'violet cream' was always one of my least favourite chocolates in the box, tasting as it did of cheap bottled perfume. But then I dare say the chocolate in question hadn't been near a real sweet violet.

A small bunch of violets does, however, impart a wonderful scented flavour to a rice pudding: simply infuse the flowers in the hot milk (or half-milk, half-cream) for 10 minutes, then proceed with your recipe.

Due to overpicking, violets are increasingly scarce in the wild. But they are a lovely garden plant, and if you want to use them regularly in your cooking you should consider growing them.

WILD ROSE OR DOG ROSE *(Rosa canina)*

The wild rose is a common plant in the hedgerow and on the edge of woods, except on very high ground. Its flowers are white or pink, and appear in June or July, lasting sometimes into August.

Wild rose petals have long been used in both the boudoir and the kitchen, to give their scent to pot-pourris and flower waters (in the former), and to syrups, jams and jellies (in the latter).

Rose water can be used as both a scent and a flavouring. It is easily made by pouring boiling water over a few handfuls of petals in a bowl. Cover and leave to steep for half a day. Strain the rose water first through a sieve, pressing through the petal juices to maximize the flavour, then through muslin or a cotton cloth. Bottle and keep in a cool place. Try adding a teaspoon to a strawberry sorbet, or a rice pudding. It is also one of the best flavourings for Turkish delight.

Rose petal jelly can be made by adding rose petals to a simple apple (or crab-apple) jelly recipe (see page 142). Add petals to the strained juice (a small handful for every 600ml/1 pint) with the sugar, leave them in during the boiling, and strain out before potting. This pleasantly scented jelly is good on pancakes, scones, waffles and milk puddings.

See also *Rosehips* (page 135).

EDIBLE GARDEN FLOWERS

As I said at the beginning of this chapter, wild food foraging begins at home. There are many garden flowers which are edible, and a fair few with a genuinely interesting flavour and texture. One word of warning: it is not advisable to eat flowers purchased from nurseries or garden shops which may have been sprayed with insecticides. And any flowers in your own garden that you may wish to eat should be raised organically, without the use of chemical sprays or weedkillers.

Here is my small selection of edible garden flowers.

BORAGE *(Borago officinalis)*
The little blue star-shaped flowers are a beautiful garnish, and have some of the thyme-like fragrance of the leaf that is used as a herb. A nice addition to summer drinks, such as elderflower cordial, or Pimm's.

CHIVES *(Allium schoenoprasum)*
The crispy blue pom-pom shaped flowers have some of the oniony bite of the rest of the plant, and look great in a salad. Attached to a couple of inches of stalk, they can be dipped in batter, deep-fried, then dipped in honey and eaten off the stalk.

COURGETTES
The large, orange-yellow tube-shaped flowers of courgettes just beg to be stuffed. I usually oblige by putting an anchovy rolled up in a large basil leaf inside each one, before dipping in batter and deep-frying. Serve on

their own as a starter, with a dusting of fresh grated Parmesan.

COWSLIPS *(Primula veris)*
If you grow them yourself, you can satisfy your curiosity as to the taste. The bell-shaped flower heads make a lovely-looking fritter. If you grow enough, you could even investigate whether cowslip wine deserved its fine reputation.

DAY LILIES *(Hemerocallis lilioasphodelus)* and others
Very crunchy and delicious, these flowers have almost the texture of iceberg lettuce – and a far more interesting flavour, with a peppery aftertaste. For salads, they are my favourite of all garden flowers.

NASTURTIUMS *(Tropaeolum majus)*
Their unusual hot cressy taste means they are a flavourful, as well as colourful, addition to a salad. They are big enough to make a decent fritter too. I like to float one on the chilled version of my nettle soup (see page 34).

PANSIES *(Viola × wittrockiana)*
Quite edible, though not a particularly distinctive flavour. But good in fritters, as the bright colours often show through the batter.

PRIMULAS (various)
The cultivated version of the primrose can be used in the same way as the wild one (see page 27), and comes in a variety of colours.

DOCK PUDDING

The ladies of the Calder Valley would no doubt be able to find fault with this recipe, but I have done my very best to accommodate their advice: if only they could agree among themselves. Anyway, the most important thing is that I think it's delicious!

SERVES 6

115g/4oz butter
I large onion, finely chopped
½ large leek, finely sliced
I carrier-bagful (about 1kg/2lb) of bistort
    leaves, washed and destalked

2 dozen young nettle tops
85g/3oz medium grade oatmeal
salt and freshly ground black pepper
6 thick rashers good back bacon

- Melt half the butter in a large heavy pan and sweat the onion and leek until soft but not brown.

- Pile in the bistort leaves and nettle tops, pour over a cup of hot water, and squash the leaves into the pot with the lid.

- Cook for a few minutes, then take off the lid and mix up the leaves with a wooden spoon so the heat is reaching all of them. Continue until all the leaves have wilted down and are bubbling in their own juices.

- Reduce the heat to a gentle simmer, replace the lid, and cook for 45 minutes to I hour until the leaves are tender. Pour off most (but not all) of the excess liquid and reserve.

- Beat the leaves with a wooden spoon, or mash with a potato masher to break up into a rough purée.

- Add the oatmeal and mix well. Season well with salt and freshly ground black pepper. Cook the mixture, stirring often, so that the oatmeal absorbs the water and thickens the pudding. If it starts to get too dry, add a little of the reserved cooking liquid.

- After about 15 minutes, you should have a creamy green purée, the consistency, as one of the good ladies so charmingly put it, of 'a fresh cow clap'. Add the rest of the butter in pieces, and mix in until melted. Check seasoning. At this point, the pudding can be transferred to a container and kept in the fridge for up to a week, or put in the freezer.

- Dock pudding is traditionally served with bacon: fry the bacon rashers in a large frying pan, remove and keep warm. Add the pudding mixture to the fat in the frying pan and cook, turning occasionally: you are not trying to fry it into a crispy cake, just to heat through and impart some bacon flavour. A generous dollop of the pudding with bacon on the side, and a good hunk of crusty bread, really makes a complete meal: breakfast, lunch or tea.

ROGER WORSLEYS'S PILGRIM SALAD
(with dill mustard dipping sauce)

In the second programme of the second series I spent a happy afternoon gleaning the hedgerow near the river Severn with hedgerow historian Roger Worsley. While I christened the Gastrobike with a goose egg and wild garlic omelette, Roger rustled up what he called his pilgrim's 'sallet'. The recipe is variable, according to what is found, but the dressing goes well with all kinds of salads.
On the day we used the following edible leaves and flowers:

dandelion (leaves and a few flower petals for
    decoration)
celandine leaves
Alexanders leaves
wild chervil
pennywort (a succulent member of the
    stonecrop family)
meadowsweet leaves
primroses (leaves and flowers)

FOR THE DRESSING:
½ teaspoon crushed mustard seed (or yellow
    rocket seeds)
I dessertspoon finely chopped fennel (or
    dill)
4 tablespoons olive oil
I tablespoon wine vinegar
I tablespoon white wine
I teaspoon honey

• Shake all the ingredients for the dressing together in a jar, before you go out to collect the leaves.

• The journeyman's way to eat this highly enjoyable impromptu leaf feast is to take the jar of dressing with you, gather the leaves and flowers as you wander, then sit down, arrange the spread of leaves in front of you, and get comfortable. Take the lid off the jar of dressing, and use it as a dipping sauce, dipping individual leaves and small bunches into the dressing and popping them straight into your mouth. No utensils required, and no litter created.

FRESH GOAT'S CHEESE WITH HEDGEROW HERBS

In South Wales, on my way to catch a rabbit, I stopped off at Mrs Norma Ackroyd's wonderful goat farm, in the hope of bartering some of my oak-leaf wine for general supplies: eggs, goat's milk, butter and cheese. She had no need of my wine, having plenty of her own, so instead she put me to work, milking, churning, and wrestling with her immensely strong billygoat, Samson. I should have cut his hair off, because he ended up dragging me into a ditch.

It was worth it though: the butter and cheese from her goats were superb, and though I never consumed the cheese on camera, I made this delicious concoction for my own supper. Mixing very fresh goat's cheese with garlic and herbs is a French tradition, and it's often served as a starter with crusty bread and crudités.

You can buy a version of fresh soft goat's cheese in cartons in the supermarket, and it will do for this recipe, though it won't be quite as good as the farm-fresh version. This dish should be prepared at the last moment and the cheese should be chilled from the fridge.

SERVES 6 AS A STARTER OR CHEESE COURSE

about 500g/1lb very fresh soft goat's cheese
salt and freshly ground black pepper
small bunches each of:
    chives
    wild garlic leaves
    wild chervil (young cow parsley)
    bittercress or watercress

You can add or substitute home-grown or shop-bought herbs:
    parsley
    chervil
    garlic
    tarragon

TO SERVE WITH THE CHEESE
batons of carrot and celery, whole radishes
    and other crudités
fresh crusty bread

- Wash, shake dry, and finely chop all the herbs. Add three-quarters of the chopped herbs to the goat's cheese in a bowl. If you don't have wild garlic, crush a garlic clove and add that to the bowl.

- Mix the herbs and cheese well together with a wooden spoon or fork. Season to taste with salt and freshly ground black pepper.

- Sprinkle the remaining herbs over the top of the cheese and take the bowl to the table with the bread and crudités.

- Serve with a good rosé or chilled Beaujolais.

FLOWER FRITTERS
(Beignets de fleurs)

Flower fritters make a surprising and pleasing dish for a small dinner party (or a romantic supper for 2). You can make a savoury version and have them as a starter, lightly dusted with Parmesan; or a sweet version, sprinkled with sugar and served as a dessert. (See illustration on page 10.)

Fritters made from either elderflowers or acacia blossoms are special enough to be worth serving on their own, without any other flowers. In both cases, the whole flower-heads are held by the stalk end and dipped in the batter, then deep-fried. They make large fritters, and 2 or 3 are usually enough for even the biggest fan. I always make them sweet, rather than savoury. With the smaller flowers, 4-6 fritters per person are usually enough.

You can use any of the wild or garden flowers mentioned on pages 24-28 for the sweet version. The savoury version can be made with a selection of flowers, shoots and leaves. The following are my favourites:

hogweed shoots and young leaves

sprigs of wild chervil

a small sprig of chives, knotted in the middle

flowering sprigs of hairy bittercress

yellow flowering rocket (leaves or sprigs in flower)

fennel fronds

sage leaves

Alexanders flowers

chive flowers

day lilies

courgette flowers

nasturtiums

THE BATTER

115g/4oz plain flour

pinch of salt

3 tablespoons olive oil

freshly ground black pepper (savoury version only)

2 teaspoons rum or kirsch (sweet version only)

150-200ml/5-7fl oz lukewarm water

1 egg white

TO SERVE

a sprinkling of caster sugar, or runny honey, warmed and thinned with a little wine vinegar (sweet version)

rock salt, grated Parmesan (savoury version)

• Make the batter: mix the flour and salt with the olive oil and either pepper or rum/kirsch, and whisk in the water by degrees, until the batter is the consistency of double cream. Cover and leave to stand in a cool place for at least ½ an hour.

• Prepare your chosen flowers by dipping them in cold water and giving them a quick shake, and lay on a cloth ready for dipping.

• In a large, high-sided pan (or a dedicated deep-fat fryer) heat at least 5cm/2 inches of good frying oil (i.e. groundnut or sunflower), until a small cube of white bread thrown into it turns golden brown in 30-40 seconds. Turn down the heat to maintain a steady temperature.

• Whisk the egg white until it forms soft peaks, then fold gently into the batter.

• Dip the flowers in batter, allowing the excess batter to drip off them, before lowering gently into the hot oil. Fry the flowers in small batches, turning once or twice, until they are puffed up and golden brown.

- Remove each as soon as it is done, and drain on kitchen paper. Keep in a low oven or on a warm plate until you have enough to serve.

- Pile on a plate, and sprinkle with sugar (sweet version) or grated Parmesan (savoury version). A sauce made by warming 3 tablespoons of honey mixed with 1 tablespoon of wine vinegar can be served with the sweet flower fritters.

NETTLE AND HEDGEROW HERB DUMPLINGS

Dumplings are a great British tradition, and a much underrated way of providing starch to accompany a good stew. They need to be nice and light though, almost like poached scones, and the secret is to use half fresh white breadcrumbs, half self-raising flour, and not to over-knead them. I made these to go with my jugged hare (see page 58), which I'd caught with long-netter Chris Green. Even though I say it myself, he was dead impressed.

MAKES 12 GOOD SIZED DUMPLINGS (2 EACH FOR A LARGE STEW TO SERVE 6)

small bunch of chives, finely chopped

small bunch of wild chervil, finely chopped

a dozen young nettle leaves, finely chopped

You can also add or substitute home-grown or shop-bought herbs:

    parsley

    thyme

115g/4oz self-raising flour

115g/4oz fresh white breadcrumbs

115g/4oz suet

salt and freshly ground black pepper

2 whole eggs

- Thoroughly mix the dry ingredients – flour, breadcrumbs, suet, chopped herbs, salt and pepper – in a large mixing bowl and make a well in the middle.

- Beat the eggs lightly with a fork, and pour three-quarters into the well. Mix with a fork, bringing the dry ingredients into the centre, and mixing to form a dough. Take over with your hands, working the dough until smooth, and adding the rest of the egg if it seems too dry. Do not knead more than is necessary to bring the dough together.

- Divide the dough into 2, then 4, then make 3 round dumplings from each quarter of the dough.

- Dumplings should be cooked on top of your stew, with the lid on, for the last 25 minutes of cooking time. Arrange them, if possible, so that they do not touch each other. If there are too many for the size of your pot, they can be cooked separately in a steamer.

NETTLE SOUP

This is my basic recipe for nettle and other green leaf soups, including fat hen, watercress and chickweed. I still think nettle is the best, with watercress a very close second. An excellent variation is to mix the nettle leaves with watercress, or with cos lettuce. I sometimes add a few fresh or frozen peas, to give sweetness and improve the texture.

When I made nettle soup for the fenland willow coppicers I used a stock made from smoked zander. It gave the soup quite an unusual taste, but not an unpleasant one: you could certainly make this soup with a good fresh fish stock.

I used to thicken my soups with potato but some varieties can have a tendency to impart a slight stickiness when liquidized. Now I generally use cooked rice or even rice cakes: these can be put straight in the liquidizer and produce a smooth creamy texture. But you can easily use a medium potato to thicken this soup: peel and dice it fairly small, and add it just before the stock. If you do use a stock cube, the best ones are MSG-free.

SERVES 6

½ a carrier-bagful of nettles, tops or young leaves
55g/2oz butter
1 large or 2 medium onions, finely sliced
1 large carrot, chopped
1 large clove of garlic, crushed (optional)
1 litre/2 pints good chicken, fish or
    vegetable stock
1 medium cooked potato, diced, *or* 2
    tablespoons cooked rice, *or* 2 rice cakes

salt and freshly ground black pepper
pinch nutmeg (optional)
2 tablespoons thick cream or crème fraîche

TO GARNISH (OPTIONAL):
small bunch of chives
few sprigs of wild chervil or bought parsley
a little extra cream or crème fraîche

• Pick over and thoroughly wash the nettles. Discard only the tougher stalks as the soup will be liquidized.

• Melt the butter in a large pan and sweat the onion, carrot and garlic until soft but not brown.

• Add the stock and pile in the nettles. If you are using rice or potato to thicken the soup, and you do not have any already cooked, you could add them at this stage (dice the potato).

• Bring to the boil and simmer until the rice or potatoes are cooked and the nettles tender. Season with salt and pepper, and nutmeg if you wish.

• Liquidize the soup in a blender (you will probably have to do it in 2 batches). Return to a clean bowl (if serving cold) or pan (if serving hot), stir in the cream or crème fraîche and check seasoning.

To serve cold: On warm spring or early summer days I love to serve this soup cold. If you have plenty of time to chill the soup before serving, simply leave it to cool then transfer to the fridge for a couple of hours before serving. For accelerated cooling, fill a large mixing basin or saucepan with ice cubes and water and place the bowl of soup in the iced water. Stir to chill, and add more ice cubes if the first batch melts. Stir well just before serving and ladle the soup out into bowls. Garnish each with a swirl of cream and a sprinkling of chopped chives and wild chervil.

To serve hot: Reheat the soup after liquidizing but do not reboil. Garnish with a swirl of cream and chopped herbs.

Note: Nettle and other green soups freeze extremely well.

SEA BEET, FENNEL AND SALMON TART

In this delicious recipe you can substitute cultivated dill for wild fennel and spinach for sea beet without any devastating loss of flavour (in other words you will hardly taste the difference!).

SERVES 6–8 AS A STARTER, 3–4 AS A SUPPER DISH

175g/6oz fresh salmon fillet, or smoked
    salmon trimmings, or gravad lax, or a
    mixture of all three
1 dessertspoon olive oil
2 tablespoons chopped wild fennel, or dill
salt and fresh ground black pepper
500g/1lb sea beet (or spinach), trimmed
    and washed

1 medium onion, sliced
55g/2oz butter
1 whole egg
2 egg yolks
300ml/10fl oz double cream
1 × 20cm/8 inch blind-baked shortcrust
    tart case

• Cut the salmon and/or smoked salmon and/or gravad lax into bite-sized pieces, and mix in a bowl with the olive oil, chopped fennel or dill, and salt and pepper: put in the fridge to marinate for at least an hour.

• Lightly cook the sea beet or spinach in a large pan with just a little salted water, then drain well in a colander, pressing out excess liquid with the back of a large spoon.

• Place on a board, and roughly chop.

• Sweat the onion in the butter until soft but not brown and transfer to a mixing bowl. Add the sea beet or spinach and mix well.

• Mix the whole egg, egg yolks and double cream with a fork, season well with salt and pepper, and pour this custard into the bowl with the sea beet and onion. Mix well.

• Arrange the fennel-marinated fish pieces evenly in the bottom of the tart case, and spread the sea beet custard over them.

• Bake the tart in a pre-heated oven, 180°C/375°F/gas mark 4 for 25-30 minutes, until set and lightly browned on top.

• Serve hot, warm or cold, with a sharply dressed simple green salad.

Variation: Replace the fish with chopped cubes of goat's cheese: marinate the cheese with fennel and olive oil in the same way, and construct the tart as above.

SORREL SOUP

This is slightly different from the nettle soup recipe, because you don't need as much sorrel to flavour the soup. The body of the soup is therefore made up of other vegetables, and lettuce.

SERVES 4

55g/2oz butter

I medium onion, finely chopped

2 medium or I very large carrot, peeled and finely chopped

2 sticks celery, chopped

I large leek, finely sliced

I small parsnip, peeled and diced (optional)

0.75 litre/I ¼ pints chicken stock

½ a small cos lettuce, washed and chopped

a good fistful of sorrel (about 30 leaves)

salt and freshly ground black pepper

TO GARNISH (OPTIONAL)

thick cream

fried bread croûtons

two hard-boiled eggs, chopped

• Melt the butter in a large pan, and sweat all the vegetables except the sorrel and lettuce for about 5 minutes, until softening but not brown.

• Add the stock and bring to the boil. Simmer until the vegetables are almost tender (5-10 minutes), then add the lettuce and the sorrel. Cook for another 5 minutes. Season with salt and pepper, transfer to a liquidizer, and blend until smooth. Return to the pan and heat through (but do not boil for more than just a minute).

• To make this excellent soup really special, I like to serve it garnished with fried bread croûtons, a swirl of thick cream, and a sprinkling of chopped hard-boiled egg.

RISOTTO OF GARDEN WEEDS AND HERBS

There are many variations to this recipe, depending on what greens and herbs come to hand from the garden or hedgerow. You need a reasonable bulk of greenery such as nettle tops, fat hen or sow thistle, then as many interesting flavours as you can muster. A particularly delicious and delicate risotto, this makes a fine starter on its own, or can be used to accompany fish or meat.

SERVES 6

a dozen nettle tops
small bunch of wild chervil
small bunch of wild chives
small bunch of yellow rocket leaves
a few wild garlic leaves
575ml/1 pint chicken, veal or vegetable stock

1 small onion or 2 shallots, very finely chopped
55g/2oz butter
225g/8oz arborio rice
1 wineglass white wine
salt and freshly ground black pepper

• Blanch the nettles in boiling water for 2 minutes, then drain, squeeze dry, and chop finely. Wash and finely chop the other hedgerow herbs.

• Bring the stock to simmering point and keep on a low burner.

• In a separate fairly heavy-based saucepan, sweat the onion or shallot in the butter for a few minutes until soft but not coloured. Add the rice and cook for a further few minutes.

• Add a ladle of the hot stock and allow to come to a gentle simmer. Cook the rice until almost all the liquid has been absorbed, stirring occasionally to make sure the risotto does not catch on the bottom of the pan.

• Continue to add the liquid by degrees, incorporating the wine towards the end of the cooking, until the liquid is all absorbed, the risotto is creamy, and the individual rice grains are tender with just a hint of chalkiness in the middle.

• Stir the chopped nettles and herbs into the risotto, which should become a beautiful pale green, flecked with tiny pieces of herb. Season to taste with salt and pepper.

• The risotto should be served not piping hot, but *tiède*, with a sprinkling of chopped fresh herbs and a trickle of olive oil on each portion. Parmesan cheese is not required.

MOULOUKHIA ALA DAJAJ
(Mallow and chicken soup)

A staple of the peasant diet, mallow is prepared in many ways in Egypt. This version is adapted from a recipe in the excellent book Middle Eastern Food: East of Orphanides, *by cook and professional bon viveur George Lassalles. With its accompaniment of boiled rice and chopped onion, it is really more of a main course dish than a soup, but by omitting the whole chicken and using just stock, you can make it less substantial and serve it as a starter, without the rice.*

SERVES 6 AS A 'MAIN COURSE' SOUP

I free-range chicken
stock vegetables: e.g. 2 carrots, I large onion,
   I stick of celery
I bay leaf
a few parsley stalks
2 teaspoons salt
2-2.5 litres/3 ½-5 pints water
Ikg/2lb mallow leaves, destalked and washed
6 cloves of garlic, crushed
I tablespoon coriander seeds

a pinch cayenne pepper
more salt
2 tablespoons olive oil

TO ACCOMPANY THE SOUP
quarters of pitta bread, baked until very crispy
boiled rice
2 large onions, finely chopped and marinated in
   2 tablespoons red wine vinegar for 2-3 hours
   (pour off excess liquid just before serving)

• Put the chicken in a large saucepan with the stock vegetables, bay leaf, parsley and salt, and cover with the water. Bring to the boil, then simmer gently, with the lid three-quarters on, for 75-90 minutes, until tender.

• Remove the chicken from the pan, discard the stock vegetables, strain the stock, and skim off some of the fat. Return the stock to a clean pan.

• Remove all the good meat from the chicken carcass and cut into bite-sized pieces. Set aside, covered with I ladle of the stock.

• Finely chop the mallow leaves, in a food processor or with a mezzaluna, and add to the stock. Bring to the boil, and simmer for about 10 minutes. The chopped leaves thicken the soup naturally as it cooks.

• While the soup is simmering, pound the garlic and coriander seeds with the cayenne and a little salt. Gently fry this paste in the olive oil in a small frying pan.

• Stir the fried garlic paste into the almost cooked soup and simmer for 2 more minutes.

• Heat through the chicken pieces in the ladle of stock and divide between 6 large warmed bowls. Pour over the soup.

• Serve with rice, crispy baked pitta bread and the chopped marinated onion. (You could stir these into the soup , but I think a nicer way to eat this dish is to use the bread to push a little onion and rice on to your spoon, and then dip it into your soup.)

WILD TARTARE SAUCE

The classic French sauce for fish and cold meats is really just a piquant mayonnaise, flavoured with chopped gherkins and capers. My wild version uses pickled flower-buds and samphire and is (though I say it myself) at least as good, if not better.

I look on the pickled samphire as a kind of gherkin substitute, and the broom buds as capers. Actually, this tastes rather different from a classic tartare sauce, but it is delicious all the same.

I egg yolk, at room temperature
I hard boiled egg, finely chopped
100ml/4fl oz olive oil
200ml/8fl oz sunflower oil
I tablespoon chopped wild chives
I tablespoon chopped wild chervil
I dessertspoon, chopped pickled broom buds
   (see page 24)

I tablespoon chopped pickled marsh
   samphire (see page 15)
salt and freshly ground black pepper
1-2 teaspoons pickling vinegar from one of
   the pickles

• In a small basin, mix the egg yolk with the finely chopped hard-boiled egg.

• Mix the two oils in a jug with a good pouring spout. Whisk the yolk and chopped egg, while pouring in the oils in a thin and steady trickle.

• Keep whisking, so the mayonnaise thickens, until you have used up all the oil.

• Mix the herbs and chopped pickles into the mayonnaise, and 1-2 teaspoons of pickling vinegar, acording to taste. Season well with salt and pepper.

• Serve with grilled fish, cold prawns and other seafood, or with cold beef or pork.

POACHER'S PROTEIN

Although I am always ready to stand up and be counted as a card-carrying carnivore, I do not eat meat every day. Frankly, I have never found a daily dose of flesh to be necessary for either my health or my happiness. For me, meat is a treat, and when I do eat it I want it to be of the best quality, I want to take some time over its preparation, and I want to really enjoy it. And I have found, over the years, that some of the carnivorous dishes I have enjoyed the most have been created from animals and birds I have killed and cooked myself.

Why should this be? Perhaps because the finding, killing, preparing and eating of an animal (or indeed a plant or fish) is, in a society increasingly obsessed with quick fixes and instant gratification, an unusually holistic procedure. It begins, more often than not, with a solitary walk in a wild place, and a rare chance for quiet reflection. There is a tremendous weight of history behind this act – not just social history, but evolutionary history. And as I walk up the edge of a wood with my gun, hoping to bag a swooping wood pigeon or a scurrying rabbit, I am aware that my motivations, like those of all our hunting ancestors, are largely connected with my stomach.

Then comes the sighting of the quarry, and in an instant the mind becomes entirely focused on the movement of the animal, the jink of its run or the arc of its flight. Perhaps there is a bit of stalking to be done – our attempts to regain the stealth and cunning of our ancestors may be pretty hopeless, but it always feels good to discover that the instinct is still there.

As you pull the trigger, the gap between you and the seemingly unreachable quarry is closed in an instant. The moment of death, as beast tumbles or bird crashes to the ground, is an emotional one that combines the triumph of possession and power with contradictory feelings of respect and regret. Then comes a period of contemplation, almost mourning, as the corpse is carried home, a pang which slowly subsides, giving way to anticipation of the feast to come.

But first the animal must be plucked or skinned, and then gutted. This is a messy, visceral task that many would find unpleasant, but which I must admit I find rather satisfying, even educational: opening, for example, the crop of a dead pigeon, finding out whether it has been fattening itself on corn, clover, elderberries or peas, and wondering how this might affect the flavour of the meat.

Then comes restoration: the transforming of the cold lifeless corpse, with wine, herbs and the magic of the oven, into something delicious, either to be savoured in a solitary session, or shared with friends. By the time it is served up, the hunter-cook has achieved a uniquely close relationship with his quarry: observing it in the wild, taking its life, handling it, preparing it, and then, the ultimate act of intimacy, devouring it. And for me that is something very special.

RESPONSIBILITY OF THE HUNTER

No doubt some people would find the above sentiments unsympathetic, or even incomprehensible. But I think it is important that those of us who choose to kill fish, birds and mammals, for sport and for the pot, are ready to explain to others why we do what we do. This is a responsibility I have always tried to meet at appropriate moments during the series. Without doubt the most controversial sequences were those in which I went in pursuit of 'poacher's protein' – ferreting a rabbit, trapping a squirrel, netting a hare and taking young rooks from their nest. As we expected, Channel 4 and I have received a certain amount of hostile mail, in particular for the squirrel sequence. But we also received supportive letters, congratulating us for having the guts to show what other programmes would have left out.

As I said during the rooking sequence, all meat is the product of a killing, and those of us who kill for the pot are merely taking responsibility for the manner of that killing. A squirrel may have a pretty, fluffy tail, and a cuteness factor that makes some people shudder at the sight of its back legs crackling on a barbecue. But if those people have ever seen young calves and lambs playing in the fields, then why have they not applied the cuteness argument to their own carnivorous habits? For I have found that most of the people who seem to be upset by the eating of rabbits, squirrels and the like are not vegetarians, but town-dwelling carnivores. Most vegetarians I know are far more sympathetic to the eating of game and other wild meat than they are to the consumption of meat produced by modern farming practices.

QUALITY OF WILD MEAT

And this brings me to the second vital point about wild protein: all wild meat comes with a unique and invaluable guarantee of quality. First, it has been fed on an entirely natural diet, selected, as nature intended, not by man but by the animal itself – no hormones, no chemicals, and no revolting and dangerous feeds made from minced-up other animals. Second, it has lived a life, however short, as nature intended, free of the many stresses that give so much cause for concern about the welfare of our farm animals. Third, if the killer is also going to be the butcher and the cook, he or she has complete control over how the meat is to be stored, butchered and otherwise prepared before cooking.

Remember that every time you go to the butcher's for a chicken or a steak, or buy meat from a supermarket, you are at the mercy of a whole chain of intermediaries: the farmer, the abattoir and the butcher himself. You have to take it on trust that all three links in the chain have done their jobs as well as you would have liked them to. If you buy wild meat, you can eliminate the first two links in the chain, and if you kill it yourself, you can eliminate all three. (Incidentally, I am all for supporting butchers and farmers who sell meat that has been naturally fed and humanely reared, but sadly they are few and far between. When you do find one, stick with them: you will no doubt find that besides a good quality of farmed meat they can supply you with excellent game and other wild meats.)

WHAT IS WILD MEAT?

Having sung the praises of wild meat, both as a quarry and as an ingredient, it's time to make some clear distinctions, both generally and for the purposes of this book.

Wild meat can be fairly simply defined as meat coming from any animal or bird that is not bred and fed by man. But there are some grey areas. Some species of game birds (notably most pheasants, some partridges and duck, particularly mallard) are reared specifically for sport. They are therefore not strictly speaking wild – but in terms of both taste and health, a reared pheasant is at the very least 'free-range' and 'corn-fed' – and infinitely preferable to an intensively farmed broiler chicken. By contrast, and contrary to the implication of some packaging, quails that you find in this country are never wild: they are always farmed, sometimes as intensively and unpleasantly as battery chickens. I tend not to buy quails unless I know they are humanely and naturally fed. Unfortunately, since they are technically classed as game, there is no statutory labelling legislation governing the use of the term 'free-range', so if you want to get hold of decent quail you will have to do some homework. Truly wild quail are native to the flat plains of Eastern Europe. No doubt they are delicious, but I have never seen them on sale in this country.

The other British game birds, pretty much guaranteed to be truly wild (and, in the hands of a good cook, pretty much guaranteed to be delicious) are: wild ducks (other than mallard, but including widgeon, teal and pintail), wild geese (including greylag, pink-footed and white-fronted), grouse, woodcock and snipe. Access to these species, for shooting, is controlled by the law (which enforces a closed season) and by the owners of the land over which they range. Much has been written about the sport of shooting game, and about the art of cooking it. I have already had my own say about the latter, in my first book, *Cuisine Bon Marché*, so I won't add to that here.

The game mammals (not including hares, which I'll discuss below) hunted for sport in this country basically comprise the deer family: red, roe and fallow. The meat of all of them is excellent eating, if properly prepared (marinating, in my view, is usually a mistake). The humane pursuit of these large animals (I do not condone deer-hunting with hounds) is the sport of stalking, which requires skilful handling of a high-powered rifle. It is something I have done and, to a limited extent, enjoyed, but again I won't elaborate on it here.

Of more interest to me in the current context are the non-game birds and mammals, generally regarded as pests, for which there is no closed season, and which may be taken by anyone, at any time, on their own land or, with the permission of the landowner, somebody else's (provided – if they are using a gun – they have a gun licence, and observe the laws of firearms – see below).

Once you have ruled out the tinier and less appetizing birds and creatures that you are allowed to control – for example, sparrows, starlings and jays, mice and rats – you are left with a short list of highly palatable and largely accessible quarry. This includes birds: wood pigeons, collared doves and rooks; and mammals: rabbits, grey squirrels and hares, and these are the species to which I devote the rest of this chapter. To them I add one further source of land-based protein, partly for want of a better place to put it, but also in the hope that it may particularly appeal to urban foragers whose access to pigeons, rabbits and the like may be somewhat limited. I am talking about a beast neither furred nor feathered, but who carries his house on his back: not your pet tortoise (though that too might be pretty tasty), but the common garden snail.

FIELD GUIDE

Unlike most of the wild plants described in Chapter I, most of the wild meat described in this chapter (with the notable exception of rooks and squirrels) can be bought from a good butcher (and live snails are available, believe it or not, by mail order). What follows in this field guide is a few thoughts on how you might get to pursue this very worthwhile quarry yourself and, failing that, how you might acquire it for the pot in some quantity, for little or no money. Should you end up getting it from a butcher or game dealer, it certainly won't cost you much – and I offer a few tips on making the right choice. Incidentally, if ever you want to buy game, including pigeons and rabbits (and even, during the autumn, squirrels) in some quantity, and you happen to live within fifty-odd miles of the Wiltshire town of Fairford, then I can't recommend any game dealer more highly than Roger's Quality Foods (tel: 01285 713254).

OWNING A SHOTGUN

By far the easiest way to kill a bird or small mammal is with a shotgun. In the hands of a skilled shot, it is also one of the most humane. But there is no point in owning a shotgun unless you intend to use it fairly regularly, and know how to handle it responsibly – and indeed, unless you can convince your local police station that you can do this, you will not be given a licence to keep a gun.

Having said that, you don't have to own vast tracts of land to exercise a passion for shooting, or even to be a paid-up member of a syndicate shoot. I have always preferred shooting alone or with, at most, one other like-minded human companion to a ten-gun, gin-and-tonic-fuelled pheasant massacre. And if the sport you intend to pursue is not the expensive and social one of shooting carefully managed game birds, but the often more challenging and enjoyable one of setting out alone to reduce the population of edible vermin, you may be able to benefit, as I have, from the goodwill of a local farmer or gamekeeper. If you are friendly with such a figure, and you can demonstrate to them that you can handle a gun responsibly, they may allow you on to their land to flight or decoy pigeons, stalk rabbits, and bag a few young birds from the springtime rookery. Similarly, if you keep a ferret, you don't have to be a poacher to enjoy your sport: if it's rabbits you're after, there are many landowners who would be happy for you to work their warrens. If such access is granted, for shooting, ferreting or even gathering snails, be aware that it is a privilege, and observe to the letter any conditions to which your access is made subject.

SHOOTING AT HOME

You are not allowed to use a shotgun in a built-up area, or within 50 yards of a public road. This means that, practically speaking, it is not feasible to use a shotgun on your own land unless you live in the country and have at least 3 or 4 acres. However, if you do have a large garden, bordering on farmland, regularly visited by pigeons, rabbits or squirrels, it may be possible to shoot on and over it in a limited capacity, but it is only sensible to do so with the understanding of your neighbours. Explain what you intend to do and ask them if they mind. Ask permission to recover any birds that may fall on neighbouring land. I used to flight pigeons from a makeshift hide in brambles at the bottom of my parents' garden. It was quite safe, and quite productive. Any birds that didn't land in the garden would fall in the field beyond, from where I had the farmer's permission to gather them. But then a neighbour bought a young pony and put it the next field. It turned out to be 'gun shy', and I gave up my pigeon flighting at her request. Now I have an air rifle...

AIR RIFLES

If you have a large garden, in leafy suburbs or a country village, which gives you a certain amount of space and relative privacy from your neighbours, you are quite within your rights to use an air rifle to shoot incoming pigeons and squirrels. (The latter can be as much of a problem for the gardener as for the farmer, owing to their devastating habit of gnawing the bark of young trees.) But if you are serious about this, you should get a decent gun, pressurized to the maximum legal level (12lb per square inch) and make sure it is properly sighted. Always use it safely, firing only when the backdrop to the target is either clear sky, or solid ground.

POACHING

Poaching has been around in this country as long as the feudal system, which took the right to hunt (and indeed to own land) away from the peasant and made it the exclusive preserve of the nobility. In its purest form, when birds or beasts are taken by stealth and cunning, not for profit but for the family pot, poaching is still a romantic notion, which smacks of social justice.

In the Norfolk programme I interviewed Barbara, a single mother who had resorted to poaching after she lost her job as a school caterer. She had some great stories, some funny, some gruesome, including one time when her accomplice (also a woman) broke her leg falling out of a tree, and Barbara had to carry her the five miles home.

Less sympathetic are the kind of poachers who arrive at night in four-wheel-drive vehicles, shoot twenty roe deer by spotlight, or clean out a whole wood of pheasants with a silenced rifle – though they would no doubt also claim that they were exercising their right to have a share of the wild larder.

In the eyes of the law, anyone who takes a bird or animal from land which is not theirs, without the owner's permission, is guilty of poaching. It is the privilege of the gamekeeper and the local police to decide when to pursue, when to prosecute and when to turn a blind eye. Personally I wouldn't advise anyone to poach when they have the opportunity to enjoy their sport with the landowner's permission. But I haven't always practised what I preach.

ROADKILL

It is worth noting one other particularly reliable and convenient way of acquiring many small mammals or birds at absolutely no cost, and with minimal effort. The motor car may never have been intended as a lethal weapon, but it probably accounts for the deaths of more birds and animals in this country than the gun. Of course, impact with half-a-ton of metal is not a particularly subtle form of despatch, and many poor creatures that meet their end like this are squashed into a hopeless state – if not by the car that hit them, then by the many that follow.

But a surprising number of roadkill animals, particularly pheasants and rabbits, are in quite a decent state. Making good use of them should be seen not as an act of desperation, but of sound ecological and economical principle. So if you see a dead pheasant, partridge, pigeon, rabbit or hare looking reasonably whole by the side of the road, it's worth stopping to take the trouble to assess its potential as food. The fact that it's there at all is a promising start: foxes, crows and other scavengers will usually make off with a carcass within a few days of its death. The briefest inspection will usually allow you to reject anything that is clearly beyond the pale. If it looks at all promising, a few further measures should allow you to rule it in or out of the pot:

1. Look very closely to see if anything moves. A maggot-infested beast or bird may appeal to some roadkill enthusiasts, but not this one.

2. Pull firmly at a leg or wing and turn the body over to check it is intact and whole. Lift it up and feel the weight: it should be as you expect, not light through dehydration. Check all sides, and feel for decent meat – on the back legs, in the case of a rabbit or hare, or on the breast, in the case of birds.

3. If all is good so far, risk a sniff. A hint of gaminess is nothing to worry about, but if it smells nasty, then chuck it (preferably off the road, for some less fussy scavenger to enjoy).

4. If it smells fine, then it almost certainly is fine. If, when it comes to gutting or skinning, it transpires that you have made a mistake, you can always chuck the carcass then.

Note also some tell-tale signs of a very fresh kill: loose feathers still blowing about the road; uncoagulated or 'wet' blood on the animal or on the tarmac; a warm carcass in cool weather; rigor mortis (onset is usually after 4–6 hours, and will last about 24 hours).

By far the best season for roadkill is late autumn or winter. In cold weather, the bacteria that breaks down meat takes a long time to get a hold, and there are far fewer flies and other insects around to infest a carcase with maggots. In really chilly weather and in the unlikely event that it remains unmolested by foxes or crows, a roadkill will stay in good condition for up to a week.

I have heard it said that you are not allowed to pick up any roadkill that you have killed with your own car. I suspect that this is lore rather than the law, but it makes sense on the basis that it discourages people from running over edible birds and animals 'accidentally on purpose'.

If you regularly drive along country roads, and you make a point of becoming 'roadkill aware', you will soon notice if a new body appears on the route. And once you have selected, butchered, cooked and enjoyed a couple of good specimens, you will no doubt find that your ability to spot and assess roadkill is rapidly reinforced by the satisfaction of the experience.

THE BEASTS AND BIRDS

RABBITS

There is no shortage of rabbits in this country, and provided we do not completely destroy our rural landscape, there probably never will be. The introduction of myxomatosis, a particularly revolting disease, though initially devastating, has had absolutely no significant long-term effect on the population. I hate to see a rabbit suffering from 'mixy', and will always try to put it out of its misery if I can. But mixy rabbits are not good eating.

There are other, far more humane methods of controlling rabbits than such grotesque biological warfare, which have the added bonus of keeping the meat in good condition. When a serious impact on numbers is required, night shooting with a hand-held spotlight, and either a shotgun or a .22 rifle, is extremely effective. Some people think ferreting is cruel, but it has never struck me as being so: the rabbit, fleeing from a natural predator, hits a net, gets tangled up, and before he realizes what's happening, he'll be dispatched by a swift blow on the back of the neck. If you want information on how to keep and look after a ferret, contact the British Field Sports Society, The Old Town Hall, 367 Kennington Road, London SE11 4PT (tel: 0171 582 5432).

Acquiring

If you want to shoot or ferret for rabbits try, as I suggested above, approaching a local landowner, farmer, or gamekeeper. If you do not already know him personally, you will want to approach gently – perhaps start by asking if he has any to sell or give away; if he ever shoots them himself (and if so, could you go with him). He may be surprised, he may even be hostile – in which case you're better off well away from his patch anyway – but if you show genuine interest, and some knowledge of your sport, you should get a fair hearing and, with any luck, the access you require.

If you don't wish to hunt rabbits but simply want to locate a ready supply, some gamekeepers will let you have them for nothing, especially if you are prepared to take the trouble of driving by the keeper's cottage to pick them up. Others will happily drop them off for you, but the least you can do is offer them a bit of beer money. The going rate wholesale is about 50p a piece, so you should always be ready to pay at least that. With rabbits obtained at such a bargain rate you will almost certainly have to skin and gut them yourself (see below).

If it comes to buying rabbits retail, any decent country butcher can get them for you, though they may be harder to find in London and the larger cities. But as well as wild rabbits, butchers also stock farmed ones. They may tell you these are better, and certainly they are plumper. A farmed rabbit can weigh up to 2.5 kg/5½lb, whereas an adult wild rabbit averages about 1.5kg/3½lb. But for flavour, I find farmed rabbits extremely bland: less interesting, on the whole, than a well-chosen chicken. The wild is far better. Wild rabbits will vary in price depending where you are, but they should never be expensive. I certainly wouldn't want to pay more than £3 for one, and would often hope to pay less than half that.

Butchers sell rabbits whole and unskinned (but usually gutted), or whole and skinned, or (especially if they are farmed) skinned, portioned and wrapped in cellophane. All too often the liver, kidneys and heart have already been discarded – a great shame, as all are excellent. If you are ordering rabbits in advance, request that this offal be kept for you: see below for a simple suggestion on how to serve it. Where possible take a whole rabbit and joint it yourself. It's worth taking the head for stock.

In the supermarket rabbit is sometimes available skinned and cut into portions; it should be labelled as either wild or farmed. If it isn't, and the label contains no warning that 'This produce may contain lead shot', then assume it is farmed.

Rabbits are best for eating when they are not breeding or feeding their young: this means from September to February.

Preparation

Gutting: Unlike hares, which are hung with the guts in, rabbits should be gutted, or 'paunched', as soon as possible after killing, either when you get home, or even in the field. It isn't difficult: with a very sharp knife make an incision, no deeper than is necessary to pierce the skin (you don't want to pierce the intestine if possible), starting at the urinary tract between its legs, and working up to the beginning of the breastbone. Pull out the stomach and intestines, carefully separating the membrane that attaches the stomach to the kidneys, so that the two kidneys remain attached to the carcass. Leave the liver and heart attached to the lungs inside the chest cavity. At the first opportunity, remove the offal, discard the lungs, but keep the liver, heart and kidneys (wrap in clingfilm and keep in the fridge) and rinse out the inside of the beast. In this state the rabbit can be hung for up to 5 days before skinning – but not so long in warm weather.

Skinning: With a pair of pruning shears or strong kitchen scissors, cut off all 4 feet above the 'knees'. Lay the rabbit on the table on its back, tail end towards you. With a very sharp knife, make a crossways slit, at right angles to and an inch or so below the cavity slit, across the belly and the tops of the thighs. Take the skin that is released, and pull it down off the thighs and turn the back legs out of the skin, pulling it inside out like a pair of socks, and down over the tail (hard to describe but really quite easy to do). Then turn the body over so that the head is towards you, get a good grip of the skin and pull down towards the head as far as it will go. Ease out the front legs, one by one. You can either cut through the neck and discard the head with the skin, or,

to keep the carcass whole and the head on, use the point of the knife to loosen the skin around the head until it can be pulled right off.

Jointing: You can roast a rabbit whole (see below), even with the head on, but almost all other recipes require it to be jointed.

First cut off the 4 legs: use a sharp knife to cut between the muscles that join the legs to the hips and shoulders, then cut through the bone with a heavy knife or cleaver. Cut away the thin flaps of meat that join the ribs to the belly. These look almost useless – but don't discard them: they contract when cooked and make very tasty little boneless portions. Cut off the neck and head (which can be used for stock, or included in your casserole then discarded). The remaining back or 'saddle' should be cut with a cleaver into 3 or 4 equal pieces.

Cooking

Many old recipes call for wild rabbits to be soaked overnight in acidulated salt water before any cooking is begun. The idea of this is to bleach the flesh and remove any 'gamy' flavour – a crazy notion, in my view, as rabbit is not a strong-tasting meat at the best of times. The idea that the meat is made more attractive by being bleached white, or more palatable by being robbed of its natural taste, is an outdated piece of dainty nonsense, and should be disregarded.

Casseroles: Rabbit is a well-flavoured, delicate meat, but it does have a tendency to dryness. Stews and casseroles are therefore among the best preparation: always brown the meat first, tossed in a little flour if you want to thicken the gravy, then put in a pot with a few sliced vegetables (try carrots, onions and celery), a bay leaf, sprig of thyme, some peppercorns. Water or stock, combined with wine or beer, can be used as cooking liquid. Cooking time will depend on the age of the beast: a big old buck rabbit is best given a long slow simmer for 1½ hours, until the meat is flaking off the bone. But a younger animal will be tender and succulent in about half that time. See page 65 for the recipe I cooked for (ex) poacher and ferreter Malcolm McPhee – 'bunny à la runny honey'.

Roasting: There is very little fat on a rabbit (slightly more in autumn and early winter), which means that any attempt to roast it will be a battle to preserve some juiciness in the meat. If this battle is won, then a roast rabbit is a very fine dish indeed. Constant basting in a moderate to hot oven (190°C/375°F/gas mark 5) is the key factor. It is sensible to remove the front legs and roast only the saddle and rather chunkier thighs.

A detailed and delicious recipe for roast rabbit, which is finished with a mustard glaze, appears on page 64.

Rabbit over the fire: A dab hand at the barbie or campfire, who can keep the meat well basted and the flames low, can do wonderful things to a rabbit. Either a whole rabbit (ideal if your barbecue has a spit attachment) or pieces can be used. Whatever you decide, the meat should be marinated first, for 3-4 hours, in olive oil with chopped wild garlic, or a few crushed garlic cloves, and fresh wild chervil or thyme. Do not use the marinade for basting, though – the oil will drip on to the fire and encourage flames which will burn rather than grill the meat. A better basting liquid is a strong, well-reduced stock (ideally of the rabbit head and trimmings) with a splash of wine and a good dollop of mustard stirred into it. Make sure your grilling rack is a reasonable height above the hot charcoal; the rabbit must cook right through without being scorched on the outside.

Rabbit offal salad: The trio of fresh rabbit offal, comprising heart, liver and kidneys, should not be wasted. Rinse all the items well, and trim the liver of any discoloured (yellowy brown) parts. Fry a little chopped bacon or pancetta, and when it is nearly ready, throw the offal in the pan. Sauté for just a few minutes, until nicely browned. Scatter the offal and bacon over a lightly dressed salad of bitter leaves – rocket, watercress and dandelion (or chicory).

HARE

The hare is a very different beast from the rabbit, which it superficially resembles: cleverer, rarer, more shy, much faster, and even more delicious to eat.

The hunting of hares by almost any method is becoming controversial. Some conservationists maintain that hares are in great decline, and should be protected. Many farmers, on the other hand, claim to be overrun with hares, and argue that without their annual hare shoots (which can bag several hundred hares at a time) they would have a serious hare problem. The truth is that both parties probably have a point: the distribution of hares in this country is very uneven. In Devon and Cornwall I never see many hares, but in Gloucestershire

and Wiltshire I have sometimes seen upwards of 50 on a short stroll. The Countryside Commission is monitoring the hare situation, but at present, 'is not concerned about overall hare numbers'.

Hares are not strictly classed as game, and do not benefit from a close season as such. But they do enjoy partial protection, in that it is not permitted to 'offer a hare for sale' from the end of March to the beginning of August. This is the time when hares are rearing their young, and given the concern that has been expressed about hare numbers in some areas, I think it is appropriate that hares should be considered off-limits during these months.

Note that there are two kinds of hare to be found in the British Isles. The brown hare, the larger of the two, is widespread throughout the country, and the only one you are likely to encounter in the south. The blue or mountain hare is common only in Scotland, where it greatly outnumbers the brown hare. The blue hare is rather skinny, and though it is fair eating it tends to be tough. The brown hare, on the other hand, is quite one of the most delicious wild creatures you could ever hope to eat.

Acquiring

Coursing: The most controversial way to pursue hares is coursing, in which greyhounds or lurchers, or other dogs built for speed, are set in pursuit of the animals. Many people regard this as cruel, but in the right circumstances I don't think it is necessarily so. One man and one dog (or sometimes two) in pursuit of a hare seems to me like a sporting hunt. The hare will often escape, and if it doesn't, it will be swiftly killed. Far more questionable is the practice of netting hares, keeping them alive, and transporting them for coursing competitions, where the main object of the exercise is not sport, or getting a hare for the pot, but gambling on the performance of the dogs.

Hares are undoubtedly beautiful creatures, and most landowners like to see a few of them on their land. Ironically, in a twist on the old poacher-turned-gamekeeper scenario, some professional hare-catchers have turned their skills to capturing live hares for restocking depleted estates.

Netting: Chris Green, one of the wiliest, and also one of the most amiable countrymen I have ever met, demonstrated on the programme the old poacher's art of long-netting – often used to catch rabbits as well as hares. I had no idea if we were going to get one, and had we not, I think we might have been in trouble: hedgerow herb dumplings on their own would have made a disappointing climactic meal to the first episode of the second series.

For more information about coursing and long-netting, contact the British Field Sports Society, The Old Town Hall, 367 Kennington Road, London SE11 4PT (tel: 0171 582 5432).

Shooting: Hares used to be regularly shot on pheasant shoots, but being such large and fast-running creatures, one can be sure that many more were wounded than were killed. It takes a skilled shot to kill a hare with a shotgun, and the pellet size used for pheasants (usually 6 or 7) is simply not appropriate. These days, if I want to shoot a hare I will set out specifically for that purpose, walking up September stubble or the winter plough, equipped with special cartridges (shot size 4) to do the job properly.

As I mentioned, many keepers now have an annual hare shoot, usually in January or early February. Traditionally the hare shoot is for other keepers and local farmers, rather than the landowner or syndicate, but if you are very friendly with a keeper, he might let you come along.

Buying

The price of hare may vary considerably according to local availability, but they are rarely expensive. At the time of writing, my local London butcher is selling them for £10 a piece — not too bad when you consider that a large specimen will feed 6 greedy people. You may get a much better price from a game dealer, and better still from a gamekeeper (you should get them for a knock-down price from a keeper just after his hare shoot).

Many butchers keep hare in the freezer. Like most game, whose meat is always close-textured, it freezes reasonably well, and a defrosted hare would make a good casserole if very slowly cooked. But fresh is preferable, and essential if you are roasting. A good butcher who deals regularly in game should be able to give you a fresh hare, well-hung, skinned and jointed, with the collected blood in a plastic tub.

Preparation

Skinning and gutting: Hares should always be hung for at least 4 days to help develop the flavour and tenderize the meat. In unusually warm weather, try to find a cool place such as a cellar. In cold weather, you can hang a hare for up to 10 days if you like it really gamy. Hares are usually hung head down with the guts still in. This makes the job of gutting them a rather smelly one — and one which I prefer to do out of doors. In many hare recipes you will be wanting to use the blood. This collects in the chest cavity while the hare is hanging, and can be emptied into a bowl when the hare is gutted. If your hare is dripping blood from the mouth when you hang it (its lungs may have been punctured by shot), put a plastic bag over its head, secured with a rubber band, to catch the blood.

Hares are often skinned before being gutted, and this is the method I prefer. The technique is as for rabbits — with the proviso that with your first cut (across the belly of the animal) you should take care to release a flap of skin without piercing the membrane that holds in the stomach contents. When the animal has been skinned, it is then a relatively simple matter to slit this membrane, while holding the hare head down over a lined dustbin, and release the intestines and stomach contents into the bin. The heart, lungs and liver will remain in the chest cavity, along with a considerable quantity of blood. It is therefore best to remove them over a bowl or bucket, in which you can collect the blood. Once you have saved as much blood as you can from these organs they can be discarded — unless you have a young hare which has not been hung too long, in which case the liver will be mild enough to add, finely chopped, to your sauce, or fry up to eat on toast.

The skinned and gutted hare should not be washed, but should be picked over for bits of fur sticking to the meat and wiped with a damp cloth. It can then be jointed (if required for your recipe) as for a rabbit — except that the back legs of the hare can each be divided (with a meat cleaver) into 2 portions, and the saddle into 4 or 5. Covered, the meat can be stored for a day or two in the fridge.

Cooking

Roasting: It is customary to roast only the saddle (i.e. the body) of a hare, removing the legs and casseroling them separately (or they can be used in the game pie recipe, see page 60). However, if you have many mouths to feed, the back legs (which have plenty of meat on) can be left on for roasting. The saddle alone will serve only 4 at most. Keep the back legs on and it should serve 6.

Provided they have been well hung, all but the most ancient of hares can be roasted. However, like rabbits, they must be well protected from drying out. Besides basting during cooking, 24 hours in a marinade (olive oil, red wine, bay leaf and sliced onions) beforehand will help to ensure the meat is tender and moist. The hare should be thoroughly wiped free of the marinade, then lightly rubbed with olive oil before roasting. Another trick is to line the inside of the hare with a few rashers of streaky bacon, and place it upside down for the first half of the cooking time. Remove the bacon half-way through the cooking, then deglaze the pan with the strained marinade and a little stock or water and use these juices to baste the hare, now right side up, for the rest of the cooking time. Roast hare can be served just a tiny bit pink, which it should be after 35-40 minutes in a fairly hot oven (200°C/400°F/gas mark 6).

Gravy for roast hare: It is easiest to make the blood gravy in a separate pan. The juices in the roasting tin – thinned with water or stock if they have boiled very dry – should be added slowly and by degrees to the blood, which you have warmed just a little in a small saucepan. Stir constantly, over a low heat, to emulsify this sauce. Add also a little of the excellent red wine that you are proposing to drink with the hare, and I teaspoon of redcurrant jelly. Heat the sauce right through, but do not allow it to boil. Taste and season if necessary with salt and freshly ground black pepper, then pour into a warmed sauceboat and serve.

Open fire: A young hare, jointed and marinated, cooks very nicely out of doors, on a rack over the hot coals of a fire, or on a conventional barbecue. The adept outdoor cook might wish to improvise a spit and roast the hare whole.

Slow cooking: See the recipe for jugged hare (page 58), one of the finest of English game dishes.

GREY SQUIRRELS

As I have said, the squirrel-cooking sequence in the New Forest provoked some hostile reactions among squirrel lovers. In one local Hampshire newspaper, a headline ran: 'Fury as TV Chef Cooks Tufty'. A woman from a local animal hospice was quoted complaining about what a bad example this set to children (as if fish fingers or sausages set a good example) and ended up by saying, 'Anyone who kills a squirrel

should be forced to eat one!' Well, I'd go along with that – although maybe 'forced' is a bit strong!

Unfortunately, so unrecognized is the squirrel as food, that it comes under very little control. And in areas where it has run amok, threatening whole plantations of young trees, people have resorted to poisoning with warfarin – another slow and unpleasant method of pest control which, like myxomatosis in rabbits, renders their meat quite inedible. I wonder if the woman quoted in the newspaper realized that the Forestry Comission has, for some time now, been poisoning hundreds of New Forest squirrels every year.

Clearly it is no more cruel or uncivilized to kill and eat a squirrel than a rabbit. The plus is that the meat is, if anything, even better than rabbit. I know one chef who occasionally, and mischievously, puts squirrel on the menu of his New Forest restaurant as 'flightless partridge', and in gastronomic terms the comparison with that delicious bird is a valid one.

The squirrels of interest to the wild cook are, of course, grey squirrels. Red squirrels are a rare and protected species, and anyway too small to be worthwhile as food.

Acquiring

Squirrels can be taken at any time when they are not hibernating, but are not really worthwhile eating in the spring and early summer, when they are fairly scrawny and busy feeding their young. They get plumper and tastier as they fatten up on fruits, nuts and berries in the autumn, and are at their best in early winter, just before hibernation.

IMPORTANT NOTE: Anyone taking squirrels should make sure that nobody in the vicinity is using poison.

Trapping: Trapping squirrels, which is what I did in the New Forest with the help of ranger Grahame Wilson, can be very effective, and has the advantage of providing meat that is not full of lead shot. Squirrel traps, baited with birdseed or nuts, catch the animals alive without injuring them. They must be used conscientiously: traps should be checked every morning and evening. Never set or bait a squirrel trap that you cannot check within 24 hours.

Squirrels can scratch and bite something rotten, so taking one out of a trap has to be done with care. The best method is to hold a coarse sack over the entrance to the trap, release the gate, and shake the squirrel into the sack. Locate the squirrel in the sack, hold it firmly, and dispatch it with a single blow on the back of the head (with a stout stick).

Squirrel traps, and information on how to use them, are available from Killgerm (tel: 01924 277631).

Shooting: Squirrels can easily be shot with a shotgun, but always aim for the head, or at least the front end. Apart from being the best way to make a clean kill, it will help to minimize the amount of lead shot in the back legs, which is where the worthwhile meat is.

Air rifles can also be effective. You can often get fairly close to a grey squirrel, especially if they are not often shot at: they tend to think they are pretty safe once they are up a tree. Always aim for the head or heart, not the belly, where you are likely to wound without killing it.

Gamekeepers are likely to be sympathetic to requests to shoot or trap squirrels on their land: they are, in the spring, voracious egg-eaters, both of song and game birds. But be aware that some people won't like you killing squirrels, and be correspondingly discreet in your pursuit.

Buying

I have never seen squirrel on sale in any butcher, which I think is a shame, given its excellent eating quality. If you can't or don't want to trap or shoot squirrels yourself, but are interested in cooking with them, try contacting a local gamekeeper or forest ranger. If you can't find a supply locally, squirrel meat is available by mail order from The Game Larder (tel: 0181 391 9000).

Preparation

Skinning and paunching: Like rabbits, squirrels should be paunched (gutted) as soon as possible after killing. They can then be hung, for up to 4 days in cool weather, though this isn't really necessary, especially with younger animals. Skinning is as for a rabbit, except harder! Older, larger squirrels can be particularly tough to skin.

Jointing: All the good meat on a squirrel is on the back legs, or 'haunches'. The best way to joint them therefore is to cut skinned squirrel pretty much in half, just above the back legs. The two haunches, still joined together, make a perfect one-person portion. Or they can be separated to make smaller portions for a casserole. The front half – head, neck, shoulders and forelegs – can be discarded, but is certainly worth keeping for stock:

roast the pieces briefly before putting in a stock pot with vegetables and herbs.

Cooking

First you need to decide whether your squirrel is young or old. Size is the best indication, but apart from being larger, older squirrels are likely to have harder, more ragged claws and longer, more worn teeth.

Frying and grilling: Young squirrels (ideally killed in the autumn of their first year) are particularly tender and delicious, and haunches of them can be simply sautéed or grilled. In the programme, I had two young haunches from our trapped squirrels and marinated them with elderberry wine (more like port in character) and a little olive oil, before cooking them over wood on the Gastrowagon's front-mounted jerrycan barbecue. They were, even though I say so myself, sensationally good.

Stewing and casseroling: Older squirrels could still be given the marinade-and-grill-or-barbecue treatment, but will be a little chewier. They are also ideal for slower cooking, and could be substituted in any casserole recipe for pheasant, partridge or rabbit. (See suggestions for casseroling rabbit on page 49.) One set of haunches approximately equals a partridge (and serves one); two or three will substitute for a pheasant or a rabbit.

A particularly fine recipe, for squirrel (or rabbit), appears on page 61.

WOOD PIGEONS

Perhaps the hardest-exercising of all the birds that are commonly killed for food, the pigeon is a little powerhouse of feather and muscle: fast-flying, hard to kill and absolutely delicious to eat. I am more pleased when I have shot a pigeon than almost any other bird – and more pleased to eat one, too..

Shooting

As I suggested for rabbits above, your best bet for some good pigeon shooting is to get permission from a friendly landowner to come and shoot pigeons on his land. You can bag a few pigeons by walking up the edge of a wood, or through it, and shooting them as they fly off at your approach. But by far the most effective techniques are decoying, where you wait for pigeons in a hide constructed next to the field in which they are feeding, with decoys to lure them in; and evening flighting, where you wait inside the edge of a wood for pigeons coming in to roost.

Both these techniques require good shooting skills and some understanding of pigeon behaviour, flight paths, etc., but skilled practitioners can achieve huge bags. The late Archie Coates, one of the greatest countrymen of his generation, became a professional pigeon shooter, and was even paid a retainer by several landowners to keep the birds off their crops. He once shot 550 in a day – a world record. His wife Prue must have cooked more pigeons than anybody else alive: I have, with her kind permission, included a couple of her excellent pigeon recipes later in this chapter.

As I said, pigeon meat is truly excellent. You may never shoot 500, or even 50, in a day, but if ever you do get a lot more than you want for your own consumption, try and give them away to anyone who you think will appreciate them: alternatively, make a very large batch of Prue's wonderful smoked pigeon pâté (see page 63), which freezes extremely well.

Sniping

The air rifle (see page 46) is a very sporting weapon with which to try and nab a pigeon or two. You have to get very close (not more than 30 yards), and you have to shoot very straight! Some air rifle enthusiasts actually climb a tree in a wood, and sit on a branch waiting for the pigeons to come in to roost. If you want to do this, don't be reckless and attempt to shin up into the canopy by free climbing and then descend in the dark. Find a good tree in broad daylight, and throw up a rope, or better still, a rope ladder, to make your climb a safe one. Go up, and find a good comfortable sitting and shooting position. And when you go back in the evening, don't change your mind about which tree to climb and where in it to sit!

If shooting pigeons with an air rifle, and the bird is facing you front-on, aim either for the top of the breast, or for the head; if the bird is side-on or has its back to you, always go for a head shot. The back and wing feathers are almost impenetrable to an airgun pellet, and you may surprise a few pigeons, but you won't kill many. A good head shot will kill the bird instantly, and a miss is likely to be a clean one.

Buying

If you can't shoot your own pigeons, you will almost certainly have to pay for them. You may be able to buy direct from a gamekeeper or farmer, if you are in touch with one who regularly shoots pigeons. Otherwise buy from a game dealer or butcher. Pigeons will certainly be cheaper if they are still feathered and undrawn rather than 'oven-ready', and since you will often be using just the breasts (see below) cut off the bone, you should take them feathered when you can. But even oven-ready pigeons should be cheap, and if you are using whole birds in your recipe you will certainly save some plucking aggravation if you buy them in this form.

Preparation

If you have shot some pigeons, or acquired freshly killed birds from a keeper or dealer, they can be cooked straight away, and should certainly not be hung for more than 4 days. If it's hot, don't hang them at all. Either pluck and draw them, put the whole birds in the fridge, and use within 2 days. Or just cut out the breasts.

This is easy, but should be done with care so as not to waste meat. Pluck away a few feathers on the breastbone, then, using a very sharp knife, slit the skin along the breastbone. Slip your fingers between the skin and the breast muscle, and pull back skin and attached feathers to expose the raw meat. Cut the breasts as close as possible to the breastbone, by slicing the meat away from the bone with the tip of the knife; cut right back behind the wing, so as to waste as little as possible. The breasts can then be wrapped in clingfilm (or, if you suspect they are old birds, placed in a simple marinade of olive oil and sliced onions) and kept in the fridge until needed, but not for more than a couple of days.

It is a shame to waste the carcasses of de-breasted birds, as they make excellent stock. You don't have to pluck the whole bird either. Once you have removed the breasts, simply take the flaps of skin, and skin the bird, turning it inside out. You can clip off the wings, feet and neck with a stout pair of kichen scissors. Then draw the guts and crop contents from the birds, and roast the carcasses for 8-10 minutes in a hot oven. Put in a stock pot with onions, carrots, celery, leek tops, bay leaf, etc., and simmer gently for a couple of hours. This stock can be used as the liquid for a pigeon pie or casserole or, strained through muslin or a cloth and supplemented with a good slosh of wine, it can be reduced right down, to make a sauce for the pan-fried breasts.

Ageing

Before you decide whether or not to de-breast your pigeons, and how you are going to cook them, it is useful to know whether you have old or young birds on your hands. Young pigeons are more tender and can be roasted whole, or the breasts cooked fast and served pink. Older birds are more suitable for pies and casseroles.

It is not easy to be sure of a pigeon's age unless you encounter the bird before it is plucked and drawn – which of course you will if you have killed it yourself. A flexible beak, a thick neck and a supple, pliable breastbone are all signs of a young bird. You may also perceive the 'flush of youth' in the fine colour of its feathers.

If the bird is 'oven-ready', from a butcher or game dealer, you still have a bit to go on; try pressing gently to see if the breastbone is supple. Does the skin look slightly rosy, as if it is stretched from beneath by a plump and youthful breast? Or is it whitish-grey, slightly wrinkled, contracting over a hard, prominent breastbone and tough, dark meat? Experience will sharpen your response to these factors, and in time you will be able to tell a youngster even through the clinging cellophane of its supermarket wrapping.

Cooking

Roasting and grilling: When you have identified a young pigeon, it can be roasted whole, with a strip of bacon over the breast, or, if you like the meat very rare, griddled whole on a cast-iron griddle.

Griddling or pan-frying the breasts: The breasts of young pigeons are dense and rich, but tender: they can be cooked fast and served pink, either on a dry cast-iron griddle (in which case brush the breasts with a little olive oil) or in a lightly oiled frying pan. Cook for 5-6 minutes, turning frequently, for breasts still just pink in the middle. Alternatively, the breasts can be 'butterflied' – slit almost in half with a knife, then flattened like little minute steaks. Just a minute on either side is then sufficient.

Breasts cooked like this are particularly delicious when served on top of a simple green salad (see illustration, page 42), perhaps dressed with walnut oil, elderberry (or balsamic) vinegar, and sprinkled with a few lardons of pancetta or bacon, and toasted walnuts. One breast, still just a little pink and bloody, cut into 4-5 slices, is a decent first course portion per person, though it would take 2 to make a really satisfying main course.

Casseroles and stews: Older pigeons, and indeed birds whose age is in doubt, should be braised or casseroled. The meat is so rich it can be thought of almost as beef, and recipes for stews and daubes adapted accordingly. Pigeons can be casseroled whole, then cut in half to make 2 portions, though very hungry pigeon fans might want a whole one. Alternatively, you can make a breast only stew, using a stock made from the roast carcasses of the birds to provide the cooking liquid (see above). Cooking for 1 ½ hours, in a slow to moderate oven (160°C/325°F/gas mark 3), with wine, and stock vegetables as well as the stock, will do the trick.

See also Prue Coates's Smoked Pigeon Pâté (page 63) and Up a Tree Pie, (page 60).

ROOKS

In many areas of rural Britain, particularly Somerset, South Wales, and the north-west, young rooks have long been rated as food. At one time they were so popular that poor country folk, who could not afford to own a gun, would shin up the trees in the rookery to remove the young 'branchers' just before they were ready to fly the nest. It was this tradition that I sought to recreate in a Lancashire rookery in the last sequence of the series. Unlike the rookers of bygone days, I was all tackled up with ropes, under the safe guidance of professional tree-climber Wally Smith. Even so, to be perched on the spindle-thin branches at the top of the rookery, swaying yards at a time in the stiff breeze, was both exhilarating and mildly terrifying. And the view over the whole chattering rookery, and out over Lancashire hills and hedgerows in the yellow-green colours of spring, was unforgettable. I got my rooks too, though not before they'd given me a run for my money, hopping about the branches just out of reach of my one free hand.

Hardly anybody climbs rookeries any more, except professionals like Wally who occasionally do it as a means of pest control. But the tradition of culling the young branchers in mid-May, as they start to leave the nest, has not entirely vanished. In Victorian times, this used to be considered a suitable sport for boys and young ladies, who would traditionally gather on the 12th of May, with their specially made rook rifles, for a little genteel sport. Today it's more likely to be done by a farmer or gamekeeper with a shotgun or .22 rifle.

Acquiring

Climbing a rookery: I can't recommend climbing a rookery without professional guidance, unless you are an expert climber yourself. But if ever you do happen to climb for young rooks, be sure to take a small backpack or drawstring bag with you. You can put the branchers in it alive, and they will stay nice and quiet until you can climb down and dispatch them quickly with a knock on the head.

Shooting branchers: If you know anybody with a rookery on their land, they may be happy for you to attempt to reduce the local rook population somewhat – they may even be grateful for an introduction to the pleasures of rook meat.

Exactly when the young rooks emerge from their nests, and wander up a branch to stretch their unused wings (hence the name branchers), will depend partly on what kind of a spring it has been. In the north it usually happens about a week or so later than in the south. But the second week in May is about the right time to start looking out for them, and they have usually all flown by the end of the month.

It's pretty easy to shoot branchers with a shotgun: apart from the odd practice swoop, they don't fly much – certainly not very fast or far. The down side is that you are likely to have a lot of lead shot in what is a rather small portion of meat. More sporting, and less damaging, is some kind of rifle, though to own anything more powerful than an air rifle you need a licence (and they are harder and harder to come by).

Young rooks do make a very challenging target for an air rifle, especially since you will probably have to allow for the swaying of the trees in the breeze.

Buying

Rooks are not available on the market, and unless you know a farmer, gamekeeper or landowner who regularly culls his own May branchers (or can be persuaded to do so) you will have to shoot them yourself.

Preparation

Apart from their tender little breasts, young rooks have very little meat on them, and they are really not worth the trouble of plucking, drawing and serving whole. However, if you really want to make the most of your rooks, it is worth saving the carcasses for stock: the process is as described for pigeons above (see page 54). This will give you a good stock to add to your rook pie, or it can be strained and reduced right down, with a good slosh of wine, to make a sauce to go with sautéd rook breasts.

Cooking

Pieing and frying: Rooks are traditionally made into a pie, and the recipe on page 60 for Up a Tree pie is a particularly satisfying one. But young rooks' breasts are delicate and tender things, and really don't need such long cooking as they get in a pie. For the series I devised a recipe of pan-fried rook breasts, served fairly pink, on a salad of hedge garlic and dandelion, dressed with the juices from the pan, deglazed with elderberry wine. I thought it was delicious, but the Lancashire farmers with whom I shared it were a bit sceptical of my trendy southern ways. Another delicious preparation for pan-fried breasts is to serve them with creamy mash, lightly steamed cabbage, and the reduced stock and wine gravy I describe above.

Barbecue and grill: Rook breasts are also good grilled or barbecued: first 'butterfly' the breasts by cutting almost in half then unfolding the breast (effectively halving the thickness and doubling the surface area). Marinate for a few hours with a light coating of olive oil, a few onion slices and freshly ground black pepper, then cook on a cast-iron griddle or over a barbecue for just a couple of minutes each side. I like these 'rook steaks' in a sandwich or bap, burger style, with fried onions and mustard!

SNAILS

No guns, nets or traps are required in the pursuit of this quarry – and I doubt that anyone has ever been prosecuted for snail poaching. But I wanted to mention snails here, because they are one of the greatest unsung land-based freebies available to everyone.

Unfortunately we are, as a nation, curiously prejudiced against snails as food – perhaps because they have come to symbolize our xenophobia against the French. Yet we don't seem to have any problems devouring sea snails by the ton: we eat a lot of whelks in this country – more, apparently, than the French. Well, snails are a whole lot easier to find than whelks, wherever you live. So why not give them a whirl?

All English snails are edible, but there are two species of particular interest to the forager gourmet. Largest, and rarest, is the so-called Roman snail, *Helix pomatia*, which was indeed introduced by the Romans as a food. These are relatively rare, but occasionally locally prolific. Although they are a classic eating snail, I do not like to kill them myself: it is such a rare pleasure to find them, and the alternative, which is just as good, is so commonplace.

My only snail quarry, therefore, is the common (or garden) snail, *Helix aspersa*, which is what the French call *petit gris*. In case you did not realize, this is the plain old regular snail, the one you squash on your garden path on a rainy night. They are not quite as impressive, size-wise, as the Romans, but the flavour is just as good, or better, and they provide a fine and tasty morsel of meat.

Gathering

As snail enthusiast Anthony Vaughan and I proved in the final London-based episode of the first series, most average-sized suburban gardens that are not mercilessly sprayed with pesticides probably have enough snails in them to make a nice starter for 2. And if you take to the hedgerow, you can find enough for a feast.

Snails hibernate, and there is not much point in looking for them until after the first spell of mild weather in March, when the young shoots that they feed on start to come up. Thereafter, snails can be gathered at any time but by far the best time to look for them is on a warm or mild day after (or during) rain.

I used to collect snails regularly as a child (for racing rather than eating), and my proven technique was to tread down the grass growing against the Cotswold dry stone walls near where I lived. They can also be found at the base of trees, underneath large leaves (such as hogweed), and, once you get the hang of it, just about anywhere that 'looks likely'.

In the garden they can be found attached to any obstacle that provides them with shelter: flower-pots, bits of wood, old house bricks. Based on these habits, another good way to collect snails is to encourage them to stay in your garden by providing them with the kind of shelter that will attract them: an empty bucket, or half a rubber tyre discarded in the long grass at the bottom of the garden.

Snail husbandry

Snails cannot be eaten as soon as found. They need to be purged, to rid them of any unclean (or unpleasant-tasting) matter in their gut. The best way to do this is to feed them on a one-item purgative diet: carrot shavings, or lettuces, are the usual fodder. This means keeping them in a cool, well-ventilated container, with space to move. I use a large plastic washing-up bowl with fine meshed chicken-wire stretched over the top. The best preparation is five days on the purgative diet, then 48 hours total starvation: this final phase clears out the gut and reduces the sliminess of the snails. If, however, you are in a hurry to eat your snails, you could give them 3 days of the purgative diet and skip the starvation.

Cooking

Once they have been purged, there are 2 basic ways to prepare snails, before finishing them in the sauce of your choice. These are more a matter of presentation than anything else.

The French way: The French usually remove cooked *petits gris* from their shells and finish them in some sauce, discarding the shells (the snails they serve in the shell are the larger Roman snails). The initial process is therefore simply to shake the snails in a bowl or sieve until they all retract into their shells, then throw them into a pan of well-salted rapidly boiling water (which may be flavoured with a few stock vegetables and a splash of vinegar). After coming back to the boil, they are simmered for just 10 minutes, then drained. When cool enough to handle, the meat is removed with a pin and a twist of the wrist (there is a knack to getting them out whole and unbroken, but you'll soon pick it up).

The Spanish way: The Spanish like to serve their snails still attached to the shell, but with the body of the snail outside the shell. This is achieved by putting the snails in a pan of unsalted cold fresh water so that they all come out of their shells. The water is then placed over a very gentle heat, so that the snails 'drop off', remaining out of their shells. The water is then salted, brought to the boil, and the snails are simmered, again for 10 minutes.

Snails prepared in either manner can then be finished in a number of ways (in all cases, allow at least a dozen snails per person).

Mussel style: Finely chop 2 cloves of garlic, and fry gently in a pan with 55g/2oz butter. Add ½ a glass of wine and a tablespoon of chopped parsley, and bring to a fierce bubble. Throw in the pre-coated snails (Spanish or French style) and allow to bubble for just a minute. Serve in warmed bowls with French bread.

Gratin: As above, without the wine, and using French style, shell-less snails. Then pile the garlicky, buttery snails into ramekins, top with breadcrumbs, and brown under the grill.

With mushrooms, on toast: Sauté some wild mushrooms (parasols, inkcaps, or fresh ceps) in garlic butter or garlic and very good olive oil. Throw in the snails. Serve on toast rubbed with more garlic.

Risotto: Add shell-less, French style snails, sautéd in butter, garlic and a little wine, to a wild mushroom risotto (see page 183) a couple of minutes before the rice is done.

For one of the best of all snail recipes, a sophisticated number practically dripping with Michelin stars, see page 182 of the mushroom chapter.

JUGGED HARE

If I had to choose a single recipe from the two series as my 'desert island dish' it would have to be this jugged hare, with herb dumplings, which I cooked for long-netter Chris Green on the Bain Marie.

I didn't have any stock vegetables, bacon or chocolate on board, and the stew turned out very nicely without them, but I would always add them given the choice.

SERVES 8–10

I large brown hare, skinned, plus its
   blood (liver optional)
115g/4oz good streaky bacon (optional, but
   advisable)
2 tablespoons olive oil
I small onion or 3 shallots, peeled and
   sliced
I large carrot, peeled and sliced
I rounded tablespoon plain flour
30g/Ioz butter

½ bottle good (aged) elderberry wine (or
   full-bodied red wine such as Merlot or
   Cabernet Sauvignon)
a few sprigs of thyme
a few sprigs of wild chervil (or parsley)
2 bay leaves
salt and freshly ground black pepper
2 squares of bitter chocolate

For the hedgerow herb dumplings, see page 33.

• Joint the hare with a heavy knife or meat cleaver, cutting off its legs and dividing the saddle into 5-6 pieces.

• Start to prepare the dish at least 3 hours before you intend to eat it. Chop the bacon into 1cm/½ inch pieces and sweat for a few minutes in half the oil in a large frying pan.

• Add the onion and carrot, and cook for a further few minutes. Transfer the bacon and vegetables to a large heavy casserole (in which the hare will also be cooked).

• Put the frying pan back on the heat and add the butter and the rest of the oil. Turn the pieces of hare in the flour, then add to the pan. Fry the hare, turning the pieces occasionally until they are nicely browned. Transfer the meat to the casserole.

• Pour over the wine, and just enough water to barely cover the meat. Add the herbs, tied in a bundle, season with salt and pepper, and bring the pan to a gentle simmer. Cover and cook over a gentle heat, or in a slow oven (140°C/300°F/gas mark 2) for 2-3 hours. The hare is cooked when the meat is quite tender and begins to come away from the bone.

• The next stage is to make a liaison of the blood, the liver and the cooking liquid. This has to be done carefully if the sauce is not to separate, but even if it does it is only the appearance, not the flavour, that is affected. Remove the pieces of hare from the pot to a warmed dish. Strain the stock through a sieve to remove the vegetables, then return it to the pan, over a low heat.

• Have the blood ready in a small basin. Spoon a little of the cooking liquid into the blood to both warm and thin it, and stir well. Add the chopped liver (optional) and grated chocolate to the pot. Then ladle in the warmed blood, a little at a time, stirring as you go. When the liaison is smooth and well blended, return to the heat and bring back to the boil. Return the pieces of hare to the pot and bring back to a gentle simmer.

• Add the dumplings to the pot – they can just sit on top of the meat. Cover the pot and leave the dumplings to steam gently for 20 minutes. Then serve the stew at once.

PAPARDELLE ALLA LEPRE

In this classic Italian version of jugged hare, the meat is taken off the bone and the sauce is much reduced, then recombined with the meat and served with fresh pasta strips, like extra wide tagliatelle, called 'papardelle'. (See illustration on page 59.)

- Follow the above recipe, omitting the flour, but browning the hare pieces without it, until you get to the end of stage 6. (You may cook the hare for rather longer than 2 hours – the meat should come easily off the bone)

- After removing the meat from the sauce, but before the liaison with the blood, strain the sauce first through a sieve, then through muslin or a cotton cloth. Add the rest of your bottle of wine (which could be a nice Barolo instead of the elderberry), then boil the sauce hard to reduce it to just 200 ml/ 7fl oz.

- Check for seasoning and adjust as necessary. Then add the chocolate, and perform the liaison with the blood, as above. The idea is to produce a rich, dark, intense sauce.

- When the meat is cool enough to handle, take all of it off the bones, picking off and discarding bits of membrane and gristle, and breaking the good clean bits into small neat pieces. Add the clean meat to the sauce, and heat through until just bubbling. Serve with strips of fresh sheet pasta (ideally home-made) or white tagliatelle.

UP A TREE PIE

This is a fairly straightforward recipe for a game pie, with the novel twist that some of the meat is chicken: not feathered, but fungal – that is to say, the very fine and meaty yellow bracket fungus known as chicken of the woods.

When I made it in the Norfolk programme, and served it up to both a poacher and a gamekeeper, it had the added satisfaction that even the wine in it came from up a tree – it was the witch's oak-leaf wine from Wales.

You could easily substitute other game, such as pheasant or rabbit, for the rooks. The quantity below makes a 30cm/10 inch pie, to serve 6.

FOR THE SHORTCRUST PASTRY
250g/9oz butter or lard, cut into small pieces
500g/1lb plain flour
a pinch of salt
iced water
1 egg yolk, beaten, to glaze

FOR THE FILLING
3 wood pigeons, breasts only
3 rooks, breasts only
salt and freshly ground black pepper

30g/1oz plain flour
2 tablespoons dripping or oil
1 medium onion, sliced
500g/1lb chicken of the woods (or other
    wild mushrooms)
300ml/½ pint strong reduced stock (made
    from bird carcasses)
½ glass oak-leaf wine (or other dry white wine)
a bouquet garni of wild or bought fresh herbs,
    e.g. chives, chervil, bay leaves, parsley,
    thyme

- First make the pastry. Rub the fat well into the flour until you have the texture of fine breadcrumbs. Add the pinch of salt, and just enough cold water (about 1 tablespoon) to bring the pastry together. Knead briefly, cover or wrap in clingfilm, and chill for 1 hour before using.

- To prepare the pie filling, toss the pigeon and rook pieces in the flour seasoned with salt and pepper, shaking off any excess. Heat the dripping or oil in a large saucepan, sauté the sliced onion for a few minutes, then add the meat and mushrooms and turn until all the pieces are well browned. Set aside.

- Roll out the pastry and line a 30cm/10 inch pie dish right to the edges. Fill to the top with the meat and mushrooms and pour over the stock, and add the bouquet garni of herbs. Brush the edges of the pastry with beaten egg yolk and cover the pie with a pastry lid cut to shape, crimping the edges with your fingers to seal.

- Brush the top of the pie with the remaining egg yolk, and bake in a preheated moderate to hot oven (190°C/375°F/gas mark 5) for 45-50 minutes.

Any extra stock can be strained, transferred to a clean pan and boiled, with an extra slosh of wine, until reduced to a good rich gravy to serve with the pies.

SQUIRREL (OR RABBIT) CASSEROLED WITH BACON

This is an excellent way to cook big old rabbits or squirrels, or ones which have been defrosted. To serve 6 generously, use either 2 rabbits, 4 or 5 squirrels, or a combination — 1 rabbit and 2 squirrels.

2 rabbits or 4 squirrels (or a combination), skinned and jointed
8oz/225g streaky bacon or pancetta, cut into thick slices
1 tablespoon dripping or olive oil
2 carrots, sliced
1 large onion, sliced

1 wineglass white wine
300ml/10fl oz stock (made with the heads and trimmings)
1 bay leaf
a small bunch of parsley
1 clove of garlic
salt and freshly ground black pepper

- Choose a pot into which your rabbits or squirrels fit neatly without too much room to spare. Cut the bacon into 2.5cm/1 inch pieces. Heat the oil in a frying pan and fry the bacon or pancetta gently for a few minutes. After it has released plenty of its fat, but before it gets crispy, remove with a slotted spoon and transfer to the pot.

- Brown the pieces of meat on all sides in the sizzling fat, then place in the pot. Add the carrots and onion to the frying pan and fry until they begin to take a little colour. Spoon these into the pot around the meat.

- Add the wine, stock, herbs and garlic to the pot, with 1 teaspoon salt and a few twists of pepper. The liquid should cover the meat almost completely, — add a little more stock or water if you need to.

- Bring to a gentle simmer, cover and cook for 1 ¼ hours. Serve each person with 1 large or 2 smaller pieces of rabbit or squirrel. Spoon the bacon and vegetables, and plenty of juice from the pot, over each portion. Serve with mashed potatoes and either braised celery or Savoy cabbage or winter greens braised for just a few minutes in a ladleful of the juices from the pot.

SLOW-COOKED PIGEONS WITH WILD CHERRIES

Once in a while it's nice to cook a dish with whole pigeons. This is a good dish for any pigeon, but particularly those which may be on the old side, or which have been frozen. I like a whole pigeon to myself, but half a bird may satisfy more meagre appetites.

SERVES 4–6

2 tablespoons bacon fat or olive oil

4 whole oven-ready pigeons

4 shallots or 1 medium onion, thinly sliced

1 rounded tablespoon plain flour

a bouquet garni

1.1 litres/2 pints stock (rabbit, pigeon or chicken)

2 teaspoons red or white wine vinegar

1 teaspoon redcurrant jelly

salt and freshly ground black pepper

225g/8oz wild (or bought) cherries

30g/1oz butter

• Heat the fat or oil in a large casserole and brown the pigeons well on all sides. Remove the pigeons and split in half down the breastbone with a heavy knife. From each half trim the wings and the backbone with a heavy knife.

• Add the shallots or onion to the fat in the casserole and fry until soft and lightly coloured. Sprinkle in the flour, stir well and cook for 1-2 minutes.

• Return the half pigeons to the casserole, packing them in closely, add the bouquet garni and pour over enough stock to cover them completely. Cover the casserole and simmer gently over a low heat, or in a slow to moderate oven (150°C/300°F/gas mark 2) for 1½ hours.

• Test with a skewer that the meat is tender (very old birds may need a further 30 minutes). Remove the birds from the casserole and place in a covered dish to keep warm.

• Strain the cooking juices through a sieve into a clean pan and add the vinegar and redcurrant jelly. Boil over a high heat to reduce to a light, syrupy consistency. Season with salt and pepper.

• While the sauce is reducing, sweat the cherries gently in the butter in a small saucepan until the juices start to run – this takes just a few minutes.

• Serve the pigeons on well-warmed plates, pouring plenty of sauce over them, and spooning the cherries on top. I like to serve this dish with warm potato crisps.

PRUE COATES'S SMOKED PIGEON PATE

Prue says, 'This is an all-time favourite and guests frequently ask for the recipe. It is a true example of "sweet and sour". The honey and lemon are just discernible through the rather strong smoky flavour of the pigeon and give it a certain lightness.'

You need a portable smoker for this recipe, but you can easily improvise one with an old biscuit tin (see page 73).

SERVES 6–8

8 pigeon breasts (4 pigeons)
5 rashers streaky bacon, de-rinded
75g/3oz chopped shallots
115g/4oz unsalted butter
75ml/3fl oz vermouth
1 teaspoon runny honey
2 teaspoons lemon juice

1 teaspoon stem ginger juice or dried ground
  ginger
1 tablespoon double cream
¼ teaspoon ground cloves
½ teaspoon mild Dijon mustard
1 pinch of dill weed
salt and freshly ground black pepper

• Sprinkle 1½ tablespoons of sawdust over the bottom of the smoker and put in the grid and drip tray. Place the pigeon breasts on the grid and then lay 3 of the rashers on the top. Slide on the lid and put the smoke box over the methylated spirits container which has been lit. Leave until it has burned out. (If less than 10 minutes, repeat for a longer smoking.)

• Sauté the shallots and remaining bacon in the butter until transparent and transfer to a food processor or liquidizer.

• Cut the pigeon breasts into 2.5cm/1 inch dice and sauté for a few seconds, stirring constantly. Take out and put in a food processor.

• Pour the juices from the drip tray into the sauté pan with the vermouth, honey, lemon juice, ginger juice, cream and the rest of the seasonings. Increase the heat and bubble furiously for a few seconds.

• Process the pigeon, bacon and shallots until really finely ground, then pour in the pan juices and blend until very smooth. Put into a pot or pots, smooth down and cover with melted butter.

• Refrigerate for 2 or 3 days to allow the flavour to develop. Serve at room temperature and not straight out of the fridge. Freezes well.

PAN-ROAST RABBIT ON A BED OF CABBAGE

A roast rabbit that is not tough or dry is quite an achievement. Marinating, then roasting in a pan with wine and juices, and regular basting, is the secret in this recipe. (See illustration on page 59.)

SERVES 6

FOR THE RABBIT
2 young whole oven-ready rabbits
1 carrot, roughly chopped
1 small onion, roughly chopped
1 bay leaf
1 wineglass red wine, plus extra for deglazing
   the roasting tin
4 tablespoons olive oil
2 teaspoons brown sugar
a few sprigs of fresh thyme

1 tablespoon strong mustard (English or
   Dijon)
salt and freshly ground black pepper
30g/1oz plain flour (optional)

FOR THE BED OF CABBAGE
1 large Savoy cabbage
2 tablespoons olive oil
115g/4oz streaky bacon or pancetta, diced
2 cloves of garlic, chopped

• Joint the rabbits. Put the heads, front legs and any giblets or trimmings into a large saucepan with the carrot, onions and bay leaf and barely cover with water. Simmer gently for 1 hour, then strain this stock through muslin or a clean cotton cloth, and reduce by boiling to a scant 300ml/10fl oz.

• Meanwhile mix the wine, 2 tablespoons of the olive oil, sugar and thyme with the mustard and pour this marinade over the rabbit joints in a dish. Turn them in the marinade to make sure they are well coated, and leave for 4-6 hours.

• Heat the rest of the olive oil in a frying pan that will fit in the oven. Remove the rabbit pieces from the marinade, wipe dry, and brown well on all sides in the pan.

• Add 4 tablespoons of the stock to the marinade and mix well, then pour over the rabbit pieces in the pan – this gives you your basting liquid. Place the pan in a preheated fairly hot oven (200°C/400°F/gas mark 6) for 30-35 minutes, basting regularly with the liquid in the pan – every 5 minutes is not excessive. Season the rabbits with salt and pepper about half-way through the cooking time.

• Prepare the cabbage while the rabbit is cooking: wash the leaves and chop into large squares (do not discard the dark green outer leaves: they have the best flavour). Blanch the leaves in well-salted boiling water for 2 minutes, then drain. Heat the olive oil in a large frying pan and fry the bacon until well browned. Throw in the chopped garlic, and just as it takes colour, add the blanched cabbage. Heat through for just a couple of minutes, tossing well to prevent it burning.

- After 30 minutes the rabbits should be well browned and glistening. Pierce the meat with a skewer. If the juices run clear, it is ready. If they are still pink, it needs a few minutes more.

- Make a gravy by deglazing the roasting pan first with a little red wine, then with the remaining stock. Scrape the tin well with a palette knife to remove any tasty morsels of browned meat. I prefer a thin gravy, but you can thicken it with flour if you like. Season to taste with salt and pepper, then strain into a warmed sauceboat.

- Arrange the cabbage on a large warm plate, and arrange the rabbit pieces over the top.

BUNNY A LA RUNNY HONEY

This is wilderness cuisine in its pure form: every single ingredient, bar the salt and pepper, was acquired during the course of the first episode of A Cook on the Wild Side. *I even churned the butter myself. You can of course substitute less wild alternatives (see my suggestions in brackets) — but please don't replace the rabbits with chicken.*

SERVES 6

2 young rabbits, skinned and jointed
a good knob of goats cream butter (or
    regular butter)
a fistful of young hedge garlic (or a clove of
    garlic)

150ml /½ pint nettle beer (see page 163
    – or use bitter)
1 generous tablespoon runny honey
salt and pepper

- Heat the butter in a casserole, and brown the rabbit pieces (fairly gently, so as not to burn the butter).

- Roughly chop the hedge garlic, and throw into the pan.

- Add the nettle beer, honey and salt and pepper, and bring to the boil. Lower the heat to a gentle simmer, put on the lid, and cook for 30-40 minutes until the rabbit is tender. (If you can only get older, tougher rabbits, it may take up to an hour).

- Serve hot, to an appreciative (ex) poacher such as Malcolm McPhee.

FRESHWATER FEAST

If you don't like fishing you can skip this chapter. On second thoughts, please don't. I wouldn't want to exclude anyone, angler or non-angler, who is at all interested in learning more about the culinary possibilities for the vast stock of freshwater fish that we are lucky enough to have in this country. On this topic I need all the allies I can get.

For unfortunately much of the angling fraternity in this country take a pretty dim view of anybody killing and eating their beloved coarse fish – and I use the word dim in both senses. The whole subject of eating coarse fish is racked with hypocrisy and bad feeling. For example, when I cooked and ate a small carp that I had caught in the Thames in the last episode of the first series, there was a rash of hostile letters and articles in the angling press. I was accused of brutality and barbarism. 'Our carp are not for eating!' ran one headline. Why not? Wrapped in foil with a sprig of fennel and a trickle of olive oil, and baked in the bonnet of the Gastrowagon, my carp was absolutely delicious. And whoever wrote that headline has perhaps forgotten that the reason this country is so chock-full of carp, is precisely because it is a good food fish. Reared in ponds all over the country, carp was once a staple fish of the British diet – especially popular among monks (whose monasteries almost always had a dedicated carp pond) for their meat-free Friday lunch.

The problem is not that anglers don't eat fish: I wonder how many fisherman who nodded in agreement with the articles attacking me, or muttered disapprovingly about our programme at their club meetings, then went home to a nice fish supper of haddock and chips. The problem is that they don't eat *their* fish. A lot of anglers are guilty of a kind of fishy racism: it's all right to kill and eat some fish (i.e. the ones they don't fish for), but not others (especially the beloved carp!). As far as I'm concerned, the criteria for whether a fish species is a candidate for the kitchen are simple. Are they tasty? Are there plenty of them (of course I don't want to eat an endangered species), and last but not least, can I catch one? (To which the answer is usually no, but I'll keep on trying!)

Incidentally, I am not necessarily opposed to the strict no-kill policy of many small still-water fisheries managed specifically for the sport of angling. I understand completely that the management want to reserve stocks, and allow the fish to reach a good sporting size. I have enjoyed fishing in such places, and even enjoyed catching and putting back large carp (my best, 14lb 10oz). Besides, most fish from such ponds and lakes are liable to taste pretty muddy (see below).

What I am less happy about is local angling authorities that forbid the killing of any fish taken from their rivers and canals (eels are usually excepted, which is certainly a small consolation). The removal of a few gudgeon, dace or minnows, and the occasional decent pike, is hardly going to decimate the eco-balance in the Thames, Trent or Severn. I am not arguing for the commercial exploitation of our coarse fish stocks (although with the right controls in place I might be prepared to). But surely all fishermen must be aware that the technique of catching fish on a baited hook with rod and line was devised originally as a means of gathering food. All I ask is for the right to line up with the other predators who like a fish supper – the herons, kingfishers, otters and grass snakes, for example – and have a go at taking my share.

Well that's enough fishy politics. Let's get on with the gastronomy.

FISH FROM STILL AND RUNNING WATER

The suitability of coarse fish for eating is not simply a question of species – almost all coarse fish are more or less palatable (the barbel and tench are notable exceptions). Almost more important than what kind of fish it is, is where it came from; and the key question is, was it still or running water? The general principle is that fish from running water will taste 'fresher' and cleaner than fish from lakes, ponds and gravel pits, which may have a tendency to muddiness. I find a hint of earthiness acceptable, almost pleasant (like freshly dug potatoes) but in some waters the muddy taste will be so pronounced as to render the fish unpalatable – I gave up fishing for rainbow trout in a Gloucestershire gravel pit because all but a very few of the fish I caught (the recent arrivals, I suspect) tasted like a mouthful of soil.

In still waters, one can never be sure how bad the muddiness problem is going to be – although it is a pretty fair bet that a carp from a small pond that is not fed by fresh water will be distinctly earthy. Larger lakes, and those that are fed by rivers and streams, will not be so bad. (I have never caught a pike in Loch Lomond, but when I do, I'm sure it will be delicious.) The quality of water in canals, the way they are fed and the flow of the water, varies considerably: some canals have the constitution of a stagnant pond, others of clean and gently flowing rivers, and the taste of the fish that you catch in them will vary accordingly.

But as a general rule, if you are fishing with a view to eating your catch, you're best off fishing in rivers and clean canals. Even then, you can never be sure: an eel taken from the freshest, cleanest, fastest-flowing water may be unpalatably mudddy in flavour, simply because he or she has just arrived in the river after living for several years in some dank muddy ditch. Obviously you can make a rough visual assessment of any water you are fishing in, but the real proof of the pudding will only come with the eating.

The muddy taste of still-water fish can be partially counteracted in the way the fish is prepared (see carp, page 70), but is almost impossible to eradicate altogether. You will just have to hope that trial and error finds you a good fishing spot that produces a regular catch of clean-tasting fish.

POLLUTION

As well as the 'natural' dirtiness of some waters that can affect the taste (but not the safety) of freshwater fish, there is the more worrying question of unnatural dirtiness: i.e. man-made pollution. Our major rivers are not supposed to be polluted any more, and most angling clubs confirm that water quality seems to be improving nationwide. But we have not eradicated the problem altogether. One could take the slightly cavalier attitude that if the pollution hasn't killed the fish then the fish probably won't kill you, but I wouldn't vouch for the scientific soundness of that principle. I certainly wouldn't advocate the eating of fish taken from waters polluted by industrial waste or agricultural chemicals, or caught near heavy sewage outlets. If in any doubt, you should make enquiries locally. And if ever you do become ill from eating a fish you have caught, in lake, canal or river, you should file a report to your local water authority. The chances are someone is putting something in the water they shouldn't.

THE FISH

(see pages 66 and 79 for illustrations)

A NOTE ON ANGLING TECHNIQUES

The following guide to my own favourite edible freshwater fish assumes a basic knowledge of fishing techniques – and doesn't attempt to add greatly to that knowledge either! An exhaustive guide to angling seriously for the dozen or so species listed below could fill a larger book than this – and I am certainly not a good enough angler to write such a volume. What I have done is to outline in brief the accepted wisdom on basic tackle and technique for each species, plus a few little tips of my own. I'll give you the first tip here: for general-purpose bottom fish, which could catch you any number of edible species, legering with a swimfeeder is a good all-round method. Swimfeeders are little plastic capsules which you can fill with maggots: the maggots escape while you are fishing, and thus act as a localized ground bait. Most swimfeeders double as leger weights, so all you need is a swimfeeder, a small swivel to stop it, and your baited hook. A size 16 hook with a double maggot on a 3-pound line is a good all-round end tackle. If you're getting bites but not hooking fish, put on a smaller hook.

Having said that, most beginners prefer float-fishing to legering, and certainly having a float to watch can make fishing more exciting. If you're new to fishing, a reputable tackle shop should furnish you with a good basic kit and a good beginner's guide will acquaint you with all the basic methods. I don't know if it's still in print, but I can't recommend a better starter than *The Ladybird Book of Coarse Fishing* – it is intended for children, but is very clear and informative, and one of the few fishing books that acknowledges that some freshwater fish are good to eat!

BLEAK

The bleak is not a particularly exciting fish for the angler – unless he or she is gastronomicaly minded. Rarely more than an ounce in weight, they are found usually in the slower flowing parts of our larger rivers – but not in Wales, Scotland or Ireland. In warmer weather bleak shoal near the surface, where they feed on small insects – fish will often jump clear of the water in pursuit of flies and midges.

I recently read of a match angler who won a competition by catching over 1,500 bleak in a session, at an average rate of one every 12 seconds. What a feast he could have prepared for his friends, if only he'd known.

Fishing

The lightest possible float tackle is appropriate. Fish a tiny hook (size 20 or smaller) just a foot below the surface, baited with a single maggot. Fly fishing with a light trout rod and tiny dry flies can also be fun – and effective. Once you have located a shoal you can keep it in your 'swim' (the anglers term for the section of water in which you are fishing) by throwing out a handful of floating groundbait or dry breadcrumbs.

Preparation and cooking

Frying: 6 or more bleak make a decent fry-up for one. Descale the fish with your fingers (the scales come off easily) and remove the gills, gut, wash and pat dry. Then toss in seasoned flour, or dip in egg and coat in breadcrumbs, and deep or shallow fry. Include with gudgeon in a small fry fry-up with red pepper ketchup (see page 86).

Grilling: Brush the fish with oil, season with rock salt and freshly ground black pepper, and grill like sprats – 2 minutes each side under a very hot grill.

CARP

Originally from central Asia, most of the species of carp found in British waters were probably introduced by the Romans, who certainly appreciated the carp as food. There are several different species of carp regularly taken by anglers, including the common, leather, mirror, crucian, koi, golden and ghost. There are also innumerable hybrids, since most species happily interbreed. All are edible, but the common, leather and mirror (and the hybrids closest to them) are the best eating. Best of all are the true common carp – relatively small fish which are found only in waters where no other type of carp has been introduced.

Carp have now colonized, or been introduced to, waters all over Britain. Many still waters are now managed specifically with the carp angler in mind – which means you will probably not be allowed to kill any carp that you catch. However, carp can also be caught in canals, and in the stiller, deeper parts of our larger rivers – and these are likely to be less muddy-tasting than pond carp anyway.

Fishing

Bottom fishing, with a float or leger, with almost any bait, but especially luncheon meat or sweetcorn, will always put you in with a chance of catching a carp – but they are shy fish and fussy feeders, and the pursuit of larger specimens has become one of the most obsessive and highly specialized forms of fishing. If you are interested, there is endless literature on carp fishing, and the angling press is always packed with articles about the latest techniques, gismos and gadgets designed to help you catch more and bigger carp. I like fishing for carp in hot weather, when you can actually see the big carp basking on the surface. They can occasionally be induced to take a fly or, more likely, a dog biscuit superglued to a size 8 hook and floated on the surface with a bubble float.

Carp of between 500g/1lb and 2.5kg/5lb make the best eating. Specimens over 5kg/10lbs are highly prized by anglers, and unless you know twenty people who would like to sit down and eat a carp, it would be a kindness to return such fine specimens to the water for other fishermen to enjoy.

Carp from the fishmonger

Carp are one of the few freshwater fish that are available from more enterprising fishmongers. They do have a following in this country, particularly in the Chinese and Eastern European communities. If you are curious to try this greatly underrated fish, ask your fishmonger to see if he can get you one – he should be able to without too much trouble. Londoners need look no further than Soho's Chinatown – the fishmonger at the end of Gerrard Street sells live carp all the year round – and live eels too, come to that.

Preparation and cooking

Carp should be gutted, descaled (except for leather carp, which have no scales) and thoroughly wiped of their slimy coating before cooking.

As to the muddiness problem, it can certainly be partially alleviated by using only boneless, skinless fillets in your recipe. My friend Mauro Bregoli, chef at the Old Manor House in Romsey, Hampshire, says that carp can be further 'de-muddied' by soaking the fish in a solution of half water, half wine vinegar and some sea salt for 15-20 minutes before cooking. I must say I tend not to bother, accepting my carp as it comes and doing my best to find the muddiness 'interesting' when I encounter it.

Most traditional recipes for carp involve baking them in the oven, either whole, or in large steaks, and though I have tried frying and grilling them with moderate success, I side with tradition on the whole. A foil parcel, or appropriate oven pot with a lid, are the best receptacles, and the carp may be flavoured with butter, sliced onions, wine and herbs (particularly bay leaf and fennel). For a fish of, say, 2-3lb, bake in a fairly hot oven (190°C/375°F/gas mark 5) for 30-40 minutes. Drain off the juices and whisk in a little butter or cream, plus more fresh herbs, to make a sauce.

For full instructions for carp baked in the car engine, see page 87.

DACE

The dace is a gregarious and attractive river fish, with a slim, cylindrical body and a preference for shoaling in the middle reaches of clean, fairly fast rivers. It's not much rated by anglers, as it is rarely over 225g/½lb in weight and often takes the bait intended for bigger species (especially chub, which frequent a similar habitat). If only, instead of throwing it back with contempt, they took it home and had it for their tea, they might have a better opinion of it. From Mrs Beeton the dace receives the distinguished compliment that, at their best (which she says is in February), dace are 'more palatable than a fresh herring'.

Dace are sometimes confused with small chub, to which they are superficially similar: the critical difference is that the dorsal fin (the one in the middle of the fish's back) is concave in the dace, and convex in the chub.

Fishing

Dace can be caught on light float tackle, small hooks (size 16 or less) and a variety of baits, particularly small worms and maggots. It is also one of the few coarse fish that will regularly take a fly, and this has to be the most fun way to fish for them.

Cooking

Fry in breadcrumbs, or grill (as for bleak, page 69). Definitely worth including in the small fry fry-up (see page 86). Dace are also good smoked in a portable smoker (see smoking eels, page 73).

EELS

I had adventures with eels of all kinds during both series, including a conger (which turned up in Cornwall in Larry McAbe's lobster pot and was promptly put to sleep by Larry's eel massage), and sand eels (which failed to catch me a bass as bait, and ended up making a third-rate breakfast instead).

But the eels which made the biggest impression on my palate, indeed, furnishing me with two of the best dishes I ate all series, were the common freshwater eels, in both adult and infant form. In Norfolk I went eel netting with farmer Robert Gaze, and ended up breakfasting on hot smoked eel and wild horseradish sandwiches – out of this world. And in Gloucestershire, on board the *Bain Marie*, I caught up with the elver migration in the company of West Country elverman and all-round rascal Hartley Everett. Same species, very different size (the eels I mean).

Eels are an extraordinary species – immensely successful and highly adaptable. They have been fished for, farmed and eaten in Europe for hundreds of years, yet still many aspects of their natural history remain a mystery. Their migratory life cycle is the inverse of that of the salmon: they live in fresh water and migrate to the sea to breed. It is widely believed (but by no means proved) that all eels breed in the Sargasso Sea (in the Atlantic, between Bermuda and the Leeward Islands) – which is pretty extraordinary when you think that the adults are distributed all over Europe.

The elver migration

Adult eels are believed to die after breeding, but the eggs, and subsequently the leaf-shaped larvae called *leptocephalus*, are borne towards Europe in the surface current known as the North Atlantic Drift. By the time they reach our shores, in late February and March, they are free swimming elvers (also known as 'glass eels'), and every effort of their 7.5cm/3 inch long transparent bodies is directed at getting into fresh water. In estuaries like the Severn, they swim upstream with the incoming tide, especially at night, and when the tide turns they hug the bank to avoid being swept back out to sea. And this is when the elvermen like Hartley Everett get their chance...

Elver fishing

You need a licence to fish for elvers, and technically anyone can apply to the local river authority. But the best elver-fishing spots, or 'tumps' as they are known, are jealously guarded: they don't officially belong to anyone, but in some cases (including Hartley's) they have been handed down through the generations. Encounters between elver fisherman and intruders on their tumps have been known to end in violence.

The technique for catching elvers is straightforward enough: a fine-meshed rectangular net, some 1.2 metres/ 4 feet long, is mounted on the end of a pole and set up to cover the edge of the river where the elvers are expected to be swimming. Escape routes under or around the net are blocked by piles of mud (confusingly also known as 'tumps'), and the net is checked every few minutes.

On a good night, an elverman like Hartley can net up to 20 kilos/40lb of elvers. But he will often draw a complete blank, or net only a few stragglers. The market for elvers is a volatile one, and this year, with elvers relatively scarce, prices were extremely high: up to £160 per kilo! The reason for this is that live elvers are increasingly in demand for stocking eel farms: because of their life cycle, eels cannot be bred in captivity, but elvers can be 'brought on' – reared in ponds, where they grow rapidly to a market weight of a few pounds. The Japanese are paying bigger and bigger sums for live elvers, which they fly to Japan and bring on in massive eel farms: eels are much in demand, both for sushi, and for a delicious traditional dish called *Unagi*: grilled eels glazed with sweet soy sauce.

Because of these crazy prices, the traditional Gloucestershire elver feast is a thing of the past. This is a great shame, as the elvers I ate with Hartley were really sensational, both his way – fried in bacon fat with a fried egg on the side – and mine (the Spanish way) – fried in olive oil with red chillis, garlic and salt.

If you want to try elvers, you could attempt to catch some yourself: but make sure you get the appropriate permissions – and try not to get into a fight.

Or you could splash out, and pay the market rate, for a once in a lifetime experience: develop a taste for them at your financial peril! You could try contacting H. G. Cook at UK Glass Eels (tel: 01452 750464 or fax: 01452 750150). Orders are subject to availability and they don't usually deal in quantities of less than 1 kilo/2lb.

Artificial elvers

The Spanish are mad about elvers – so much so that, in the face of extortionate prices for the real thing, they have in recent years begun to produce artificial elvers (*angulas falsa*). These are an extruded fish product, a bit like the dreaded 'ocean sticks', but rather more worthwhile: they look like elvers and taste pretty good – especially fried up with chilli and garlic (see my recipe below). They are easy enough to find in Spain, and worth bringing back as a culinary curiosity. You can occasionally find them in Spanish and Portuguese delicatessens in this country, either vac-packed or frozen. Ask for 'gulas'.

Preparation

Elvers need to be cooked while still alive, though a few dead ones in a batch (known as 'white eyes' for obvious reasons) won't hurt, as long as they're fresh.

Like adult eels, elvers are slimy things, and the collective slime which bubbles up in a bucketful of live elvers, like the head on a pint of beer, is known as 'vomp'. This must be washed off: clean the elvers in a sieve, in batches, in cold water under a tap, until all the vomp is gone. Then they must be thoroughly dried: several cotton tea-towels will be required, and the wriggling little elvers should be rubbed and massaged between 2 cloths until dry (but just a little tacky) to the touch.

Cooking

A kilo/2lb of elvers will give 4 people a fairly decent plateful, 8 a sampler portion (of the kind some might find frustratingly small). As you are unlikely to be getting experimental with an excess of elvers, I suggest you do them either my way or Hartley's — or half each.

My way: (I say 'my way' — this is actually a classic Spanish recipe which I learned from my friend Helena Rey. She makes it with 'artificial eels' — see above.) For ½kg/1lb of elvers you need 2 large cloves of garlic, finely chopped, ½ a small red chilli, finely chopped, a generous tablespoon of olive oil, and 'big salt' (either flaky sea salt or large crystals of rock salt). Heat the oil in a large heavy frying pan and throw in the garlic. As soon as it starts to take colour, add the elvers. Cook fast, tossing and stirring, until all the elvers are dead, and heated through. Add the chilli, and cook for a couple more minutes *if* you want a few of your elvers to be crispy. Sprinkle generously with 'big salt' and eat at once.

Hartley's way: Fry a couple of rashers of good bacon (traditionally smoked back from a Gloucestershire Old Spot pig) in a large frying pan until done to your liking. Remove the bacon and keep warm. Throw the elvers into the hot bacon fat and stir-fry for a few minutes until all the elvers are dead and cooked through (longer cooking for crispier elvers). Move the eels to one half of the pan and fry an egg (preferably goose or duck) in the other half. Eat the elvers with the bacon and egg on the side.

Catching adult eels

Adult eels are among the most resilient and adaptable fish around. Their ability to tolerate a vast range of water conditions, and even to wriggle miles across fields to colonize new areas, means they can be found in almost every conceivable kind of water, from the Thames estuary to the tiniest stream, from the lowliest ditch to the biggest lake. And they can be caught in all of these places, by a wide range of methods. Eels are largely nocturnal creatures, and whatever method you employ to catch them, success is most likely to be had at night. Eels can be caught all the year round, but are said to be at their best for eating in the autumn and winter.

Babbing: In small rivers and slow streams, one traditional method of catching eels (which I tried briefly, and without success, in the Norfolk programme) is called babbing. This requires a rod (a long bamboo cane will do) and line, but no hook, and relies on the eel's known penchant for earthworms. Up to a dozen worms (the larger the better) are threaded on to a length of worsted wool, using a darning needle, so that the wool passes right through the middle of their body. The threaded worms are then gathered into a ball, and tied to the end of the line. The ball of wool-mounted worms is then lowered into an eely stretch of water, until the first bite is felt. Then the clever bit happens: the eel, whose mouth is lined with tiny backwards-pointing teeth, bites through the worm and into the wool, the fine fibres of which, in accordance with the velcro principle, catch on to the eel's teeth. A skilled practitioner (which I am not) then draws the eel smoothly out of the water and with one firm shake drops it into a waiting receptacle (traditionally, an up-turned umbrella).

Trapping: Eel traps come in various shapes and sizes, and are mostly used in rivers and streams. The general principle is the same, and a variation on the lobster pot idea: it's a lot easier to find your way in than out. But eels being somewhat cleverer than lobsters, so eel traps are a touch more sophisticated: a series of long, cone-shaped nets (or, in days gone by, wicker baskets), of diminishing size, are fixed one behind another; there is only one entrance, and each net or basket leads inevitably to the one behind; the last net or basket is the one with the bait in it (usually a rotten chicken, a piece of liver, or a sock full of pet food). Once the eel has got to the bait, it's a long way back against the grain of the net. Chances are he'll stay put till you haul him out.

Traps of this design vary greatly in size. Hartley Everett has one for commercial eel fishing on the Severn, with an opening some 30 metres/90 feet wide. Such a trap, laid out over a couple of days, could catch hundreds of eels (plus a few salmon or sea trout if you're lucky).

Smaller traps, with an entrance of just a few feet across, are relatively easy to handle. If you have access to a stretch of water where you suspect an eel trap might be effective, it's well worth investing in one. Try contacting a local tackle shop: they may be able to order one for you.

Fishing with rod and line: Catching eels on a rod and line is not difficult, provided you are prepared to be nocturnal. Fairly strong tackle is required (especially if fishing in tidal estuaries and fast water, where you will need some weight to hold the bottom). Legering a dead sprat, or a strip of liver or bacon, is a good method. The Thames is full of eels, as are most of our major rivers. Fishing the tidal zone of our bigger rivers can often be productive, especially when a high tide coincides with darkness. On such occasions, I have sometimes fished for eels from the towpath near Hammersmith Bridge – and never come away empty-handed.

Killing

If you are going to eat an eel, you may as well kill it as soon as you have caught it: a live eel of any size is a difficult beast to handle, and a quick dispatch will save you a lot of grief and sometimes a very bad tangle. The first rule is to use a dry cloth for handling an eel, and if possible to lay it on a bit of newspaper: the dry surface tends to stop them wriggling. Unhooking eels can be extremely difficult, especially if they have swallowed the hook right down. In such cases the sensible thing is to cut the line straight away – you can retrieve your hook when you skin and gut your eel. In order to subdue an eel, the best thing to do is to whack it, not on the head, but on the tail: hold it firmly with a cloth or gloved hand at the head end, and bring the tail down sharply on a heavy object, such as a log or stone. This should stun it. The next best step is a gory but effective one: cut its head off, just behind the gills. Unfortunately, eels being the remarkable creatures they are, it may continue to exhibit apparent signs of life, the headless body squirming slowly or rolling on to one side. Don't be distressed: the eel really is dead; it's just that its nervous system doesn't quite know it yet. Just cover it and go back to your fishing. It should be quite still by the time you get it home.

Skinning

Unless they are going to be smoked (in which case the skin helps to keep in the rich and flavoursome fats), eels should be skinned before cooking. The vital tool for this job is a pair of pliers: the skin is tough, and clings hard to the body, so good leverage and a strong pull are essential.

Use a sharp knife to release a flap of skin at the (severed) head end of the eel. Gripping the body hard with a cloth, use the pliers to work the skin back down the body towards your gripping hand. When you have skinned enough of the eel to get a grip on the skinned head end (i.e. a few inches), move your grip to this end and, pulling your hands away from each other, peel the skin off the middle and tail: it should come off in one tubular piece.

Cooking

Smoking eels: Portable smokers, which work by smouldering oak or other sawdust over a meths burner, are useful for cooking all kinds of fish, but the results with eel are particularly fine. But whenever you are using such a smoker, you should be aware that this is 'hot smoking', which means you are really cooking your fish, not preserving it in the manner of smoked salmon. (Traditional smoked salmon is salted, then cold smoked, for up to 12 hours. See page 80 for notes on how I smoked a zander up the chimney of the *Bain Marie*.)

A portable smoker can be bought relatively cheaply in most fishing tackle shops and other country stores, but you can also make your own. You need a meths burner, a large biscuit tin or high-sided tin baking tray with something that will fit over as a lid (e.g. another tray), a wire rack that fits inside the tin or tray, and some oak sawdust or other smoking wood. Sprinkle a couple of tablespoons of sawdust on the bottom of the tray and place the wire rack over the top. Put the fish (or several lengths of eel) on to the rack, and put the lid loosely (it should not be airtight) over the tin. Then prop up the tin on a couple of bricks (or similar), light the meths burner (a small sweet tin half-filled with meths will do) and put it underneath the tin. The sawdust will soon start smoking, and your fish will begin to cook in the hot smoke.

Most smokers, homemade or otherwise, have a tendency to burn out before the fish is done. If necessary, add more sawdust and relight the burner. Most small fish will be done in 10-15 minutes, but anything over a couple of pounds will take upwards of half an hour.

I like my hot smoked eel straight from the smoker, oozing fat into fresh brown bread, with either grated wild horseradish or rocket leaves (see picture on page 84).

Frying: Sections of small eel are delicious dipped in breadcrumbs, deep- or shallow-fried, and served with a piquant sauce (see page 84). They can also be part of the small fry fry-up (see page 86).

I am not much of a one for eel pies and jellied eels, but sound recipes for both can be found in *Mrs Beeton's Book of Household Management* – one of the few cookbooks to do justice to the culinary merits of our freshwater fish. My other favourite eel recipe is fillets simply fried in butter, and served with the wild herb sauce described on page 83.

GUDGEON

These little bottom feeders of our rivers and canals are greedy fish, and easy to catch – once you're into a shoal, it seems like you can go on catching them all day. This is good news, because they are one of the best of all freshwater fish to eat (rather like the little red mullet you find in the Mediterranean). Gudgeon are definitely worth pursuing until you have enough for a really good fry-up. I often take a second light rod when I go pike fishing: staking out a dead bait for a big pike can be a long waiting game, and occasionally draws a complete blank. If I can catch a few gudgeon while I'm waiting, I know I'll have something to look forward to when I get home.

Catching

A size 18 hook or smaller, baited with one or two maggots, fished right on the bottom with either a float or a light leger, should produce results. Gudgeon are often found very close to the bank, sometimes right under your feet. But if you don't encounter them straight away, a little ground bait should help bring the fish to your swim and keep them there.

Preparation

There is no need to descale gudgeon, but they should be gutted, and the rather spiky gills should be removed.

Cooking

I only ever fry gudgeon, tossing them in flour, or sometimes egg and breadcrumbs, or a simple batter, for extra crunch. The small fry fry-up (page 86) wouldn't be the same without them, and I often make it exclusively with gudgeon.

MINNOWS

Minnows may be the proverbial small fry of our rivers, smallest of the small, in fact, but they're not half bad to eat if you can get enough of them. They are not as ubiquitous as some would have it, preferring cleaner water, in the upper reaches of rivers and in stony well-oxygenated lakes.

Catching

Minnows will take a bait, if the hook is small enough, especially maggots, bread and small worms. But the best way to catch them is either with a fine-meshed net, when you see them shoaling, or with a minnow trap of the kind I used in Wales to produce 'battered minnows' for coracler Bernard Thomas. This is easily made with an old brandy bottle, or any kind with a deep dimple in the base: a sharp tap with a hammer on a screwdriver placed in the dimple usually knocks out a neat hole (though you may have to waste a couple of bottles before you get it right). This forms a lobster-pot-style entry hole. The bottle, weighted with a handful of small stones and baited with bread or chopped worms, should be lowered into the water and left for an hour or so, or overnight. If there are any minnows in the water, some should certainly be in your trap by the time you return. Put back the really tiny ones alive, and take the plumper fellows home to the kitchen.

Cooking

There is no need to gut or descale minnows. They should be floured, battered or breadcrumbed, fried quickly in hot oil, and munched up heads, tails and all.

PERCH

Perch are beautiful fish, fun to catch (putting up, ounce for ounce, a fine fight) and very good to eat – though I must confess a prejudice, as the first fish I ever caught and ate, aged 6, was a magnificent 1.2kg/2½lb perch, from Loch Corrib, near Galway, in Ireland. It probably remains my single most impressive fishing feat – a perch of that size is really a specimen fish.

Perch are found in a great variety of waters, but particularly in lowland lakes and ponds, and larger, slow-flowing rivers. They were all but wiped out in the seventies by a mysterious 'ulcer disease'. Happily the disease seems to have run its course, and perch are bouncing back, though bigger fish are still hard to come by.

Catching

Perch are greedy, and can be caught by a variety of methods. They often gather in shoals around underwater obstacles, walls and canal lock gates, and these are the places to try first. The depth at which they feed varies, so float-fishing is probably the best bet. Maggots and worms are the standard bait, and hard to improve on, though small minnows, dead or alive, and spinners, will catch the larger fish, if there are any about.

Preparation

Perch scales are big and hard, and must be removed before the fish can be cooked. The fish should then be gutted – and the spiny dorsal fin can be cut off with scissors.

Cooking

Perch have nice firm curds of tasty white meat that stand up to all kinds of cooking methods. Fish of just a few ounces are good simply fried or grilled, but if ever I get one of any size (more than 225g/½lb), I like to bake them as for salmon and sea-bass (to which they are related) – in a foil parcel with butter, fresh herbs, and a trickle of wine (see Salmon, page 77).

PIKE

Pike is the king predator in fresh water, and has a large mouth of viciously sharp teeth to make the point. When hungry, they will tackle any fish that comes their way, as well as ducklings, frogs and water rodents. Young jack pike are not infrequently found drowned, with another fish bigger than themselves jammed into their jaws. The point is made nicely in Ted Hughes's wonderful poem, 'Pike', in which he refers to pike 'so huge that past dark I dared not cast'.

Pike are found in rivers, lakes and canals: most waters, in fact, from which they have not been deliberately excluded. But despite their undoubted prowess as predators, and contrary to their historical reputation as a destroyer, experts now regard them as well adapted, and largely in harmony with their surroundings. Left to their own devices, they will not over-reproduce, and rarely have an adverse effect on the numbers of other species. (The same cannot be said of its alien relative, the zander. See page 78).

Catching

Artificial lures, such as spoons, spinners and plugs, take a good number of fish, and this is certainly the most active way of fishing for them. Strong line, a reasonably stout spinning rod, and a robust fixed spool reel is the best outfit for lure fishing.

The other tried and trusted method of catching pike is what I call the stake-out: a whole dead fish, usually a sardine, small mackerel or herring, is tossed out with a couple of treble hooks in it, a lead to keep it on the bottom, and the waiting game begins. I sometimes stick a polystyrene float inside the deadbait, to lift it off the bottom. Livebaiting, with roach, gudgeon, dace or other small fish, can be deadly, but it is not allowed in some waters: and those that do allow it usually specify that the bait must be caught in the same water you are fishing in. Goldfish, which I wanted to use to catch my zander, are therefore usually off-limits – but I'm sure they'd make a great pike bait

if I ever got the chance. For dead- and livebaiting, a fairly heavy rod capable of casting some weight is required, but for the best possible sport when piking, always fish the lightest tackle that will do the job.

Fly-fishing for pike, with large sparkling streamer flies, is a new technique just being developed now, but has the potential to offer great sport.

Incidentally, I have always wanted to try a bizarre experiment: fishing for pike with a clockwork duckling. I had meant to do it in the last series, but never quite got round to it. One day...

Preparation

Pike should be gutted and descaled, washed well of any slime, and patted dry.

Cooking

River pike tend to make better eating than lake or pond pike, owing to the muddiness factor (see above, though pike from the Scottish and Irish lochs, and the great Cumbrian lakes, should taste clean).

Pike's great virtue as an eating fish is its flavour, which is excellent, and quite distinctive (curiously unlike any other fish). Its downside is its bones, which are small and numerous, and distributed evenly throughout the meat.

For this reason a whole baked pike may not be the right fish to serve to the Queen Mother, but for patient fish enthusiasts, who don't mind picking the odd bone out of their teeth, it is definitely a worthwhile preparation. Follow the recipe for baked salmon on page 77, adding perhaps a few sliced shallots to the parcel for extra flavouring.

For those who prefer not to take their chances with bones, the solutions lie in a number of preparations which have become classic for pike: mousses, quenelles, and fishcakes. In such dishes the flesh is mashed to a pulp (easily done in a food processor) and then rubbed through a sieve, which breaks down the smaller bones and catches the larger ones.

For perfect pike fishcakes, mix 500g/1lb of processed, sieved pike fillet with 500g/1lb of well-seasoned mashed potato, ½ a large beaten egg and some chopped herbs, such as chervil, fennel or tarragon. Brush with the rest of the beaten egg, coat in breadcrumbs, and shallow-fry in hot oil, turning once. Serve with red pepper ketchup (see page 86).

For the great pike classic (and surely one of the finest fishy testaments to the wild larder) *Quenelles de brochet, queues d'ecrevisse, sauce Nantua*, see page 88.

ROACH

The ubiquitous roach, another fish beloved of the match angler, is common in still waters of all kinds, as well as the slower-moving parts of larger rivers. It is certainly caught more often than any other fish in Britain. It's no great shakes as an eating fish, but perfectly palatable all the same, especially when caught in cleaner moving waters.

Catching

When other fish are sulking at the bottom in cold weather, or off the feed during the brightest part of the day, roach can usually be relied on to come and take your bait. They bite tentatively, and are quite adept at cleaning a hook, so a good catch rate requires a well-timed strike. But roach are usually so persistent that even a clumsy fisherman will catch a fair few. A light float-fishing rig is best, with a double maggot fished at varying depths until the fish are found.

Preparation

Descale, remove the gills, and gut.

Cooking

Small roach can go in a fry-up, battered, floured or breadcrumbed, and anything over about 225g/½lb (a good fish) can get the carp treatment – see above.

SALMON

I decided not to include salmon as a quarry during my on-screen exploits, in rather the same spirit that I omitted pheasants, grouse and other game birds from the hit list. As the object of (often very expensive) sport and the subject of gastronomy, the salmon is famous the world over. For many, the pursuit of this fish is a life-long passion, and for some (friends of mine included) an obsession that leaves little room for thinking about anything else at all! So much has been said and written about the fish that I decided to leave it on one side, and focus more on some of the unsung fishy heroes (and villains) of our rivers, lakes and canals.

Having said that, I do fish for salmon whenever I get the chance, and provided I don't have to pay ludicrous sums of money for the privilege. And since salmon fishing, for me at any rate, usually means hours or even days of fishless casting, my preference is to fish in locations which, if they usually fail to satisfy the blood lust, are always guaranteed to stir the soul. Due to the kindness of one salmonophile friend, most years I get a chance to fish on the River Findhorn, north of

Inverness. Here we have honed the process of not catching fish into a fine art: long days on the river are punctuated with frequent breaks for picking mushrooms, gathering blaeberries and watching the ospreys catch the fish that we can't move. Bliss.

One of the nicest places to fish for salmon, and certainly the best place for beginners to go, is Ireland. Fishing rights on all but a few of the major salmon rivers are not privately owned, and access to genuinely good sport can often be had by just paying a few pounds at the local post office. The expense (which in some places is certainly worth paying) comes if you want to hire a local gillie to show you the best way to fish the river. Because salmon fishing is open to everyone in Ireland, there is much less snobbery and élitism about the sport. Those who are not adept at casting a fly can spin or even use worms (a technique which, the locals will assure you, requires no less skill than the fly).

Buying

Wild salmon is available in fishmongers, but is usually outrageously expensive. If you want to buy a whole large fish to cook for a party, your best bet might be to try to contact a wholesaler and see if he can include you in his round of deliveries. Or go for sea trout, which is always wild, every bit as good, and usually much cheaper.

A note on farmed salmon

Farmed salmon is cheap and readily available, and could of course be used for any salmon recipe in this (or any other) book. But I have mixed feelings about this product. It is not so much the quality of the fish that worries me: farmed salmon is not as good as wild (it lacks the richness and depth of flavour of wild fish recently returned from the sea, where they feed on crustaceans and small fish) but it is a legitimate product and deserves a fair chance in the market. More worrying is the way that salmon farms are being run – often without regard for their environmental impact, and their effect on the stock of wild fish. The waste from huge numbers of caged fish is contaminating lochs, and diseases against which farmed fish can be inoculated are passed on to wild fish. I know that many Scottish fish farmers are working to improve the situation, but until I am confident that the good guys are in the majority I will remain a reluctant and occasional buyer of the farmed product. Having said that, I do occasionally buy a whole large farmed salmon for making gravad lax: a dish in which the magic combination of salt, sugar and dill compensates admirably for the slight insipidness of farmed fish.

Cooking

There must be thousands of recipes for salmon, and I suppose now that there is so much cheap farmed salmon on the market there might be an argument for getting a bit experimental with this fish. But I've said my bit about the farmed product, and I can't say I'm much inclined to expand my limited repertoire for preparing the wild fish. A fresh wild salmon is such a beautiful raw ingredient that it hardly requires any fancy preparation. If I catch one (and I am not faced with this dilemma as often as I would like), there are only two choices for me: bake it the same day or make it into gravad lax.

One of the factors in making this decision is how 'fresh' the fish is — not in the sense of hours since death, but of time spent in the river. Running fish just in from the sea may be identified by their fresh silvery colour, full plump bodies, the possible presence of sea lice, and the absence of any hooking in the jaws. Fish in such good condition (including almost all fish caught before the end of April) are likely to be full of shrimpy flavour and nicely barded with a natural layer of fat. Any such fish of less than 4.5kg/10lb is a prime candidate for baking in a simple foil parcel, as follows.

Baking a salmon (also large trout and sea trout): Lay the fish on a double layer of foil, the inside layer lightly buttered. Place in the cavity a bay leaf, a few parsley stalks, maybe a sprig of fennel and a large knob of butter. Season the fish, inside and out, with salt and freshly ground black pepper. Dot with more butter, and just before sealing up the parcel, trickle over a tablespoon of white wine. Always wrap a fish loosely to allow hot air to circulate around it. Bake in a very hot oven (220°C/425°F/gas mark 7) for 15 minutes per kg/8 minutes per lb — but start testing any fish of 2kg/5lb or more after 40 minutes. Test the fish by pushing a thin blade into it along the lateral line to the bone at the thickest part. The fish is done when the flesh is opaque right through to the bone — but err on the side of underdone. Serve with the juices reserved from the foil parcel, with perhaps a little chopped wild chervil, chives or fennel stirred in.

Alternative cooking methods

Fish which have been several months in the river and are getting close to spawning are darker and leaner, showing plenty of red in the sides and back. They have not been feeding for months and so lack the fat reserves and rich flavour of a sea-fresh fish. They are still worthwhile eating though: baked, they have more the flavour of a river trout. But best of all, I like to make them into gravad lax. This takes out almost all the water from the fish, concentrating the flavour of the flesh and mingling it wonderfully with salt, sugar, and the incomparable aroma of fresh dill (or, if you prefer, wild fennel). For the full recipe, see page 82.

TROUT

Trout, both rainbow and brown, are great sporting fish, and trout fishing has understandably become an immensely popular and highly commercial sport. Many fisheries have been set up with the trout fisherman in mind, and lakes, ponds and gravel pits have been stocked to the brim with farmed rainbow trout, providing easy and accessible sport. I would hazard a guess that there are now few places in Britain where you are more than an hour away from a day-ticket trout fishery. However, what is good for the fisherman is not necessarily good for the gourmet. Many, probably most, still-water trout fisheries are overstocked with fish that adapt only slowly (if at all) to a natural diet and, without benefit of flowing fresh water, retain the unpleasant, dull and muddy taste that characterizes farmed fish.

I really hate catching trout that then turn out to be almost inedibly muddy, and for this reason I restrict my still-water trout fishing to a few fisheries where the eating quality of the trout is consistently good — or to larger lochs and lakes, usually river or stream fed, that sustain a healthy resident population of trout.

Fishing for trout in rivers and streams is an entirely different matter. Rivers where the magnificent brown trout thrives wild come more or less with their own guarantee: if they weren't clean and fairly fast-flowing, the brown trout would not tolerate them. Such rivers are also often stocked, of course, with farmed rainbows. But they too will thrive in the clean, well-oxygenated water, adapting quickly to a natural diet of insects, small fish and larvae. And their succulent, clean-tasting flesh will bear witness to their much improved lifestyle.

Catching

Fly-fishing, with a rod, reel and heavily weighted line specially designed for the purpose, is still the most popular, most exciting and often most effective way to catch trout. Casting a fly is an aquired skill, and before you attempt to deploy the technique in a potentially fish-catching situation, it is as well to take a lesson or two – either formally, from a professional, or informally, from an experienced friend. The first time you feel the determined tug of a feeding trout on your line is a moment to cherish: if that doesn't get you hooked on fishing, nothing will.

In most British trout rivers, fly-fishing is the only method allowed. But in some purpose-stocked fisheries, and a few of the larger lakes where other species are also fished, controlling authorities operate an 'any method' policy. Under such circumstances, artificial lures, such as plugs and spinners, can be effective, as can float-fishing or legering with maggots and worms. Large rainbows, and the great cannibal brown trout (known as *ferox*) of the northern lakes and some Scottish sea lochs, may fall to small trout, used as live or dead bait, and slowly trolled at some depth behind a boat.

The **sea trout** is (and don't let anyone persuade you otherwise) a brown trout that has decided, for reasons best known to itself, to go to sea. It has always struck me as an eminently sensible thing for a sea trout to do. They come back to the river a little older, a little wiser, and a whole lot tastier. Sea trout are, in my view, better eating than either salmon or trout.

They can be caught, on fly or spinner (where allowed), in estuaries, rivers and lochs which empty into the sea. Keen sea trout ethusiasts cast their fly after dark, when the sea trout run up-river and are most inclined to take.

Cooking

There is no great difference in approach between the cooking of trout and sea trout and that of their relative the salmon, except that trout and sea trout will often be just a pound or two in size, making them well suited to a quick grilling on an impromptu river- or lakeside barbecue or fire. For just such an eventuality, one of those folding, fish-shaped wire grill trays can be a useful item in the tackle bag. And some fire lighters.

Truite au bleu: This is the classic French treatment for a very fresh wild river trout. It only works really well with smallish fish (max. 500g/1lb) that are only a few hours dead. The fish should be gutted, but not wiped, and dropped straight into a rapidly boiling court bouillon flavoured with wine, a splash of vinegar, peppercorns and bay leaves. For fish of 250-500g/½-1lb, boil for 6-10 minutes, drain, and serve with melted butter, or a wild sauce tartare (see page 41).

Smaller fish are of course also suitable for grilling and frying. They can be pan-fried in butter, but really small trout (especially the little 'quarter-pounders' you get in Scottish lochs) are particularly good tossed in seasoned flour and deep-fried in very hot oil.

In my kitchen, larger fish tend to get the salmon treatment: either baked in foil (see above), or dill-pickled as for gravad lax. Incidentally, freshwater trout, such as rainbows, are just as good as salmon and sea trout for the gravad treatment, provided they are large enough (1.5kg/3lb would be about the minimum viable).

ZANDER

The only freshwater predator remotely to rival the pike, the zander is not native to this country but was introduced in 1878 to the lake at Woburn Abbey by the ninth Duke of Bedford. Since then it has spread, and has been most successful in colonizing the East Anglian fens.

The population I caught up with was living happily in a stretch of the Birmingham canal – introduced, allegedly, by two anglers who had a grudge against the Birmingham and Coventry Anglers Association. If this is true, their prank certainly had the desired effect: local anglers are complaining that their sport is in decline, and the highly effective hunting skills of the fast-growing zander are thought to be largely to blame.

Whether or not the zander is a dangerous menace may still be open to debate, but that it is a first-class eating fish is, as far as I'm concerned, beyond dispute. Having watched Wayne Northall take great pleasure in throwing a zander over the hedge, I was delighted to help reduce the population a bit further, and much enjoyed my first experience of electro-fishing with British Waterways.

Catching

Zander populations are very localized, so to stand any chance of catching one you must first be sure that they are there. Local information, from a tackle shop or the appropriate angling authority, should set you right. Tactics for catching zander are more or less identical to catching pike (see above), except that zander show a marked preference for cloudy water and are more active hunters. Livebaits (mainly gudgeon and small roach) are reckoned particularly effective, and deadbaits should be fished mid-water, on a float.

Preparation

Like their cousins the perch, zander have large tough scales which must be thoroughly removed before the fish can be cooked.

Bleak

Brown Trout

Carp

Dace

Eels

Elvers

Fishing for Elvers

Minnows

Pike

Salmon

Sea Trout

Zander

Cooking

The zander has excellent firm flesh, appropriate for all manner of treatments. As with most fish of a good size, I find it hard to improve on my favoured technique of baking it whole and on the bone in a foil parcel, with herbs, butter and wine (see salmon above). But zander also offers the cook excellent fillets, which I prepared on camera simply on a griddle, and served with a juniper sauce. See page 85 for the recipe.

After the electro-fishing I had a great surplus of zander, and decided to smoke a few up the chimney of the *Bain Marie*'s wood fire. This, somewhat to my surprise, was a great success, producing, after a couple of hours up the chimney, an effect somewhere between a portable smoker and a traditional cold-smoking smoke hole — more like smoked haddock than smoked salmon. I therefore decided it could use a little further cooking, and when I braised it with a little wine, a few sliced onions and a bay leaf, it was absolutely sensational: the oaky, smoky flavour had thoroughly permeated the chunky curds of fish, and the final texture was somewhere between smoked salmon and poached salt cod: and that's a pretty interesting place to be, if you're a texture.

The experience has convinced me that it is well worth experimenting, putting fish up chimneys of almost any kind, for varying lengths of time, where possible with oak sawdust sprinkled on the embers of the fire. Even if the fish requires further cooking afterwards, the resulting flavour makes the exercise entirely worthwhile.

And finally, we come to a creature that is not a fish at all (though it goes by that name). No survey of the culinary possibilities of our inland aquatic life would be complete without our largest resident freshwater crustacean:

Crayfish

The native freshwater crayfish is a close relative of the marine lobster (which it closely resembles), and its typical habitat is the shallower reaches of clean, fairly fast-flowing rivers and streams. They live under stones, in holes in the bank, and among the submerged root systems of waterside trees. They are found only in hard water, as soft water is lacking in the calcium and other minerals necessary to build the creature's protective shell.

The native crayfish was once prolific, and remains so locally in well-maintained clean rivers. But in its general distribution it has declined greatly in the past few decades because of pollution, and the over-zealous dredging and bank-clearing of many of our rivers and streams.

As water quality has improved in recent years, one might have expected an increase in crayfish numbers. But in many areas they now have a new menace to contend with: their own kind. For some time now, the American signal crayfish, larger, more adaptable and more voracious than its English cousin, has been farmed in this country to supply the restaurant trade. Escapees have begun to colonize our river system, and in certain areas they are rife. They are ruthlessly efficient 'ethnic cleansers', making a quick meal of any natives they encounter and quickly supplanting them in the habitat. Their environmental impact is thought not to end there, either. Like the zander, they are a predator out of tune with the natives they prey on. Their favourite food, once the native crayfish have been wiped out, is fish eggs. Angling clubs in areas under invasion by the signal are complaining of decimated fish stocks.

Despite the beating they are taking from the signals in some areas, there is probably no harm in fishing for native crayfish in places where they are still prolific (the trout streams of Wiltshire and Hampshire, for example). And catching the alien invaders such as the American signal can only be an environmental good turn. The chances are, sadly, that in areas where the signal attaches itself to your bait, you have little chance of catching a native. At the present time there is no official strategy in place on the part of the National Rivers Authority for either protecting the native crayfish, or removing the signal.

Catching

Crayfish hibernate, and though they can occasionally be lured out of their hole to investigate a bait during winter months, you will catch them in far greater numbers from April onwards. If you want to know whether crayfish of either species can be caught in a given stretch of water, local anglers are probably the best people to ask. But in the absence of good local information, you'll just have to dip a bait in the water and see what bites.

When the water is warm and crayfish (of either species) are on the hunt, they are so voracious that they are not difficult to catch. I was introduced to the voracious signal in the series by Oxford narrow-boat dweller and all-round wheeler-dealer Steve Walsh. He had no trouble in persuading me that we would only be doing the local ecosystem a favour if we removed and ate as many signals as we could catch. The technique is much as for catching crabs off a harbour wall. Steve's preferred bait is a chicken carcass. He ties it to a piece of string, lowers it into the water to the river bed (right under the bank, by a tree, is often a good spot), and waits for a crayfish to grab hold. And grab hold they do – so forcefully that you can actually feel them tugging, trying to make off with the meat. They can then be hauled up on to the bank – though some kind of landing net is a useful extra, as they will occasionally drop off as you lift them out of the water.

Crude traps can also work well, and mean that you don't have to be permanently attached to the other end of your string. A square or circle of chicken wire can be attached by three or four strings at the edges to a stout cord in the middle. Tie a bait (a chicken carcass, piece of bacon or fish skeleton) in the middle, and lower the trap into the water. Check the trap every 15 minutes or so: haul it up smoothly and swiftly, and any crayfish feeding on the bait will not have time to jump off. If you want to catch crayfish in some numbers, several traps, placed at intervals along a river bank, and checked regularly over the course of a few hours, can produce good results.

Baited pots of the kind used for Dublin Bay prawns (see page 105) will also be extremely effective. Tied with a strong cord to a peg, or to the branch of a tree, they can be checked every few hours or left overnight.

Crayfish can be kept alive in a well-ventilated box in a cool place for about 48 hours. A dead crayfish should be thrown away, never cooked.

Cooking

Native crayfish are rarely more than 10cm/4 inches long, though signals can be much bigger – up to 25cm/10 inches, and weighing almost 500g/1lb, in exceptional circumstances. If you are lucky enough to catch such a creature, follow the guidelines for cooking a lobster.

Boiled: Like lobsters and prawns, crayfish should be cooked alive. The best technique is to drop them into a large pan of rapidly boiling, well-salted water, and give them just 5 minutes. (Larger signal crayfish might take 8-10 minutes , in which case put them into the water a few minutes before the rest of the batch.)

Freshly boiled crayfish can be peeled and eaten as soon as they are cool enough to handle. As with larger prawns, remove the dark vein than runs along the back of the tail. Relative to, say, langoustine or prawns, the flavour is subtle, so a good way to perk them up is to dip the tails in chive or garlic (wild or otherwise) butter, or the wild tartare sauce described on page 41.

The claws have a good little morsel of meat that is worth extracting in all but the smallest specimens.

Fire/barbecue: There is probably no more satisfying way to cook crayfish than over the hot coals of a fire or barbecue, pitched next to the river from which you took them. On a wire rack, over charcoal or wood embers, crayfish will take between 5 and 15 minutes, depending on heat and size. As with boiled crayfish, garlic butter or a spiked mayonnaise will make a nice accompaniment.

There are many elaborate recipes for crayfish, mostly derived from France, where the creature is very highly esteemed. Gratins of crayfish and sliced truffles, mousses and timbales, bisques and beurres: get hold of a *Larousse Gastronomique* and you can try them all. But of all the crayfish classics, the one I feel is really worth offering to you in this book is the truly sensational partnership of crayfish with its old enemy of the river, the pike. (See page 88.)

Crayfish tails are traditionally used as a garnish.

GRAVAD LAX
(and Gravad trout, sea trout and mackerel)

Anybody who goes fishing regularly for any of the above-mentioned fish should have this recipe down pat. The combination of dill, salt and sugar is not so much a happy marriage as an outrageous mènage à trois.

When wild fennel is abundant, and in the fine frondy stage (early summer, usually) it can be used very successfully instead of cultivated dill. On the other hand, every kitchen-minded fisherman should have masses of dill growing in the garden. (The glass-forced supermarket pot-plants can be very weak in flavour.)

I whole salmon, sea trout, or large trout
  2.2-2.8kg/5-6lb

FOR THE CURE
125g/4oz rough sea salt crystals
250g/8oz caster sugar
30g/1oz freshly ground black pepper
2-3 large bunches fresh dill
(This quantity should be increased
proportionately according to the size of your
fish. It is also sufficient for about half a
dozen average size mackerel. Fish too big to

fit in the fridge can be cured in a cool cellar
or outhouse – provided it never exceeds 6°C.
Failing that, you'll have to make two parcels.)

FOR THE SAUCE
I tablespoon chopped dill or fennel leaves
I tablespoon chopped chives
I tablespoon English mustard
I teaspoon caster sugar
2 tablespoons sunflower oil
I teaspoon wine vinegar

- Gut and wipe clean the fish then take 2 large fillets from each side, as close to the backbone as possible (use the carcass for stock or soup).

- Roughly chop the 2-3 large bunches of dill and mix thoroughly in a bowl with the salt, sugar and pepper.

- Lay out a sheet of foil or clingfilm about 4 times the width of a salmon fillet.

• Spread a quarter of the cure mix over a fillet-sized area on one side of the foil, with a good 15cm/6 inch margin for folding over.

• Place one fillet, skin side down, on top of the cure mixture and cover with slightly more than half of what is left. Place the second fillet on top, skin side upwards, to make a sandwich. Scatter the remaining cure mixture over the skin.

• Wrap up the parcel tightly, tucking in the ends and edges of the foil underneath the fish.

• Put the package on a tray and place a similar-sized tray, or a plank of wood, on the top. Weight it down with a brick or two or anything else handy (the contents of the fridge?). Turn the package daily for at least 5 days, and no more than 8. Do not discard the liquid that oozes from the package, unless it threatens to spill over the side of the tray.

• At least 1 hour before you wish to serve the fish, combine all the ingredients for the dressing in a jar, and shake well together. Leave to stand, and shake again to emulsify before serving.

• To serve: unwrap the gravad lax, and wipe off excess liquid. There is no need to scrape off the dill pieces, though, as some recipes suggest. Slice fairly (but not too) thinly, and serve with the sauce, and buttered brown bread.

• Unused gravad lax can be rewrapped in clean clingfilm or foil, and kept in the fridge for up to 5 days.

Mackerel variation (for the same quantity of cure): Cut the heads off 6 mackerel, gut them and wipe clean. Split each one and remove the backbone (as described on page 97) so that you have 6 double fillets. Lay 3 of the filleted fish skin side down, each on a separate, large square of clingfilm or foil. Spread a third of the cure mixture on each fish, then lay another split fish, skin side up, on top of it. Wrap up each double fish parcel in the clingfilm, put them next to each other on a tray, and put another tray (or piece of wood) over the top. Weight them as for the salmon version. Turn every day. These mackerel will cure rather quicker than the salmon – 4 days is usually enough. Serve as for gravad lax, with the dill mustard sauce.

WILD HERB SAUCE FOR FISH

You can also add basil, parsley and cultivated chervil to this highly adaptable but delicious green emulsion. Serve with eel and freshwater fish, simply barbecued or pan-fried over a fire.

a small bunch of wild garlic
a small bunch of wild fennel
a small bunch of wild chives
a small bunch of wild chervil

4 anchovies (optional)
1 teaspoon crushed yellow rocket seeds
1 tablespoon pickled broom buds (see page 24)
olive oil

• Finely chop all the ingredients, and mix with enough olive oil to make a thick emulsion. A jar of the sauce keeps for a few days in your pocket or backpack – longer in the fridge!

CAR ENGINE CARP
(and other fish)

Cooking on the car engine is not as daft as it seems. If you are on the move, or if the weather is not conducive to a barbecue or campfire, or if what you really need for the dish you have in mind is an oven, then the engine of your car (or Land Rover, van or truck) may provide the answer.

The key to cooking on a car engine is that whatever you cook should be well wrapped in a reasonably leakproof foil parcel. Because it is so well suited to this kind of cooking, and because the cooking time is relatively short, the perfect item with which to begin your career as a car bonnet cook is a fish.

My choice for the series was a carp — because that's what I caught, in the strangely soupy backwater of the Thames by the Lots Road power station (in fact, my carp was practically cooked already). I won't give you an itemized recipe for your manifold mackerel (or whatever). There are plenty of suggestions in the main text for ways of flavouring fish in a foil parcel. The important thing is technique:

- *Know your engine:* The important thing is to place your parcel on a part of the engine that is (a) hot (for obvious reasons), (b) secure (in the sense that it won't fall off or get squashed by some moving part), and (c) safe (in the sense that it won't interfere with the engine's function). The place that worked for me (in my 28-year-old long wheel-based ex-army Land Rover) was a snug little shelf next to the oil-filler. But car engines differ greatly and I leave it to you to find the optimum cooking spot for your make and model (in this regard, trial and error really is the only way).

- *Make a good parcel:* Brush your first sheet of foil with oil, and lay your fish on it (for beginners, I suggest a whole fish, of no more than 750g/1½ lb. Season well with herbs (e.g. fennel, chervil, parsley), salt and pepper, maybe a clove of garlic, and a squeeze of lemon or trickle of wine. Wrap it well with at least 2 sheets of foil; the seal should be tight, but the parcel itself loose enough to allow air to circulate inside around the fish.

- *Always preheat your oven:* If necessary, drive around for 15 minutes or so with the parcel next to you on the passenger seat (you don't have to talk to it, though). Stop in a safe and legal place to open the bonnet, and fix your parcel securely in the favoured niche. I suggest you give your first fish at least ½ an hour before checking it. Eventually you will develop your own sense of timing that works for your make of car.

- Remember, a fish is done when it is hot, and opaque, right to the bone — test with a knife or skewer in the thickest part. My carp took only ½ an hour — in a slow-moving London traffic jam, on a hot day. It really was perfectly cooked — and being a Thames fish, not at all muddy.

- Good luck (with the fishing, as well as the engine).

FILLETS OF ZANDER
(or perch, bass or bream) with juniper sauce

I made this on the Bain Marie on about the wettest day during the filming of either series. And then my zander man, Wayne Northall, didn't even turn up to eat it. He'll never know what he missed. But you can...

SERVES 4

4 x 175g/6oz fillets of descaled zander, plus the head and bones of the fish, as available

1 carrot, roughly chopped

1 stick celery, chopped

1 small onion, chopped

a faggot of wild herbs (chervil, chives, nettle tops)

6 bay leaves

1 teaspoon fennel seeds

a dozen juniper berries

1 glass birch-sap wine (or white wine)

150ml/5fl oz double cream

• Make a stock with the fish head and bones, vegetables and faggot of herbs, plus 2 of the bay leaves, but be sure to simmer only gently, and not for more than ½ an hour. (Zander makes excellent stock.)

• Heat a cast-iron griddle pan until very hot, then scatter over the fennel seeds until they crackle. Lay the remaining 4 bay leaves on the grill, and place the 4 fish fillets skin side down on top of the bay leaves.

• While the fish is cooking, heat a large frying pan and ladle about 300ml/½ pint of the stock into it through a sieve (muslin or a cloth if possible). Add the juniper berries, and boil the stock to reduce by two-thirds. Add the wine and boil again.

• Keep an eye on the fish fillets. Turn after about 5 minutes, and transfer to a warmed plate.

• When the sauce has reduced to a scant 100ml/4fl oz (3-4 tablespoons), add the cream, and boil again for just 2 minutes until nicely emulsified and thickened. Pour the sauce over and around the fish fillets, making sure everybody gets some juniper berries.

• Serve straight away, under an umbrella if wet.

SMALL FRY FRY-UP WITH RED PEPPER KETCHUP

You don't have to give the fish the full crumb treatment — simply tossing them in flour will do. But for that extra bit of crunch...

gudgeon, bleak, dace and other small fry
plain flour, seasoned
2 eggs, beaten
breadcrumbs
oil for frying (groundnut or sunflower)
chopped chives and sprig of fennel (optional
   garnish)

FOR THE RED PEPPER KETCHUP:
(No wild ingredients in this, I'm afraid, but I include the recipe because it's such a good sauce for freshwater fish — especially the crumb fried gudgeon.)
2 red peppers
12 cherry tomatoes
1 teaspoon red wine vinegar
a little olive oil
salt and freshly ground black pepper

• First make the sauce. Roast, grill or barbecue the peppers until they are nicely blackened. Put in a bowl, cover, and leave to cool.

• Slice the tomatoes in half and grill until browned. Rub through a sieve.

• Peel the blackened skin off the peppers, remove and discard the seeds. Finely dice the flesh.

• Mix the pepper flesh with the sieved tomatoes, vinegar and olive oil, and season to taste.

• Prepare the fish: clean, gut, descale (not gudgeon) and remove the gills.

• Roll the fish in flour, dip in the beaten egg, and coat thoroughly with breadcrumbs.

• Heat at least 0.5cm/¼ inch of oil in a pan (or more in a deep-fat frier), and fry the fish until crispy and golden brown.

• Drain on kitchen paper, season with rock salt and garnish with the chives or sprig of fennel. Serve with the red pepper ketchup as a dipping sauce. Smaller fish can be eaten whole, bones and all — with larger ones, you may wish to nibble round the backbone.

EELS IN GREEN HERB SAUCE
(Anguilles au sauce verte)

This is another French classic, though much more of a country dish. This version, using wild herbs (if at all possible), is particularly satisfying.

SERVES 4

4 slices, 2.5cm/1 inch thick, from a slightly
   stale baguette
2 tablespoons olive oil
85g/3oz unsalted butter
450g/1lb eel fillets
a fistful of sorrel leaves, finely shredded
½ tablespoon finely chopped wild chervil (or
   parsley)

85g/3oz lightly blanched sea spinach (or
   ordinary spinach), squeezed dry and finely
   chopped
150ml/5fl oz dry white wine
juice of ¼ lemon
¼ teaspoon salt
salt and fresh ground black pepper
1 large egg yolk

• Fry the bread slices very gently in the oil until golden brown. Drain on kitchen paper and keep warm.

• Pour off some of the oil, add half the butter, and fry the fillets of eel until they are just cooked through. Remove and keep warm.

• Add the rest of the butter, the herbs, spinach, wine and lemon juice, and bring to a simmer, cooking until most of the liquid has evaporated. Season with salt and pepper.

• Beat the egg yolk with a teaspoon of water. Take the pan off the heat and cool a little. Stir the egg yolk into the sauce, heating gently until the sauce thickens. (Do not boil or the egg will curdle.)

• Arrange the eel pieces on the 4 slices of fried bread, spoon over the sauce and serve.

Smoking eels by the river, for a hot smoked eel and rocket sandwich (see page 73)

QUENELLES DE BROCHET, QUEUES D'ECREVISSE, SAUCE NANTUA

This French classic is a truly great dish, albeit a rather time-consuming and delicate one to prepare — but just imagine the satisfaction of creating such a delectable and decadent concoction with pike and crayfish that you've caught yourself. I've only done it once without cheating (by cheating, I mean using a pike caught by somebody else, or substituting prawns for crayfish), and I felt like a gastronomic god when I served it up.

Since the pike fillet is completely puréed in this dish, you could be forgiven for keeping it in the freezer, in expectation of the crayfish. And if the crayfish are hard to come by, you can, like I have, cheat by making your sauce Nantua with either Dublin Bay prawns or large shell-on Atlantic prawns.

My recipe is adapted from Raymond Blanc's version of the dish. He is lucky enough to be able to pull both pike and crayfish from the river Windrush, just a mile or so from Le Manoir.

SERVES 4

16-32 crayfish (4-8 per person, depending on size and availability)

FOR THE QUENELLES
150g/5oz unsalted butter, softened
175g/6oz fillet of young pike
1 teaspoon salt
2 pinches of cayenne pepper
3 eggs
100ml/4fl oz double cream

TO GARNISH
tails from the crayfish, de-shelled

FOR THE SAUCE NANTUA
100ml/3½fl oz sunflower oil
1 clove of garlic, lightly crushed

1 sprig of thyme
¼ bay leaf
8 tarragon leaves
2 sprigs of wild chervil or parsley
1 small carrot, washed, peeled and finely diced
2 sprigs of wild fennel leaves, finely chopped
1 tablespoon chopped fresh chives
½ celery stalk, washed and finely diced
1 small onion, peeled and finely diced
225g/8oz tomatoes, peeled, deseeded and chopped
4 tablespoons brandy
200ml/7fl oz dry white wine
heads, claws and tail shells of the crayfish
500ml/18fl oz cold water
200ml/7fl oz double cream
salt and freshly ground white pepper

- Plunge the live crayfish in boiling water and remove after 30 seconds. Drain and leave to cool.

- Cream the softened butter until smooth and free of lumps.

- Extract any small bones running down the middle of the pike fillet with a pair of tweezers, then roughly chop the fish and purée in a food processor with the salt and cayenne pepper.

- With the motor running, add the eggs one by one, finally adding the creamed butter, and process until the mixture is completely smooth. Turn out into a mixing bowl, cover and chill for 30 minutes.

- Place the bowl on ice and slowly incorporate most of the cream. Taste, check the seasoning, then rub the mixture through a fine sieve. Cover with clingfilm and put back in the fridge.

- Remove the heads and claws from the crayfish, and crack with a rolling pin or hammer. Peel the tails and set aside, covered. Add the tail shells to the pile of heads and claws.

- To make the sauce, heat the oil in a large pan and sweat the garlic, herbs and diced vegetables for a few minutes to soften. Add the crayfish shells and stir for a minute or two. Add the chopped tomatoes and cook to reduce a little. When the pan is almost dry, but before it catches, deglaze with the brandy and wine. Pour over the water and bring to the boil. Skim, and simmer for just 20 minutes.

- Strain this stock, pushing it through a sieve into a bowl (you can grind it in a liquidizer before doing this, but not so fine that bits of shell get through the sieve). Pass again through a finer sieve or chinois, into a clean saucepan. Boil and reduce to just 100ml/4fl oz. Add the cream, and boil for 2 minutes until nicely reduced and thickened. Set aside in a warm place.

- To cook the quenelles, have ready 2 tablespoons in a jug of warm water. Half fill a large saucepan or deep frying pan with lightly salted water, bring to the boil and reduce the heat to a barely discernible simmer. Using a warm tablespoon, scoop out a large spoonful of mousse and use the second spoon to mould an egg shape or quenelle. Form all the mousse mixture into quenelles and poach gently for about 4 minutes, turning carefully once during cooking. You can cook them in 2 batches if your pan is not wide enough. You should aim for 8 large or 12 small quenelles, depending on the size of your spoons. As each batch is ready the quenelles can be put on kitchen paper to dry.

- Lightly brush an ovenproof dish with a film of butter. Arrange the poached quenelles in the dish, leaving some space between them (they will puff up in the final cooking). Pour the sauce over and around. Cover and cook in a preheated oven (190°C/375°F/gas mark 5) for 15 minutes. Add the blanched, peeled crayfish tails, between the quenelles, for the final 5 minutes of cooking.

- Bring the dish to the table, and serve the quenelles and crayfish tails in front of your guests, lifting them carefully on to warmed plates. Spoon the sauce over and around. If they are not suitably impressed, never invite them to your house again.

THE EDIBLE SEASHORE

The coastline of the British Isles is nothing less than a national treasure. Although we have not escaped our share of horror stories concerning insensitive coastal development and scandalous pollution, we could certainly have had it worse, and even today the vast majority of our shoreline still consists of clean beach, virgin rocks and cliffs, natural estuary or tidal wetlands. This combination of terrains is the nearest thing we have in this country to a true wilderness – land unaltered by man – and provides a diversity of habitats unmatched by anything you will find in the interior. The tidal zone in particular is a rich haven for life, a substantial proportion of which is both bountiful and edible – making a good beach both fascinating from the point of view of the amateur naturalist and highly productive from the point of view of the chef. I like foraging for free food in all manner of places, but I'm simply never happier than when doing it on a beach.

In the tidal zone itself there are at least half a dozen seriously worthwhile shellfish to be gathered with no more specialized apparatus than a net, a rake or a good right hand. For those prepared to go a little beyond the beach, either with mask or snorkel, or by putting out pots, another dozen species come into play. Nor is the feast exclusively carnivorous: many species of seaweed offer unusual textures and flavours, not to mention extremely fine nutrition, to the adventurous chef.

In the second part of the field guide that follows, I will list the most worthwhile species that are to be found on and just off the seashore, with tips on how best to collect, prepare and cook each of them. But first I will describe the basic methods of acquiring these goodies.

BEACHCOMBING

I think we have a natural instinct for beachcombing. Put any child of toddling age on a rocky beach at low tide, and pretty soon he or she will be scrambling over the barnacled boulders, probing and peering through the bladderwrack, dabbling in pools and prodding the flotsam and jetsam. After a while they begin to specialize: some collect empty shells, others driftwood or pebbles; many young kids set about creating a seaside menagerie in a bucket, only to release the temporary exhibits at the end of the day (once you have persuaded them that they can't keep them as pets).

Sadly, many people seem to lose their beachcombing instincts as they drift towards adulthood. Those who do are missing out – not only on the charmed and innocent joy of chuckling at the sideways gait of the claw-waving shore crab, and marvelling at the symmetry of the medusa-like sea anemone, but also on the very real possibility of returning home at the end of the adventure with the ingredients for a fabulous seafood feast. If your beachcombing skills are a bit rusty, then it's high time you held a bucket in your hand and got some salt water between your toes.

CHOOSING A BEACH

There are many different kinds of beach, providing many different habitats for sea creatures and seaweeds, edible or otherwise. Very few beaches are barren of life, but the least rich hunting grounds are certainly long stretches of beach comprised of smooth pebbles gradating to loose shingle at the low-tide mark. Without permanently anchored rocks for weed to cling to, and without fine sand to provide the organic base from which the whole food chain spirals upwards, pebbly beaches have little to offer the forager in search of a free meal. Be aware, however, that what appears to be a barren, pebbly beach at high tide may, at low tide, reveal rocky reefs, sandy patches, and all kinds of opportunities for the beachcomber.

Beaches of pure sand at first appear to be unpromising flat deserts, but sand can often be rich in planktonic foods, especially if mixed with a little mud, and there may be rich pickings lurking beneath the surface. Worm casts are a sure sign that there is life a few inches down, and an indication that more palatable sand-dwellers may not be far away. Muddy, slightly shingly sand is a likely habitat for cockles, razor fish and other clam species, especially when fringed by weedy rocks, whereas cleaner 'yellow' sand may harbour shrimps at the low-tide mark.

The biggest variety of habitats, and therefore of potential food, is provided by classic rocky beaches, of sandstone or granite reefs or broken rock, gently gradating towards the low-tide mark, with plenty of weed-fringed rocks and rock pools, ideally interspersed with or edged by patches of sand. Here you will find all kinds of edible shellfish and crustacea, from prawns and small crabs to mussels, winkles and limpets – not to mention a whole variety of edible seaweeds. You may even be lucky enough to find a lobster lurking in a hole. (This has happened to me once, on my favourite rocky beach near Osmington Mills in Dorset, but he wedged himself so firmly under a rock that I eventually broke the handle of my shrimping net trying to get him out.)

Sheerer rocks dropping straight into deeper water will not be so productive, but they should still provide a home for limpets, winkles and sometimes mussels.

WHEN TO GATHER

It goes without saying that the time for beachcombing is at low tide, and a tide chart is the first vital piece of equipment for anyone with a mind to make any kind of harvest from the sea (including anglers). Two hours either side of the low tide will give you a good 4 hours' foraging, and if you want to spend maximum time at the lowest possible mark it helps to know exactly when the tide will turn (usually about 20 minutes after the given time for low tide). Habitually, the bigger mussels, larger winkles and limpets seem to be found nearer the low-tide mark. I have always assumed that this is because they spend more time under water, and therefore feeding.

Remember that the height of tides varies greatly throughout the year, the biggest (i.e. highest and lowest) spring tides occuring when the moon is either full or new, the smaller neap tides occurring in the middle of the lunar cycle. Some beaches, for example those where rocky reefs are usually below the low-tide mark, only come into their own as gathering beaches during spring tides.

POLLUTED BEACHES

Our shores are by no means free of pollution, especially in populated areas of the coast where sewage is still, in some places, pumped out into the sea fairly close to the shore. Local authorities (and local fishermen) should be able to tell you which beaches are considered clean, and which not, but as a general rule sheltered bays near houses, enclosed harbours and populated estuaries are likely to experience and retain contaminants, whereas remote and exposed beaches will be a safer bet. Cooking will take care of many harmful bacteria, but not all — especially since good cooks like to err on the side of underdone with shellfish (particularly mussels). It is therefore worth making enquiries to establish the hygiene credentials of your chosen beach. If you want to eat your shellfish raw (and why shouldn't you?) such enquiries are essential.

SNORKELLING

Many people only bother to put on a mask and snorkel on foreign holidays, in the assumption that the British coast doesn't have much to offer the snorkeller. Big mistake. I have had as much fun snorkelling in Britain (particularly in Cornwall and the west coast of Scotland) as anywhere else in the world. The visibility here, particularly in sheltered bays during late summer and autumn, can be absolutely superb, and the rocky reefs, especially those just below the low-tide mark, are often teeming with life.

Of course the down-side of snorkelling in this country is the water temperature (almost never more than about 65°F). Such are the distractions of the undersea world that cold and fatigue can creep up almost unnoticed on the snorkeller, so that suddenly you may find yourself chilled to the marrow, exhausted, and some distance off shore — a dangerous situation for even a strong swimmer to be in. So if you are planning to go snorkelling for more than just a few minutes you should certainly consider wearing a wet suit, of at least 5mm thickness.

A wet suit will also greatly increase your buoyancy, and thus help counteract the effect of fatigue. On the other hand, if you need to make regular duck dives of more than a couple of metres (which you will if you are looking for crabs and lobsters), you will need a couple of kilo weights on a weight belt to counteract the buoyancy.

Most of my snorkelling forays are 'just for fun' — to look rather than hunt — but there are some species that will regularly fall to the snorkeller which usually elude the beachcomber. Sea urchins and razor clams are a case in point, since they are rarely found above the low-tide mark except on the lowest tides. Similarly crustacea, most of which do everything within their power to conceal themselves from predators when exposed at low tide, will venture out with more confidence when they have a few feet of water over their heads. Consequently, spider crabs, shore crabs, velvet swimming crabs and even the occasional lobster can be taken by sharp-eyed, duck-diving snorkellers.

Snorkelling is also a particularly good way to gather seaweed — see below.

SPEAR-FISHING

Spear-fishing, with a spear gun powered by strong rubber bands or air canisters, turns snorkelling into a single-mindedly predatory sport. While this can no doubt be a very challenging way to take good edible fish such as bass and mullet, I have been rather put off it by the attitude of many of its proponents. In general I have found spear-fishermen to be a highly competitive bunch intent on killing as many fish as possible, with little interest in putting their catch to good use in the kitchen. (One particularly hapless victim of the sport has been the ballan wrasse — a fish not known for its eating qualities. In some areas of coastline, wrasse of any decent size have been wiped out by competitive spear-fishing, their broad flanks and marked reluctance to stray from their home territory making them easy targets.)

For this reason, spear-fishing is not the sport for me — though to those who pursue it on a non-competitive basis, and who eat what they kill, I say 'good luck'.

DIVING

Scuba diving is a specialized sport which requires expert tuition. The two best ways to learn are either to join a local club – most are affiliated with the British Sub Aqua Club (BSAC) – or to do the basic PADI (Professional Association of Diving Instructors) Open Water Diver course (which can usually be done in about 5 days of intensive tuition), either in this country or on holiday abroad.

Few sports divers plan dives specifically around the acquisition of food, but if you dive regularly in this country you will certainly encounter many edible creatures on your adventures. As a general rule it is considered perfectly acceptable for divers to remove the odd lobster, crab, or half a dozen scallops that might be encountered during a dive, to take home and eat. And certainly no one should begrudge you any number of whelks and large hermit crabs (both of which you will encounter in abundance).

However, on some well-known dive sites, wrecks and the like, divers are requested to observe a voluntary 'no goodies' policy, which means not removing anything, alive or dead, from the water. Such policies, however unofficial and unenforceable, are intended to maintain the quality of diving for everyone, and should be respected. Some 'residents' on such wrecks – conger eels, large wrasse, lobsters even – are well known to regular divers and practically have the status of pets. You would not be well regarded if you swiped them!

If you can find a like-minded dive buddy (diving alone is not countenanced by either the BSAC or PADI, and is not advisable under any circumstances for non-professional divers), there is no reason why you cannot plan 'foraging dives' in pursuit of lobsters, scallops and the like, over ground where you think they may be found. As with putting out pots (see below), it is as well not to cross swords with others involved in such activities on a commercial basis. If you think you may be infringing on somebody's patch, make enquiries first, and don't take more than you need for your own consumption.

Incidentally, spear-fishing with scuba apparatus is illegal in this country, as in most.

PUTTING OUT POTS

If you live near the sea, or regularly holiday on the coast, a couple of lobster pots and/or a string of prawn pots can be great fun to work and can supply you with a surprising array of crustacea and other shellfish, unbeatably fresh and free to boot.

The fruits of the sea are available to everyone, and contrary to what you might hear in some areas, you do not need a licence to put out lobster pots – provided the catch is strictly for your own consumption. But if you are going to give potting a whirl it is important to bear in mind that there are others who are struggling to make a living at the same game. The chances are that local potsmen have already established an unwritten gentlemen's agreement about who will throw their pots where, and before you throw your own pots you should take steps to ensure you will not further complicate the local fishing politics (which may already be sensitive enough).

There is certainly no point in making enemies by being defiant about your right to throw pots: in any contretemps with the local fisherman it is you, the 'tourist', who is sure to come off worst. If you do put your pots where they are not welcome, you are likely to find out about it pretty soon. Chances are the local boys will be up and out on the water well before you are: if you are experiencing a mysterious lack of success, it may well be because they are generously 'checking' your catch for you. And if your pots simply disappear, well then, you really have managed to piss somebody off!

The best thing you can do therefore is to go to the port nearest to where you are thinking of throwing your pots and make direct contact with the local fishermen themselves (it is the lobster and prawn men whose territory you are most likely to impinge on, as most of the serious crabbers now fish on deep reefs a long way offshore). Explain exactly what it is you want to do, and ask them if they can suggest an inshore reef or piece of rocky ground where you might pick up the odd lobster and spider crab, or a few prawns, without annoying anyone. If you are only throwing a few pots (no more than three lobster pots, I would suggest, or half a dozen prawn pots) and are seen to be taking the trouble to bait and check your pots daily, they shouldn't begrudge you a modest catch. It might be a smart move to buy some bait off them as well.

Alternatively you could go and have a chat with the local harbourmaster. He will know all the local fishermen, and should be able to advise you on the best way to get your pots in the water without antagonizing anyone.

BAITING YOUR POTS

You can bait lobster and prawn pots with just about anything, from a scrap of bacon to a lump of cat food tied up in the foot of a pair of tights, but the preference of all commercial potsmen is for fish baits. Some fishing ports have a shared bait pool for the potsmen, consisting of fish skeletons (usually flatfish which have been filleted) and unsaleable fish like wrasse and dogfish, which have turned up in nets (or indeed pots). You may be able to buy a supply of bait from such a pool, or ask for rejects and skeletons from a fishmonger. If you are an angler as well as a potsman, it is worth keeping any wrasse and small pollack that you catch as pot baits.

Brown crabs are said to prefer fresher bait to lobsters, but that doesn't mean you won't get lobsters on a fresh bait or crabs on a smelly one.

Exactly how a pot is baited will depend on the design of the pot (which varies according to where you are in the country), but almost all pots have some kind of device to allow for quick and secure baiting, such as a rubber or nylon noose or a wire mesh clip. You should always rebait a pot every time you haul it, even if the old bait appears to be intact. A new bait will create a fresh scent trail, which is essential to lure a good catch to your pot.

BUYING POTS

There are only a few places where you can buy lobster pots new, and they are expensive (about £80 a pot). However, if you think you will be able to use them for at least several weeks a year, and for many consecutive years, it may be worth investing in a few new pots. New lobster and prawn pots can be ordered from Delmar Engineering, Shellfish Gear Manufacturer, 20 Church Road, Selsey, West Sussex PO20 0LS, (tel: 01243 605123).

The obvious choice is to buy second hand pots — which turns out to be harder than you might think. First, and understandably, a working potsman is likely to want to throw and maintain as many pots as he can — and will no doubt want any spares to cover for losses. Second, the innumerable spare pots one does see lying around (apparently discarded) in fishing ports and harbours often turn out to be not so 'spare' after all. They always seem to belong to someone who's 'not yet in the water' but is apparently coming back for them in some unspecified number of days, weeks or years. I have found, however, that persistence may be rewarded in the end. If you keep going down to the boats, and chatting with the fishermen, you may finally find yourself introduced to someone who's not entirely averse to the idea of selling you a pot or two. Snap them up — and whatever you do don't ask him if he'll take a cheque.

THROWING YOUR POTS

Before throwing your pots for the first time, make sure each is securely attached by a good strong line (at least 1cm/½ inch for comfortable pulling) to an easily visible floating marker – this can be anything (a white plastic container, for example) provided it is strong, buoyant and doesn't leak. The line should be long enough to show on the surface in the depth of water you expect to throw your pots in, bearing in mind that the tide can rise as much as 12 metres/40 feet from low to high, but not so long as to drift too far off the mark. About 25 metres/80 feet should usually be ample for most inshore work.

You don't need a great big motor launch to throw and maintain two or three lobster pots – though if you are a 'boat person' with your own craft you will obviously have the advantage of range and a bit of seamanship. But provided the weather is reasonable, you can throw your pots from the most modest vessel – I have regularly fished half a dozen pots in Scotland from a tiny inflatable powered only by a couple of paddles and launched from the beach. The only struggle is to get the pots out in the first place, and bring them in at the end of my stay – 6 pots in the boat leaves little room for me. But once they are in the water, they come up only one at a time, so there's no space problem. So in a sheltered bay (which is anyway a perfect place to throw a few pots) you really need nothing more glamorous than my little inflatable.

In some places it is quite possible, and worthwhile, to throw pots without any kind of boat. A few years ago I went to stay with a friend of mine on the Isle of Wight. He is a keen fisherman who has a couple of pots, but for the week I was there, his boat was grounded for repairs. Undeterred, we fished his pots every day 'on foot' – walking out on the reef at low tide to the pots, which we had lowered into a few feet of water at the end of a rocky outcrop. We never drew a blank, and in the course of the week had some really good-sized lobsters – on the last day, a monster of over 2kg/4lb, which we made into a very fine lobster thermidor.

In terms of choosing where to throw your pots, the only essential is that it should be on, or at least very close to, rocky ground – ideally a reef (this does not apply to Scottish prawn pots – see below). This is the natural habitat of the crustacea you are hoping to tempt into your pot. To this end, there is an advantage in throwing your pots for the first time at low tide – in shallower water it will be easier to see what kind of bottom you are over. If the ground looks good there is no reason not to throw your pots very close to the shore, or only just below the low-tide mark, in just a few metres of water.

Pots are best left for 24 hours, then checked and rebaited daily (first thing in the morning, if you want to minimize the possibility that other passing craft have been there first). Whether, and how far, you move them each day will depend largely on how well, and what, they are catching. Any one throwing lobster pots (which are the same as crab pots, by the way) over inshore reefs is taking pot luck (sorry) on what might turn up, but the casual potsman doing it for fun need not be so fussy as the commercial fisherman. I know that a few velvets and a spider crab will give me a fine meal (at least a great soup), so if that's all I'm catching, I won't feel bound to move my pot in search of the big lobster. (Besides, lobsters are wanderers, and you never know when one might turn up.) Eventually, however, you will want to vary the ground over which you throw your pots, even if only by 50 yards at a time.

For more details on techniques for throwing pots, see under Lobsters, Crabs, Prawns, etc., below.

SEA ANGLING

I have decided not to include much detailed information on angling for or cooking sea fish, as the list of species that can be caught from shore and boat in our waters is a long one, and unlike our freshwater fish, most sea fish are available commercially in the fishmonger and have been covered well in the culinary literature. (Incidentally, the best all-round book on fish and shellfish is *North Atlantic Seafood* by Alan Davidson – it provides a brief natural history for each creature as well as being witty, wise and largely comprehensive about the whole delightful subject of fish cookery.)

Of course, one of the great pleasures of sea angling, both from shore and boat, is that just about every fish you are likely to catch will be superb eating and flappingly fresh. For beginners and holiday anglers hoping to hook 'one for the pot', I can highly recommend the book *Shore Fishing* by veteran sea angler Trevor Houseby. Meanwhile I will mention just a couple of fish in my field guide.

SHORE FORAGER'S FIELD GUIDE

MACKEREL

I include the ubiquitous mackerel because even a complete novice can fish for them with every chance of success and, when as fresh as only a self-caught fish can be, they are fantastic eating.

Catching

Almost everyone who has been on a seaside holiday has paid to go on a mackerel fishing trip at least once, and many will have hauled up a 'full house' – 6 mackerel on 6 feathered hooks, on either a hand line or an iron poker of a rod intended for shark and conger fishing. It's fun, but the novelty soon wears off. If you want some real sport, try taking your own tackle on a mackerel fishing boat (or on your own boat). A light spinning rod and just a couple of feathers or reflector (hok-eye) lures, or a single fairly heavy (28g/1oz) wobbling spoon, such as a Toby, will always catch fish if the fish are there. When mackerel are feeding close to the surface, they can even be caught on a fly rod. You need a sinking line and a sinking fly (the flashier the better). Now that's fishing.

Mackerel shoals tend to come inshore as the water warms up during the summer months, and in late summer and autumn can often be taken from piers or rocky points dropping off into deep water. Again, the most sporting rig is a spinning outfit, light but with good casting power, and either a 2 or 3 hook feather rig (the modern alternative to feathers, the hok-eye rigs, are even better) or a single fairly weighty spinner or spoon.

If the mackerel are out of reach of shore points, you will need to get on a boat to find them. If you have your own boat (or access to one), and want to know where to find the mackerel shoals, ask the local fishermen. Shoals move, of course, but fish are also creatures of habit, and there will often be regular 'hot spots', which will vary with the tide and season.

It is often possible to haul in vast catches of mackerel, filling several buckets before one has even stopped to think what one might do with them all. There's no sense in wasting good fish, so be ready to call it a day when you have enough. And if you are a fan of pickled fish, you will find the recipe on page 83 for gravad mackerel a fine way to deal with the excess of your catch.

Preparation

Mackerel should ideally be eaten the same day they are caught, or, if refrigerated as soon as possible after landing, no later than the following day. Being oily fish, they freeze reasonably well, but a defrosted mackerel still bears no comparison with fresh, and if I am going to prolong their kitchen life, I prefer to preserve or pickle them in some way (see page 128).

Mackerel are easy fish to gut, and particularly easy if you cut the head off first (just behind the pectoral fins), which I prefer to do. The head will take most of the guts with it, and the cavity can then be slit open to remove the rest of the stomach contents. I usually gut my catch on the boat on the way back into port, tossing heads and guts overboard for gulls and other fish. That way I can get cooking as soon as I get home, and enjoy my mackerel even fresher.

Being a very round-bodied fish, almost sausage-shaped in fact, it can take quite a while to cook a whole mackerel right through, particularly a larger fish. I therefore prefer to split fish down the middle, cutting beyond the natural cavity towards the tail of the fish. Turned skin side up, the fish can then be pressed flat with the palm of the hand and, when turned over, the backbone can be easily lifted out, giving you a nice flat slab of fish like a double kipper fillet that cooks in just minutes. This method is also the perfect way to prepare this fish for a dish of gravad mackerel: they can then be marinated in pairs (see page 83).

Cooking

Prepared as above, and seasoned with sea salt and black pepper, the mackerel can be placed skin-side down on a very hot barbecue, grill pan or lightly greased heavy frying pan. Cook until you can see that the fish is almost cooked right through (the flesh is turning opaque), then turn over for just a minute to finish off the inside. Apart from the salt and pepper, the only seasoning I regularly use for mackerel is a bay leaf or two, placed under the fish during frying, barbecuing or grilling. Its affinity with this much underrated fish is quite uncanny.

Fresh mackerel cooked simply like this hardly cries out for an accompaniment, but it can be very good with either a salsa verde (green herbs pounded with garlic and anchovies) or a fruity chutney (such as plum or rhubarb). I prefer a few simply boiled and lightly buttered potatoes to chips.

Another way to enjoy mackerel, almost raw, is described on page 128.

BASS

I mention the bass (often called sea bass) because it is my favourite of all sea fish, both to pursue and to cook – though I have to say I have had a great deal more success in the latter department (cooking bass caught by other people) than I have in the former.

Rod-caught bass are taken by boat and from the shore by all kinds of methods, but especially spinning, livebaiting with sand-eels, and beachcasting with worm and squid baits. The pursuit of bass is a specialist form of angling, and one at which, as I've said, I can't claim a great deal of success to date. I therefore won't tell the secrets of my technique, in case you are cursed with the same 'luck' as me. Had I caught one in the Cornish episode of the series, I would have grilled it over a fire of dried fennel twigs (see page 21). As it was, after fishing all night I had to make do with a meagre breakfast of sand eels – my leftover fishing bait.

CRUSTACEA
(see pages 99 and 119 for illustrations)

BROWN (EDIBLE) CRAB

The brown or edible crab is, commercially speaking, one of the most important crustacea harvested in our waters, and it is taken by potsmen (in boats known as 'crabbers') in vast quantities. These days the best catches are mostly made over deep reefs a long way offshore, but they do occur on inshore reefs, and can be taken in pots placed beyond the low-tide mark, and even occasionally by beachcombing.

Crabs do not enjoy the same culinary status as lobsters but only, I suspect, because of the relatively portionable meatiness of the lobster's fat tail. Being a great fan of the brown meat (inside the carapace), which others scorn, if anything I prefer crabs.

There is a minimum keeping size for brown crabs – 12 cm/4½ inches across the widest part of the shell. This doesn't strictly apply if you are not offering crabs for sale, but it is as well to observe it for conservation reasons in areas where crabs are regularly fished. Females carrying eggs should always be returned.

Catching

For information on catching crabs in pots, see principally the section on throwing pots above, page 96. The brown crab does not share an identical habitat to the lobster, though they certainly overlap. As well as on reefs, and among rocks, brown crabs can also be caught on a 'mixed' bottom, of muddy sand, rough ground and shingle. They will come to just about any bait, but are said by some fishermen to prefer white fish to oily (such as mackerel) and fresh to smelly.

Young edible crabs are regularly found hiding under weedy rocks at low tide, and also in holes on muddy, shingly beaches. Crabs of a decent size found in such places are a rarity, but some beaches (for example around Brancaster and Hunstanton in Norfolk, and the Helford estuary in Cornwall) are known for producing the occasional monster. Locals like to try their luck by 'chinking' – a technique that takes its name from the sound of metal on stone. A chinking iron (usually a metre or so/2 or 3 feet of broom handle with a hand-sized metal hook attached to the end) is thrust into likely-looking holes and used to hoik out any crabs that may be lurking at the back.

Killing

There is an officially sanctioned technique for humanely killing crabs: a sharp spike or small screwdriver is pushed through the mouth, between the eyes, and into the head at the top of the carapace. A second point, which should also be spiked, is the ventral nervous centre. Lifting the tail flap of the crab reveals a cone-shaped patch – the

1. Lobsters
2. Brown Crabs
3. Velvet Crabs
4. Dublin Bay Prawns
5. Shore Crabs
6. Hermit Crabs
7. Squat Lobsters

spike should be driven into the centre of this. It is also, in my view, quite humane to submerse a crab quickly in a large pan of rapidly boiling water, which will kill it almost instantly. The principal reason this is not the commercial practice is that the crab will tend to shed its legs and claws. This may make them harder for a fish-monger to sell, but for those which are going to be eaten at home it really doesn't matter.

Cooking

Crabs should be plunged into a large pan of rapidly boiling sea water. (Alternatively, add 30g/1oz salt to every 1 litre/2 pints of water). Most fishmongers over-cook them. After coming back to the boil, 12 minutes is enough for any crab up to about 750g/1½lb, 15 for anything up to 1kg/2¼lb, 20 for up to 1.5kg/3½lb, and 25 for anything larger than that.

There is no reason not to eat just-boiled crabs still hot (but just cool enough to be handled for cracking), either with home-made mayonnaise, garlic butter, or just plain melted butter with a little squeeze of lemon.

Boiled crabs that you want to eat cold and dressed should be left to cool naturally in a well-ventilated place. Most recipes for crab begin with cold, cooked crab.

Getting into a crab

There are only two bits of a crab that you shouldn't eat: the inside and the outside. Only kidding. Once you have pulled the carapace away from the main body of the crab, the most obviously dodgy bits are revealed at once. The gills (or 'dead men's fingers') are the grey spongy bits cling-ing to the main body. Pull them off and discard them. In the centre of the carapace itself, attached to the mouth parts, are the stomach and connected organs: break off the mouth part and the stomach will come with it. Throw this away. Everything that is left, the rich creamy brown meat inside the carapace, and the fine-grained white meat inside the legs, claws and body, and any other pink bits of coral or brown soupy bits, is edible, so waste nothing!

Once you know what not to eat, it's really up to you to choose any method that appeals, brutal or subtle, to wheedle out all the meat. My own preferred tools are a hammer and a chopstick.

Dressed Crab: There are many ways to dress cold crab, but my favourite is to mix the brown meat with a good blob of mayonnaise, a little mustard and freshly ground black pepper and a chopped hard-boiled egg, and serve it next to a pile of the white meat, absolutely plain. The only

other accompaniments are buttered brown bread and a wedge of lemon (which I use only extremely sparingly).

Crab Thermidore: Follow the instructions for lobster thermidore, page 104.

Crab baked in the shell: As for spider crab, page 103.

Crab soup: See page 126 for my favourite fishy soup of all.

SHORE CRAB

Soft-shelled crabs

It is widely thought in this country that the common shore crab (sometimes called the green crab, although coloration varies widely) is not edible. This is not true, and in fact it is exactly this species of crab that is prized in Italy (Venice in particular) when in its soft-shell state (immediately after shedding its carapace – a necessary moulting which allows the crab to grow).

In this country 'softies' (as they are known) have commercial value only as fishing bait: bait collectors make special 'softie-traps', usually out of old tractor tyres, which provide just the kind of shelter they need during the vulnerable moulting stage. When the traps are exposed at low tide, the crabs are collected in large numbers and deep-frozen.

There is no theoretical reason why British soft-shelled shore crabs of a decent size cannot be prepared in either the Venetian (stuffed and baked) or American (floured and fried) manner, but to do so would require some dedication. The crabs are truly 'soft-shelled' for only a matter of hours before the shell starts to harden (as opposed to the bait collectors' 'softies', checked only once a day, whose new shell, though still flexible, is usually already too hard for gastronomic purposes). This means that for a decent supply you need to keep a lot of crabs in a well-maintained cold-water marine vivarium, and catch them just after they moult.

Preparation and cooking

If you should find a decent sized shore crab, just moulted, and want to give it the soft-shelled treatment, you will need to prepare it so that, once cooked, all parts are edible. (For the following authentic procedure I am indebted to Alan Davidson's *North Atlantic Seafood*.) First cut off the crab's 'face' with a pair of scissors, on a line just behind the two eyes. This will kill the crab. Then lift up just enough of the skin to give you access to remove the gills (dead men's fingers). Then cut off the triangular tail flap that folds under the body. Removing the legs and claws is optional (after cooking, they can be crunched up, or sucked out and discarded). Rinse the crab well in cold water and pat dry. Toss in seasoned flour, and fry in a hot pan in plenty of clarified butter. Serve on lightly toasted brown bread with tartare sauce . (Try the 'wild' tartare sauce described on page 41.)

Hard-shelled crabs

When in the normal hard-shelled state, shore crabs are also quite edible. Whether or not they are worthwhile depends on their size, and your own patience. But you shouldn't dismiss them till you've tried them.

Shore crabs can be found at low tide hiding in the bladderwrack and under rocks, and those of a decent size are most easily gathered by chinking (see above, page 98). Larger shore crabs often congregate in harbours, at the bottom of sea walls, and around the concrete piles under jetties. They are easily caught by lowering a decent bit of bait (squid or bacon are always a good bet) on a weighted handline to the bottom, and waiting till you feel an aggressive tug. These feisty crabs are usually so reluctant to let go of the bait that they can easily be pulled to the surface and dropped into a bucket. A landing net is useful if you need to hoist them any distance through the air, as once they leave the water they are inclined to drop off.

Shore crabs will often turn up in pots, and those that do will tend to be of a reasonable size.

Preparation and cooking

Shore crabs need just five minutes in boiling sea water. As with the brown crab, remove and discard (or at least, do not eat) the gills (dead men's fingers).

I like to have a couple of good-sized shore crabs on a seafood platter, just for variety – any meat you can extract from their little claws is quite fine, and the brown meat from under the carapace, though sometimes a little watery, is sweet and tasty.

However, these crabs are probably most useful as soup-fillers or stock flavourers (see the recipe for crab soup, page 126).

VELVET SWIMMING CRAB

With their purplish colour, flat paddle-shaped legs, and the fine velvety covering on their shells, these are an unusual and I think rather beautiful species of crab. They are by no means uncommon, and are often caught by the dozen in lobster pots. Being in the same size range as the shore crab, they have been of little commercial interest – until recently. Whereas they were once either thrown back or killed for prawn pot bait, velvets are now an important constituent of the crustacea export market. Most go to the South of France, where they are a principal ingredient of Provençal fish soup, which is produced in increasingly huge quantities.

Catching

Since they tend to live below the low-tide mark, velvet crabs are rarely found on the beach, though they frequently turn up in pots and are likely to be seen if you are snorkelling or diving below the low-water mark.

They can also be caught occasionally on a baited crab line lowered from a pier, sea wall or jetty (see shore crabs above).

Preparation and cooking

Five or six minutes in boiling sea water is sufficient to cook through an average size velvet, and any extra large ones could be left in for an extra minute or so.

These pretty crabs, a very bright orange when cooked, look good on a seafood platter, and the fine flavour repays the effort of picking out the white meat from the little claws. Crabs of this size are of course fiddly, but the up side is that once you have removed the legs and carapace, and taken off the gills, the main inside body of the crab can be crunched up, shell and all, if you don't mind spitting out a few little splinters.

The velvet, along with larger shore crabs and undersized brown crabs, also goes very well on the seafood beach barbecue (see page 121).

HERMIT CRAB

Of all the creatures of the seashore, hermit crabs are among my favourite – not so much to eat (although they can be very good, if a decent size) but to look at, and to laugh at. Despite an impressive claw and well-armoured legs, the hermit has the misfortune among the crustacea to have been created entirely naked below the waist. His tender pink abdomen is, if you've ever seen one exposed, revealed to be one of the most tempting little morsels any predator could ever hope to find. And the hermit's lifelong mission, besides feeding himself and making little hermits, is to protect his sweet behind by keeping it well buried in the shell he has adopted as his temporary home. Any attempt to pull him out of it will be met by fierce resistance, motivated – I like to think – not simply by the survival instinct, but also by the determination that the embarassing secret of his nether nakedness should never be revealed.

Catching

Any hermit crab you encounter on the beach is unlikely to be of a size worth eating, but below the low-tide mark larger creatures can be found, sometimes in profusion. Most of the hermits I have cooked and eaten have been Scottish: they either turned up in pots intended for Dublin Bay Prawns (see page 105), or were encountered while diving or snorkelling in search of scallops, over rough ground (a mixture of small rocks and silty sand). And every single one of them, if I remember rightly, was living in the former residence of a whelk.

I have also known large hermits turn up in Cornish lobster pots, but I suspect all but the largest generally fall through the holes when the pots are being retrieved.

Preparation and cooking

The best way to prepare hermit crabs is to coax them out of their shells, after which they can be boiled, grilled or fried like large prawns. But unfortunatly the battle to tug a hermit crab out of his home is one in which there are usually two losers: the head end comes off, leaving you with just a modest clawful of white meat, while the main prize is entombed for ever up the dark end of the whelk shell. You can try smashing it out, but you are unlikely to succeed without doing so much damage to the tail as to spoil it for cooking.

A more subtle approach can sometimes succeed. Once hermit crabs have been out of water for a few hours they have to consider their options: one of these is to leave the shell (perhaps on the basis that without it they might be able to move a bit faster). You will know when they are in this decisive stage because they start to hang rather sluggishly out of their shells, testing the air with their antennae. Hermit crabs in this state are sometimes vulnerable to a bit of gentle persuasion. Pick up the shell, take the claw or head between finger and thumb, and try and wiggle them out. You can tell straight away if they are locked tight (in which case give up, and try again later) or starting to weaken a bit (in which case gentle perseverance will soon be rewarded). This is what I did with the hermit crabs seen garnishing the crab soup on page 127.

Hermit crabs very gently heated in a pan of sea water will also sometimes leave their shell — and sometimes they won't. If they do they can be instantly trans-ferred to a second pan of water on a full rolling boil, or to the grill or frying pan in which you intend to cook them. Three minutes is enough to cook them through.

The alternative is to cook them inside their shells, in which case I prefer not to boil them, but to grill them or cook them over a fire or barbecue. Once cooked, they can sometimes (but again, not always) be pulled whole from their shells. If you do end up with a cooked hermit crab that won't come out of its shell, you'll have no option but to take a hammer or rock to it. But try and crack it gently, or by the time you get to the meat it will be full of shards of whelk shell — and that, I can tell you, will considerably reduce the pleasure of consuming the fruits of all that labour.

Eating

Once you have succeeded in cooking your hermit crab, you will find they have several worthwhile morsels: the white meat of the larger claw (and, on a particularly big specimen, the smaller claw as well); a little nut of sweet brown meat just inside the head; and the contents of the plump little leathery pouch that he has been hiding from you all this time: it is a peculiar mixture of fine-grained white meat with brown 'sauce' — a winning combination I assure you, and worth all the trouble the little blighter has given you.

A simply boiled hermit crab makes an exotic (and comment-provoking) addition to a seafood platter, and an amusing garnish to a bowl of shellfish soup. At least I find it funny.

SPIDER CRAB

The extraordinary looking spiky-shelled spider crab is often covered in barnacles, and sometimes even sports seaweed and anemones (self-planted, according to some authorities, to create a good camouflage for its winter hibernation, from which it usually emerges in May). With its eponymously arachnid and rather hairy legs it is not, in appearance, the most appetizing of creatures. But crustacea, like books, are not to be judged by their covers. Spider crabs are great eating, as I was able to demonstrate in the Cornish programme of the first series. My own lobster pot, which had enjoyed a fine tour of inland Britain sitting on top of the Gastrowagon, finally made it into the water, courtesy of Helford estuary potter Larry McAbe, who took me out on his boat. While Larry's pots tempted a number of undersized lobsters, and a rather ferocious conger eel (which he proceeded to put to sleep with a firmly administered back massage), I came up trumps with a couple of enormous spider crabs – the perfect base for a wonderfully fresh crab soup.

Catching

Spider crabs have a preference for warmer water (they are particularly prevalent on the French and Spanish Atlantic coasts), so in Britain they are far more common in the south than in the north, and are only very rarely encountered in Scotland. From May to December they crop up often in the lobster pots of the south coast, particularly those fished inshore on reefs and rocky ground.

While chinking or generally beach foraging, you may occasionally encounter a spider crab hiding in a hole on a reef at low tide. But apart from putting out pots, your best chance of acquiring a spider or two is by snorkelling or diving over a shallow reef. Swim slowly and look carefully, or you may mistake your potential supper for a lifeless rock.

Buying

Unfortunately, due to the continental demand for spider crab, and our own ignorance, most of these fine crustacea go for export, and they are rarely seen in this country on a fishmonger's slab. Near the coast where they are caught, however, you should be able to order them from a local fishmonger or fish merchant. Don't mess around with one or two, but order half a dozen or so, and you should get a good bargain. Better still, try buying direct from the boats as they come into port.

Preparation and cooking

Spider crabs should be cooked exactly as for brown crabs, in a large pan of boiling sea water (or salted fresh water). The timing, by weight, is the same (see page 100).

When the cooked crab is cool enough to handle, the carapace can be removed and the stomach and dead men's fingers removed, in the same way.

Dressed spider crab: In my view, the large amount of brown meat inside the carapace of the spider crab is better even than that of the brown crab. Cold, it can be served as for dressed brown crab above, with the legs and claws, and something to crack them with, presented on the side.

Picking the white meat out of the legs and claws (which on the spider crab are no thicker than its spindly legs) is laborious, but worth the trouble: the thin slivers of white meat are extremely sweet and delicious.

Baked spider crab: The carapace of the spider crab is deep and strong, and makes an impressive receptacle in which to serve the baked crab meat. Once you have extracted all the brown and white meat, mix well together in a bowl. Finely chop a shallot or ½ a small onion, the white part of a leek, and ½ a large peeled carrot. Sauté this *mirepoix* in 2 tablespoons of olive oil until the vegetables are softened, then add a glass of wine, a pinch of cayenne, and a good teaspoon of tomato purée. Simmer hard to reduce the liquid, then mix this with the crab meat. Pile into the carapace, and top with breadcrumbs mixed with chopped fresh parsley and a little grated Parmesan (optional). Bake for 6 minutes in a very hot oven (220°C/425°F/gas mark 7). One decent-sized crab (750g–1kg/1½–2lb), thus prepared, serves two. So it's one shell, two spoons, and a fight to clean out every last scrap of delicious meat.

LOBSTER

For a long time now the lobster has been the king of the crustacea, symbolizing, along with oysters perhaps, the sheer luxury and indulgence of seafood gourmandizing. They are notoriously expensive, which means that getting one for nothing is a particularly good cause for celebration. Why not spend the £20 you saved on a nice bottle of Puligny Montrachet?

(Actually, a number of tiresome individuals have pointed out to me that by the time you have bought a few pots and kitted out a seaworthy vessel to throw them from, just about anything you catch in them is probably costing you about £50 a lb minimum. I refer these spoilsports to my paragraphs above on throwing pots: you really don't even need a boat to do this.)

Catching

Those who regularly scour beaches for crabs, prawns, winkles and other edible quarry will, once in a blue moon, happen on a tide-stranded lobster – and what a thrill that will be. Divers and snorkellers stand a rather better chance of encountering lobsters – especially if they dive at night. But by far the best chance of landing a lobster belongs to those who throw pots. See page 94 for tips on how to get started in this game.

Preparation and cooking

Lobsters are primitive beasts, with nothing in their heads that could be reasonably described as a brain. Their nervous system runs in a lateral line from head to tail; this means that there is no specialized manner of delivering a swift dispatch, and the officially sanctioned manner of killing them is to put them straight into a large pan of rapidly boiling water (from the cook's point of view, ideally sea water, but alternatively fresh water with salt added in the ratio of 30g/1oz to 1 litre/2 pints). Cooking times are, by weight, just a little longer than those for crab: 12 minutes for a minimum sized lobster of 500g/1 lb, 15 minutes for anything up to 750g/1½lb and an extra 5 minutes for every 500g/1lb after that.

Many lobster recipes require you to start with a cooked lobster – if you are following such a recipe remember that the lobster meat should be added to whatever sauce you have prepared only at the end, and just reheated, so as not to overcook the meat (it will become tough, chewy and lose succulence). If your recipe suggests anything to the contrary, then take the liberty of adapting it.

There are many ways to enjoy lobster, some romantic, some classic, and some deeply indulgent. The white meat is so rich and robust that it stands up to all manner of spicing and sophisticated sauces – so much so that I have rather a soft spot for lobster curry. But many lobster eaters make the mistake of eating only the white meat – from claws and tail. There are plenty of other goodies: the creamy meat inside the head, the browny green liver inside the body, and the pink coral that often lines the shell of a female lobster. The only bits you can't eat are the dark gut that runs along the top of the tail (and is easily removed), the small gritty sac just behind the mouth, and the gills (similar to dead men's fingers in a crab, but smaller).

As long as it is very fresh, and not overcooked, I enjoy lobster just about however it comes. But when I cook it myself I generally favour one of the following 3 methods, and I don't cook lobster so often as to be bored of any of them yet.

Beach-fire grilled: Not advisable for really big lobsters, but anything up to 1kg/2lb will be fine. Do not pre-boil the lobster, but you can, if you have scruples about grilling a live lobster, plunge it into boiling water to kill it before you put it on the fire. Over hot embers, a lobster up to this size, turned at regular intervals, will take between 12 and 20 minutes. It's done when the bend in the tail has stiffened. The most appropriate way to eat a lobster thus cooked is to tear it apart with your bare hands as soon as it is cool enough to handle. The only essential accompaniment is a cold beer. But for a little

extra luxury you could dip it in a wild herb butter: simply stir a few spoonfuls of finely chopped chervil, chives and/or wild garlic into a pan of melted butter, and dip in morsels of the lobster. (See page 121 for more on the beach-fire seafood grill.)

Simply boiled: A simply boiled lobster can be eaten either hot or cold. If hot, you could serve it with the wild herb butter described above, if cold, with a home-made mayonnaise, or better still, with a wild version of tartare sauce (see page 41).

Thermidor: Of all the famous chefs' treatments for lobster, the thermidor is easily my favourite, and the only one I regularly cook myself. Classically, white wine and a little butter are reduced in a pan with a chopped shallot and a little chopped tarragon and parsley, then stirred into a couple of tablespoons of thick béchamel, with a little extra cream, English mustard and a pinch of cayenne. The lobster meat (white, brown and coral) is mixed with this sauce, piled into its empty half shells, and topped with Parmesan and breadcrumbs. It's then baked for 5 minutes in a very hot oven, flashed under the grill, and served bubbling and brown. Last September I made a fine wild version of the thermidor, using oak-leaf wine, and substituting wild fennel and chervil for the parsley and tarragon, chopped chives for the shallot, and the pounded seeds of yellow flowering rocket for the mustard.

Crab can be cooked in exactly the same way, for a dish with a softer, moussier texture and a sensational flavour.

CRAWFISH

Also known as crayfish and spiny lobster, this is a species that causes some confusion: it is not the same as the freshwater crayfish (see page 80) – though it is of course related. The crawfish is comparable in size to the lobster, indeed often rather larger (crawfish upwards of 3kg/6lb are not unusual), but lacks the big claws which are such a marked feature of the lobster. It is a reddish brown colour, in contrast to the blue-black of the lobster, and its tail is rather wider and fatter in proportion to its length.

Preferring warmer water, they are common in the Mediterranean, the Red Sea and the Indian Ocean where, in the absence of the true lobster, they are often referred to by that name. But they do occur regularly in British waters, particularly where the Gulf Stream brings in their planktonic larvae, off the west coast of Scotland, and in Devon and Cornwall.

Catching

On marks where they are known to be present (usually on offshore reefs, but sometimes inshore), crawfish are eagerly sought by potsmen, as they fetch a high price in the market, particularly in Paris. Populations tend to be localized, but they may turn up from time to time in any lobster pot.

At one time, crawfish were taken in fairly large numbers by divers: their extremely long reddish whiskers protruding from under a rock will often give away their hiding place. A skilled diver can clean out a reef of its crawfish population in just a few dives. In Cornwall, lobster potters (such as my friend Larry McAbe) blame fairly intense diving for crawfish during the seventies for the scarcity of the creatures today. And John Montgomery, with whom I dived for scallops on the east coast of Scotland, says he has seen some real monsters, but prefers to leave them there as breeding stock.

Preparation and cooking

Preparation is exactly as for lobsters, and the flavour is similar, though perhaps a little less sweet.

SQUAT LOBSTER

There are several kinds of squat lobster, but those you are most likely to encounter are the spiny squat lobster and the long-clawed squat lobster. As the common part of their name implies, these are little chaps (smaller often than a large prawn), but their flat tails, which they carry folded under their bodies, do contain a tasty morsel of meat — not enough to make them commercially viable, but definitely enough to bring a smile to the face of a hungry seafood forager.

Catching

The spiny squat lobster can be found hiding under rocks and in crevices on rocky beaches at low tide. If you hear a flapping noise when you turn over a rock, the chances are that it is made by a spiny squat lobster trying to make its escape. Another good place to look — and you may find a torch useful for this — is underneath jutting rocks and overhangs, where squat lobsters often cling upside down.

The long-clawed squat lobster lives below the low-tide mark, but is easily caught in prawn pots thrown over rough ground, especially in Scottish sea lochs. Scottish prawn potters regard 'squatties' as a nuisance, and an irritating reminder that they have cast their pots over the wrong ground (the Dublin Bay prawns they are after prefer it muddy — see below). I have sometimes found over a dozen in a single pot, and I

always eat them — a small but nevertheless tasty compensation for the lack of large prawns.

Preparation and cooking

Just a couple of minutes in boiling sea water, or well-salted fresh water, will cook a squattie through. On the long-clawed variety, all that is worthwhile is the tail, plus a tiny nugget of brown meat in the head. Anyone who has not seen a squat lobster before will be quite intrigued to find one on a seafood platter.

DUBLIN BAY PRAWNS

Also known as the Norway lobster, and commonly in the restaurant trade as a langoustine, the Dublin Bay prawn is very much between the lobster and the prawn in terms both of size and of armour-plating. On average between 10 and 20 cm/4-8 inches long (not including the claws), the Dublin Bay prawn has a hard shell of a pretty orange colour which, unlike any other crustacea, scarcely changes when the creature is cooked. The shelled tails of Dublin Bay prawns, often crumbed or battered and deep fried, are what traditionally go by the name of scampi. (Though in recent years a lot of other less worthwhile things have gone by that name, including, I suspect, processed fish morsels.) Incidentally, the name comes not from the fact that Dublin Bay has a population of the prawns, but because they first became known in this country from the fishing boats of Dublin Bay, which often caught them while trawling for other species.

Their merits have only relatively recently been recognized in our gastronomy. Before the 1950s they were barely known in Britain (except in Dublin, of course). Now they are among the most sought-after, and expensive, of all our crustacea. And quite right too, since their juicy tails have almost the firmness of lobster, and all the sweetness and flavour of the best shrimps.

Catching

This species of prawn lives on a muddy, sandy sea bottom, or on rougher ground provided there are sandy patches to burrow in. They spend daylight hours buried in the mud with just their antennae protruding, and emerge at night to feed. These nocturnal habits mean that the only practical way to catch Dublin Bay prawns is to throw pots for them.

The distribution of Dublin Bay prawns is from Iceland all the way to Morocco and the Mediterranean, but in Britain the best catches are made off the coasts of Scotland and Ireland. For those who live or holiday near waters where the Dublin Bay prawn is found, casual potting can be great fun. The pots specially designed to catch these prawns are relatively light, and can easily be pulled by one person in strings of three or six. I suspect there are many sea lochs and calm bays on the west coast of Scotland where fair catches of prawns could be made by throwing a few pots. The important thing is to be sure you are on the right kind of bottom: if you are catching a lot of squat lobsters (see above) it is a sure sign that you are on rough or rocky ground. Once you get bored of eating squat lobsters, you can throw your pots over fresh ground.

It is one of the joys of putting out pots for Dublin Bay prawns that even if you don't get any of the intended quarry, all kinds of other things are likely to show up in your pots, almost all of them edible. I have made a fine meal from the contents of one pot that didn't include a single prawn. What I did get were half a dozen velvet crabs, a few large hermits, 2 enormous whelks, a small conger eel – and about 20 squat lobsters. All of it went to very good use.

Preparation and cooking

Boiling: Plunged alive into rapidly boiling sea water, or fresh water salted with 25g/1oz of salt for every 1 litre/2 pints of water, Dublin Bay prawns will take between 3 and five minutes after coming back to the boil, depending on size. They can then be eaten hot or cold, with melted butter, mayonnaise or, better still, the wild herb butter suggested for lobster above, or the wild tartare sauce on page 41. They are the best thing on a seafood platter, and I never know whether to eat them first or last.

Beach-fire grilling and barbecuing: This is my favourite way to cook Dublin Bay prawns. Turn frequently, and over hot embers they will take about 10 minutes. They are done when the bend in the tail has stiffened.

Soup: I also like a couple of prawn tails to garnish a shellfish soup – especially the crab soup on page 126. Shells and heads make excellent shellfish stock.

PRAWNS

The common prawn of inshore waters is a fabulous little creature for which I have a large and enduring soft spot: this curiously translucent creature was probably the first wild creature I ever stalked for food, armed as I was, at the age of three, with a rock pool net and a little yellow bucket. Twenty-eight years later I find the same activity equally engaging, and the feast that follows it better than ever.

Catching

I've never been able to work out exactly what it is that makes some rocky beaches prime prawn-hunting territory and others relatively prawn-free. I have known beaches scattered with hundreds of prawny-looking weed-fringed rock pools – from which I have drawn a complete blank; others where just a few shallow pools have yielded a fine harvest. A combination of rocks, muddy sand and plenty of sea lettuce and other green weeds seems to be productive, but I have also had success in rock pools that appear on sand- and mud-free limestone reefs exposed at the low tide. I suspect there are good prawn beaches all around our coast, but I have had my most productive hunting in the south and south-west – particularly on the coast of south Wales, Dorset and Devon. Common prawns seem to be very scarce in Scotland.

When you arrive at a new hunting ground, one fairly quick way to ascertain how good the sport is likely to be is to knock a few limpets off the rocks, mash them up with a stone, and throw the juicy mess into a likely-looking rock pool. Blennies, gobies and small crabs will certainly go for them, but within a couple of minutes prawns, if there are any in the vicinity, should arrive to investigate the smell.

On a good prawny beach, you will catch prawns by wading through rock pools and simply running a fine-meshed net along the edges of weed-fringed rocks, and underneath little underwater overhangs. Choice of net is important: shrimping nets, with their wooden bar at the front for pushing through the sand, are not suitable for rock pool work. The best prawn net I ever owned had a diamond-shaped opening, the pointed end of which was ideal for poking into little corners. I wonder what happened to it.

My favourite technique, however, is to stalk individual prawns, again using the ubiquitous limpet as bait (or a small shore crab, with the carapace ripped off). Place the bait in your net and sink it in the bottom of a rock pool. Any prawns will soon start to approach. When a decent specimen is right in, or over, your net, lift it up smoothly and quickly. Should you twitch the net prematurely, your prawns will shoot backwards out of range; but let it settle, and they'll soon creep cautiously back. If you are patient, and efficient, you can often get 2 or 3 at a time. Using this method, it may take all the time that the tide allows to get enough prawns for tea for two, but it's hard to imagine how to have more fun on a beach – with your clothes on, at any rate.

Prawn traps

There are various nets and traps especially designed for catching common prawns. It seems they are mostly used by anglers collecting prawns to use as bait (live prawns are deadly for pollack and bass), but there is no reason why they should not be deployed by those with culinary motives. Most useful is a circular drop net, with either a nylon or collapsible wire mesh. A drop net should be baited (e.g. with a fillet of mackerel or a handful of chopped limpets) and then lowered on a line into deep rock pools, off the end of reefs, or from jetties and harbour walls where prawns are known to congregate, until it touches the bottom. Every few minutes the net is pulled up, swiftly and smoothly, so the prawns do not have time to swim up and out. You can buy a drop net from most seaside tackle shops, or make your own from the rim of an old bicycle wheel.

Common prawns are also caught commercially on strings of prawn pots, baited with crab or fish and thrown, like lobster pots, on inshore reefs. If you can get hold of two or three, they can usefully extend the range of your prawn hunting: marked with a buoy on a line, they can either be dropped from a boat or thrown from the end of a reef. They should be checked every day, or at every low tide. Small collapsible prawn traps, built on the same 'they can check in but they can't check out' principle, can also be bought from some tackle shops, and can be fished in strings, if weighted with an anchor and marked by a buoy, or simply anchored in a good rock pool for the duration of a tide. Pots and traps dropped below the low-tide mark will often tend to catch the larger prawns.

Preparation and cooking

Live prawns should be dropped in boiling sea water (or fresh water salted at the rate of 30g/1oz for every 1 litre/2 pints of water). Two minutes is all that is required to turn them pink and cook them through, unless they are unusually large, when 3 minutes may be allowed. I like to eat them as soon as they are cool enough to peel without burning my fingers. The tails are obviously where the meat is, but the heads are definitely worth a suck. Freshly boiled prawns really need no accompaniment, but if you want a little extra something then a home-made mayonnaise, melted butter, or a dipping pool of olive oil can be nice, especially if flavoured with a little chopped garlic (either wild or tame) and black pepper.

Cooking prawns on the beach

Just-caught prawns are never better than when cooked straight away on the beach. But bringing a large pot of sea water to the boil over a beach fire can be tiresome and time-consuming. I have two more convenient methods.

The first is to place a frying pan right on the hot embers, with just a little oil, until it is very hot. I then fry the prawns — in small batches so that the heat kills them at once — for just a couple of minutes until they are pink and cooked right through.

The second is to cook them over the beach fire on a grill. This is best done with larger prawns, which can be mounted several at a time on saté skewers. (See also the seafood beach barbecue, page 121.)

BROWN SHRIMPS

Although superficially similar to the prawn, the lifestyle and habitat of the brown shrimp is distinctly different. While the prawn swims freely over and around rocky reefs, the shrimp spends most of its life either on, or just under, the sand. Likewise, in a curious way, the taste is somehow similar but different. I couldn't tell you whether I prefer eating shrimps to prawns, only that I like eating them both very much indeed.

There is no shortage of sand around our coast, but to support a large population of shrimps the sand has to be of just the right quality — a little bit muddy, but not too much — and also have the right relationship with the tide and currents. For this reason the presence of shrimps in inshore waters is fairly localized. The beaches and bays of Norfolk, the Severn estuary and in particular Morecambe Bay have all been known for the quality and abundance of their shrimps, but a once extensive fishery is now in steep decline thanks to overfishing, and perhaps also to pollution. I was lucky enough to go out trawling for shrimps with one of the last shrimp men working out of Morecambe, Raymond Edmondson. It was a tremendous experience, but the relatively small haul of shrimps didn't exactly bode well for the future. It is Ray's hope, and one can only share it, with fingers crossed, that the decline in the industry will gradually lead to a recovery in shrimp numbers.

Catching

Commercial shrimp fishermen use various customized drag nets, all of which operate on exactly the same principle as your common or garden shrimping net: a heavy pole or bar is pushed (or dragged) through the sand, forcing the shrimps up out of the sand so that they can be scooped by the net that comes behind. Ray uses large scaffold poles on a chain, dragged behind a special boat which, drawing only a foot or so, can be used in very shallow waters. Others drag their shrimp nets behind tractors, specially adapted to drive through a few feet of water. And until fairly recently, horses were also being used to trawl for shrimps.

Casual but 'serious' shrimpers also pull customized drag nets (usually fronted by a short length of scaffold pole) over their shoulders. It's very hard work, but productive when the shrimps are in. You could, if you are good at that sort of thing, make your own drag net.

The rest of us will have to content ourselves with a good old-fashioned shrimping net mounted on a stout pole. I suggest you buy the largest (i.e. widest) and strongest you can find. Shrimps can be fished in sand pools (as opposed to rock pools) left by the tide, and also on sand flats in a couple of feet of water, at any stage of the tide, but especially on a rising tide. Simply push your shrimping net, with the bar an inch or so under the sand, along through the water, checking every few yards to see if you have caught anything. You should not expect to see your quarry before it ends up in your net.

As I have said, most shrimp populations are fairly localized, so it may pay to ask around before you start optimistically pushing your net through any old bit of sand. At the same time many sandy beaches that are never fished commercially have small resident populations of shrimps, which can be caught at low tide in sand pools,

and occasionally in the shallows on the shoreline (but only if there is very little surf) – so it never hurts to have a go.

Preparation and cooking
The sandy grey, semi-translucent shrimp turns pinky brown when cooked. As with prawns, sea water is best, and should be boiling when the shrimps are thrown in. They will be cooked just 2 or 3 minutes after the water comes back to the boil.

Eating
Some like to eat shrimps whole, head and all, others eat only the tail, but still in its shell. Still others (the majority of us Brits, I suspect), remove the tail, peel it, and eat only the peeled morsel. I tend to eat them whole until I am bored of the sensation of crunching shells, then go for the peeled tail option.

Like prawns, freshly boiled shrimps need little accompaniment, but it would be a sin not to mention the shrimp's amazing affinity with butter. Peeled shrimps can be tossed in melted butter to which has been added a pinch each of mace, nutmeg and cayenne pepper. They can then be eaten straight away, or 'potted' and refrigerated for later consumption, either hot or cold.

I took a little dipping sauce on board Ray's boat – a phial of olive oil mixed with finely chopped wild garlic leaves, chopped wild chives, and a few drops of elderberry wine vinegar. I thought it was great, and to my delight Ray was rather taken with it too.

MOLLUSCS
(see pages 110 and 119 for illustrations)

Before describing the collectable edible molluscs, it seems in order to issue a mild warning about the small risk of food-poisoning that consuming them may entail. It has long been said that shellfish, particularly oysters and mussels, should not be harvested and eaten unless there is an 'r' in the month – thereby excluding the summer months between May and August. There is a certain logic to this guideline, but not one widely understood. There is no mysterious poison that arises seasonally in these organisms. It is rather that, in the summer months, when the waters are warm, most molluscs have their breeding season, which already puts them partly out of condition. This is also a time when, due to the higher water temperature, naturally occurring bacteria, and also those introduced by organic pollutants such as sewage,

are greatly on the increase. Under this combination of conditions, the ability of some shellfish (cockles, mussels and other bivalves in particular) to filter out dangerous toxins may be impaired.

But provided you take your shellfish from clean waters, and follow a few simple rules in their preparation, you can safely eat molluscs all the year round. (Having said that, you might like to consider, for considerations of conservation rather than safety, not knocking them too hard when the poor little blighters are trying to make babies.)

So the full set of safety rules is:

I. Never collect shellfish (bivalves especially) from close to human habitation, from near busy ports and harbours, or near a sewage outlet.

2. Always rinse well in clean water before cooking.

3. Always check your shellfish are alive immediately prior to cooking. Bivalves should close tightly shut when tapped with a finger or run under a cold tap.

4. In particular, any shellfish that you suspect might be even mildly contaminated should not be eaten raw.

COCKLES

The cockle doesn't have the sweetness of the mussel or the subtlety of the scallop, but these plump, heart-shaped shells provide a tasty morsel of meat all the same. Populations are found all around the British Isles, but are localized where conditions are just right: cockles prefer a mixture of sand, mud and sometimes fine gravel.

Collecting

First find your cockle ground: local knowledge may point you in the right direction, but finding a new cockling patch is a cause for great satisfaction, so always be on the lookout for a profusion of empty cockle shells – a natural sign that living progeny may not be far away. Cockles occur usually between the mid- and low-water marks, but some cockling patches are revealed only at the lowest tides (during full and new moons), so this may be the best time to try out new hunting grounds.

You will occasionally encounter cockles just sitting on the sand waiting to be plucked, but most will be found an inch or two under the surface. The essential tool for exposing them is an ordinary garden rake – or a customized cockler made by banging a few 10cm/ 4 inch nails through a bit of wood and fixing a handle to it. Rake backwards and forwards over the sand and see what comes up. Where cockles are regularly raked you may have to work hard for every shell, but if you are lucky enough to strike on a new patch, you can often fill a bucket in half an hour.

Preparation and cooking

Cockles can often contain quite a lot of sand. The best way to purge them of it is to rinse them well, then leave them in a large bucket of clean sea water, in a cool place, for several hours and rinse again before cooking.

Steaming: One of the best and simplest ways of cooking cockles is to steam them open in a shallow court bouillon of wine brought to the boil with butter, garlic and a few herbs. Throw in the cockles, in batches if you have a lot of them, and remove each batch with a slotted spoon when they have opened. If you want to serve the liquor with cockles (and you should: it is delicious), then it is a good idea to strain it through a cloth to filter out any sand that may remain.

Beach fire: Good size cockles can be cooked in their shells in the embers of a beach fire, or on a wire rack above it, until their juices boil and their shells pop open. No finer thing...

The flavour of bacon and pancetta goes well with cockles, and is an important ingredient in the cockle chowder on page 124.

CLAMS

There are almost 20 species of clam found around the British coast, some more easily encountered than others, depending on their habits. All are edible, and some are delicious, though some (like the little pink tellin) are often too tiny to be viable. Perhaps the best find is the carpet shell clam (what the French call *palourde*), which can be raked, like cockles, from gravelly sand at low tide, sometimes rather closer to the high tide mark. Their presence is indicated by two little dimples in the sand, between 1-3cm/½-1 inch apart. They are outstandingly good.

Also worthwhile, though on the small side, is the wedge shell or bean clam. These have a triangular, but not quite symmetrical shell, and are found right at the low-water mark: their patches are often only rakeable at the lowest low-water marks, during spring tides. The meat is a little chewy, but very pleasantly sweet.

Preparation and cooking

All clams can be steamed open, like mussels, in a court bouillon of wine and/or water, butter, herbs and, optionally (but highly recommended), garlic. They are ready when all, or at least the vast majority, are open.

Small clams such as the wedge shell, steamed open and mixed with a piquant tomato sauce, make a classic 'vongole' sauce for spaghetti.

Clams collected from clean water are great to eat raw – especially the wedge shell.

RAZOR CLAMS

These distinctive members of the clam family deserve, I think, their own entry, partly because they are very underrated, partly because there is a specialized and highly effective technique for gathering them, but mainly because I actually succeeded in collecting some in the series – with a little bit of help from Norfolk mollusc enthusiast Tim Venner.

1. Mussels
2. Scallops
3. Limpets
4. Winkles
5. Cockles
6. Whelks (and a Hermit Crab!)

Anyone who has kept their eyes open on a beach will have seen the long empty shells of this creature, so resembling the eponymous cutthroat razor, but few have ever seen one alive. Still fewer have had the distinct pleasure of eating one.

Collecting

Razor clams are found on sandy beaches at, and just below, the low-tide mark. Generally it is only practical to gather them on the lowest spring tides. But when conditions are right, and provided you have the tools for the job, a good number can be collected in a fairly short time.

Like most species of clam, the razor lives a few inches below the surface of the sand, but if disturbed, or sensing danger, the powerful muscular foot of this species can quickly pull him 2 or 3 feet under. The secret of luring him out is to irritate him, and the best way to do this is to pour salt down his burrow. Tim Venner has developed a particularly effective technique, in which he puts a very strong warm saline solution in a gardener's backpack-mounted weedkiller spray can. The razor clam reveals its place in the sand by a single dimple, about an inch wide, in the centre of which is his blow hole. Into this hole, Tim inserts the nozzle of the spray can and gives a good squirt of very salty water. Within a minute or two (sometimes longer, and occasionally not at all) the razor clam will shoot to the surface, sometimes with impressive speed, and usually protruding from the sand by a good few inches, allowing the collector to pluck it easily. In areas where razor clams are plentiful, Tim likes to walk along the low-tide mark, squirting a couple of dozen holes, then turn back on himself to pick up the razor clams that have emerged during the preceding minutes.

Preparation and cooking

Razor clams can be a bit sandy, so it is a good idea to purge them – just rinse them well, and leave them in a bucket of clean sea water for a few hours. Rinse again before cooking. Thus purged, the entire contents of the razor shell can be eaten, though the muscular foot is the sweetest morsel. Pulled away from the rest of the meat, this little chunk can be eaten raw, and makes excellent sushi (though Tim wasn't convinced).

Steaming: Their elongated shape notwithstanding, razor clams are prepared much as any other clams: steamed open in a shallow court bouillon of water, wine, butter, herbs – and of course garlic.

In the programme, I cooked my razor clams with wine, garlic, cream and slices of Alexanders, and creamed sea

spinach on the side. They weren't bad (though again, Tim was sceptical), but in all honesty if I did it again I would leave out the Alexanders, which imparted a slightly camphorous taste. Or rather, I would cook the Alexanders separately and serve them as a starter (see page 12).

On a beach fire: Their size and shape make razor clams well suited to the beach fire grill: lay on a wire rack above the hot coals, and cook until tender and bubbling in their own juices.

OYSTERS

One of the most surprising and delightful experiences I had during my first journey was on the island of Mull, where third-generation crofter Linda MacGillivray took me to a weedy beach and introduced me to the gentle art of guddling. As the camera set up, we watched a pair of otters breaking mussels on a stone, and actually feeding them to each other. Needless to say, just before the camera was ready to roll the otters slipped quietly into the water and swam away.

But Linda and I guddled most successfully: wading in the thigh-deep crystal clear water just below the low-tide mark, we were spotting fat oysters, some the size of coffee saucers, just lying on the gravelly sand waiting to be picked up. These were the true wild oysters, the 'natives' which fetch such a high price, and in half an hour we must have collected 3 dozen.

Linda wisely made it a condition of filming that we didn't reveal the exact location of this oyster beach: a cynic could make a quick killing by harvesting sackfuls of them. Where you do find beds of wild native oysters (in calm, shallow bays, estuaries and brackish creeks), take as many as you and your friends can eat at a sitting. But leave it at that, and you will stand a better chance of enjoying them for many years to come.

Natives are farmed in this country, but not as much as the fast-growing Portuguese or 'rock' oyster. Escapees of this widely cultivated variety occasionally seed themselves on rocks and reefs near to where they are farmed: they are almost impossible to prise whole and undamaged from the rocks, but they can be opened and the meat collected or, more probably, eaten on the spot.

Opening

I have eaten my fair share of oysters, but I'm still rather bad at opening them. I'm getting better, though: for both species, it's flat side up in a gloved or clothed hand, and the blade (which should be short, stout and not too sharp) goes in, pointing slightly downwards, at the hinge. That's all I can say, except that practice makes ... well, competent, if not quite perfect.

Eating

I like my oysters raw with a twist of freshly ground black pepper and a tiny drizzle of olive oil (a tip from my French friend Alex – thanks, Alex). So no lemon for me (though millions of other oyster fans enjoy it), and Tabasco, Worcester sauce and shallot vinegar are all out – too powerfully flavoured for my liking.

Those who have a problem guzzling raw oysters by the dozen, who think, perhaps, that they don't like oysters, should try them cooked – either steamed open like mussels, in a marinière-style bouillon, or placed over a barbecue or beach fire until the shells open.

Grilled: Steamed oysters can be put back in the half shell, on a little bed of steamed spinach, covered with a spoonful of cheesy béchamel and a sprinkling of breadcrumbs, and flashed under a grill until browned and bubbling.

MUSSELS

On our shores, mussels are one of the most prolific of the bivalve species, and one of the most well distributed. There's probably not 10 miles of British coastline without a clump of mussels on it somewhere. How nice, then, that they just happen to be so delicious.

Collecting

As far as I am concerned, the bigger the better: even the biggest English mussel is never more than a mouthful. The keen mussel-hunter is therefore ever in search of new pastures, where bigger, fatter mussels may be found. Mussels will grow on just about anything (as mussel-farmers have shown rearing seed mussels on wooden stakes, scaffold poles and heavy ropes). Experience shows that larger mussels are often found nearer the low-tide mark, and logic suggests that this may be because they are submerged for longer, and so spend more time feeding. There are anomalous exceptions, and occasionally you will find a lush clutch of plump mussels growing near the high-tide mark, sometimes among a bed of their rather tiny cousins.

Mussels can simply be pulled from the rocks or other obstacles to which they have anchored themselves. If you are collecting a large number, a stout gardening glove (or similar) is a distinct advantage because the shells can be sharp, as can the barnacles which cling to them.

Some mussels, and sometimes whole colonies of mussels (mainly those which have to filter a lot of sand) can be gritty, as they contain tiny pearls spun around irritant particles to protect the mussel's sensitive gut. This does not make them inedible, but it can be a bore spitting out the little pearls. If you can't hack it, it's time to move on to fresh, pearl-free pastures.

Where mussels are really plentiful, and you're spoiled for choice, it's best to avoid heavily barnacled or very dirty ones, as they will only give you more work later.

Preparation and cooking

Before cooking, mussels should be well rinsed in fresh water (scrubbed if they are very dirty). The beards (the wiry hairs that hold the mussels to the rocks – and often to each other) should also be removed. These are easily torn away either with a light pair of pliers, or if gripped between your thumb and a blunt knife.

If your mussels are going to be presented in their shells, thorough cleaning and scraping off of barnacles is particularly important. But if you are planning to remove the meat from the shells and present it in some other way (see mussel and sea beet gratin, page 125), then as long as mud and loose dirt is removed, you don't need to scrape or de-beard them. The beards can easily be removed from a cooked mussel, and if you want to use the liquor as the basis of a sauce, it can be strained through muslin or a cotton cloth to filter out any loose grit.

Steaming: The simplest way to cook mussels is to throw a glass of wine, a glass of water and a good knob of butter into a pan, add two crushed cloves of garlic (or a few finely chopped leaves of wild garlic), and bring it to a fierce boil. Add the mussels, put on a lid, and shake well every minute or so. Check progress after about 3 minutes. Mussels should be cooked as lightly as possible: remove the mussels as soon as a good three-quarters of them are wide open. Discard any that fail to open. Never overcrowd the pan (not more than three mussels deep, I always say), and if you have a lot of mussels, cook them in batches: each batch can be removed with a slotted spoon, and the liquor brought back to the boil before the next batch is added.

Grilling: Good-sized mussels can be grilled on a barbecue, a rack over a beach fire, or in hot ashes, until the shell opens.

Raw mussels: Good-sized mussels from very clean water are delicious raw: a little less meaty, but much sweeter, than oysters. Try dressing with just a few drops of very good olive oil, a twist of freshly ground black pepper, and the tiniest squeeze of lemon.

SCALLOPS

One of the biggest thrills of the series for me was diving for scallops in Lochaline Bay on the west coast of Scotland, with part-time scallop diver John Montgomery. And the moment I enjoyed most was when I reached out to pick up a scallop off the sea bed and to my amazement he (and she, to be precise, since scallops are hermaphrodites) shot away from my grasp, opening and shutting his (and her) shell like a pair of clacking castanets. I had heard that they could do this, but never expected to see it.

Collecting

Scallops are gregarious, living in beds on firm mud, sand and gravel, often close to kelp forests (which provide the necessary cover for the tiny young scallops). Dedicated snorkellers may find a few scallops in water shallow enough to duck-dive for them, but their usual range is 10-40 metres/30-130 feet, and only qualified divers will regularly enjoy the privilege of a free scallop feast.

Scallops are very occasionally stranded by exceptionally low tides, and research may reveal when and where this is likely to happen. But generally speaking, non-divers will have to pay for their scallops: if you want a decent number, you will get a far better price if you can contact a scallop diver and buy direct than you ever will from a fishmonger. I always like to buy my scallops alive and in the shell, as a guarantee of freshness.

Dived scallops are far more ecologically sound than dredged: dredging has rendered whole areas of sea floor into near deserts, and in my view should be banned.

Preparation

The scallop contains a really exquisite puck of sweet white meat (the adductor muscle), which must be separated from the rather gloopy guts and surrounding organs (including upwards of fifty eyes that fringe the shell, although the 'fringe' of eyes can be included in soups and chowders).

To clean a scallop, hold it vertically on a board, hinge end up, with the flat side of the shell facing towards you. Insert a knife blade into the gap in the shell just below the hinge, and slice down, as close as possible to the flat side of the shell. The shell will spring open and you can snap off the flat side at the hinge: all the meat and organs will be left sitting in the deep side of the shell. Then run a sharp flexible blade under the adductor muscle, to release it from the inside of the shell. With the tip of the knife, cut around this muscle, freeing it from all the attached organs except the plump pinky orange organ known as the coral, which may be left attached, as it is also edible. (If the coral is withered, discoloured or otherwise in poor condition – a seasonal occurrence which does not affect the quality of the muscle meat – then discard it with the rest of the offal.)

Very large, fat scallops can be sliced horizontally in half to create 2 discs of meat that will cook through in a mattter of seconds. But don't slice through the coral – leave it whole and attached to one of the two halves.

Cooking

There are dozens of ways to cook a scallop, and dozens of ways to overcook them – this is a great mistake, as one of the sweetest and most pleasant-textured of all shellfish is quickly rendered rubbery and bland. I don't like elaborate scallop dishes, both because of the danger of overcooking and because I don't think they are conducive to enjoying fresh scallops at their best.

I like to cook scallops for between 30 seconds or a minute either side, on a hot griddle, heavy frying pan or barbecue, and I prefer piquant dressings and salsas to creamy sauces. See page 120 for a super and simple scallop dish.

Scallop sashimi: One good way to be absolutely sure you don't overcook scallops is to eat them raw. You should prepare this dish with only the freshest scallops, and use only the white adductor muscle, not the pink coral. Slice thinly and arrange on a plate. Dress with just a trickle of toasted sesame oil, a few drops of light soy sauce, and a bit of wasabi mustard on the side. Serve with a sea lettuce salad (see page 118), and thin strips of cucumber marinated with rice wine vinegar.

LIMPETS

Limpets don't have much of a reputation as food, but if prepared well they can be quite palatable. According to Alan Davidson (and he knows everything about shellfish), there was once an international trade in tinned limpets. An enterprising Cornishman pickled and tinned them, sending them off to his homesick limpet-loving friends who had recently emigrated to the limpet-less neighbourhood of Chicago. So they can't be all bad.

Collecting

Stealth is the key. Once a limpet is made aware of your intention to dislodge it, it will clamp itself to the rock even harder – like a limpet, no less. But if you approach carefully, without vibrating the rock to which the limpet is attached, they can easily be dislodged by a sharp tap with a stone (or a neat kick of a booted foot). Seriously clamped-on limpets are not absolutely unremovable – a flexible blade slid between rock and shell should do the trick.

Cooking

Boiling: Boiled limpets tend to be tough and rubbery, and lose much of their flavour to the water: better to cook them like mussels, steamed in a shallow liquor of butter, wine, crushed garlic and parsley (or wild chervil and wild garlic). Cook for 5-10 minutes, until the meat is loose in the shells.

Baking and grilling: In the embers of a fire, or just above it on a wire rack, limpets can be placed upside down in their shells, so they bubble and simmer in their own juices. They are certainly quite tender like this, and take on a nice smokiness from the fire.

Alan Davidson records a delightful Scottish recipe for limpet stovies, in which cooked limpets (originally boiled, but I suspect the recipe might be improved if the limpets are steamed in wine as I suggest above) are layered in a pot with sliced potatoes and plenty of black pepper. A couple of ladles of cooking liquor goes over the top, then a few dots of butter, and after being brought to the boil the pot is covered and baked in the oven for an hour. I have only ever had it once, cooked by a friend, and it really wasn't bad: crude but tasty.

WHELKS

Whelks are one of the larger species of sea snail in our waters, and are extremely widespread, living on carrion on mud, sand and rocks all around the British coast.

Whelks seem to divide seafood enthusiasts: some dismiss them as uninteresting rubbery lumps, others rave about their chewy texture and a flavour which has been described as 'between lobster and chicken'. Once siding with the sceptics, I am now a recent convert to whelks which have been properly prepared.

Catching

The common whelk lives mainly below the low-tide mark, but smaller whelks can be found in (and gathered from) rock pools near the low-tide mark. A smaller species of whelk, known as the dog whelk (with whitish, yellow or brown-banded shell), feeds on mussels and barnacles and is often found among them on rocky beaches at low tide. It is also edible.

Larger whelks are easily caught in baited traps dropped on the bottom below the low-tide mark and marked with a buoy. Traditionally large wicker baskets with simple lobster-pot-style entries were used, especially on the prolific whelk fisheries off Grimsby, East Anglia and Whitstable. Now nylon and wire mesh traps are more common. You can easily fashion your own whelk trap from fine-mesh chicken wire wrapped in a tube shape, sealed at one end, with a crude, inward-pointing entrance at the other.

Whelks can also be taken in lobster and prawn pots (though the smaller ones may fall through the large mesh of an average lobster pot). Commercial lobster and crab fisherman (and in Scotland, prawn potters) tend to throw away the whelks they catch. If you ask nicely, and take the trouble to meet them at the port, they may be happy to hand them over to you for nothing, or next to it. And while you're at it, why not ask them to keep any squatties and hermits too...

Whelks have a tendency to concentrate toxins in their gut, and should only be taken from waters in whose cleanliness you have complete confidence.

Preparation and cooking

If not absolutely fresh (i.e. alive), and if poorly prepared (they are often over-boiled), the off-taste and rubbery texture of whelks can be enough to put anybody off for life. For this reason, I rarely buy cooked whelks in England (though the French cope with them rather more reliably). I prefer to catch them alive and cook them myself.

Cleaning: Whelk shells can be very dirty and silty, and the animals have a tendency to exude slime from their shells. To minimize both problems, whelks should be well scrubbed, then placed in a bucket of cold sea water for a few hours, then scrubbed again.

Boiling: They can then be boiled in clean sea water, or well-salted fresh water to which you have added plenty of freshly ground black pepper and (optionally) a halved onion, 2 bay leaves and a large carrot, sliced. Such stock vegetables can help bring out the whelk's unusual savoury flavour. Whelks take about 10 minutes at a merry simmer – traditionally they are ready when the 'operculum', a scaly disc which seals the creature in its shell, comes away from the meat of the foot.

I like to eat just-boiled whelks still warm with a good home-made mayonnaise (to which I sometimes add chopped chives). Pull them out with a pin and dip them in. (Like winkles, the last part to emerge from the shell, though it is edible, can be separated from the firm meat of the foot, and discarded.)

Beach fire: Whelks are very good grilled in their own shells over a barbecue or fire. Either place them on a rack above the embers, or put them directly in hot ash. They will take 10-20 minutes depending on their size, and the heat. If they look a little slimy or underdone when removed from their shells, discard the shell and toast the meat directly over the fire for another couple of minutes, turning occasionally.

Whelks will eat just about anything, and I suspect that the occasional bad apple that crops up in an otherwise good bunch may be the result of a particularly undiscerning meal. If on first bite I find a whelk tastes a bit iffy, I simply spit it out, take a large gulp of wine (usually a chilled rosé) and move on to the next one.

WINKLES

You've got to hand it to a sea snail who gave his name to an item of fashion footwear. Apart from this claim to fame, winkles are the beach forager's favourite stand-by – not the most subtle or sophisticated of seafoods, but dead easy to collect and fun to eat all the same. On almost every rocky beach you will find them in rock pools, on and under rocks, and especially underneath the bladder-wrack.

Collecting

If you can't find a winkle on a rocky beach, then I can only assume that you are extremely short-sighted, and have forgotten your glasses – or there has been a nuclear catastrophe. You should be able to gather dozens of winkles at low tide in a matter of minutes. Having said that, it is worth a little wander to find an area where all the winkles seem to be of a good size – usually near the low-tide mark.

Preparation and cooking

Winkles are usually fairly clean, needing only a thorough rinse under the tap or in clean sea water. From some localities, however, they may be a little gritty: they can be improved by soaking in cold fresh water overnight.

Their flavour is brought out if they are cooked in salted water flavoured with a few herbs and stock vegetables: try a bay leaf, quartered onion, large carrot, a few parsley stalks and a lot of freshly ground black pepper. Simmer this little stock for at least ½ an hour before adding the winkles.

Warm or cold, the winkles thus cooked are removed from their shells with a pin (the original winkle picker) and eaten plain, or dipped in shallot vinegar or mayonnaise. The only non-edible bit is the scaly 'door' to the shell – easily removed with your pin – though some people also like to discard the 'trail' (the last half centimetre or so that emerges from the shell) as it can be a little gritty.

Winkle eggs: Try tossing a couple of dozen picked winkles into a pan of hot bacon fat, frying them for a minute or so, then cracking in a couple of eggs and a small knob of butter. Stir until cooked to your taste, and then pile this 'scrambled omelette' on to toast and serve with the bacon you fried up initially on the side.

SEA URCHINS

There are many foods alleged to be aphrodisiac, but just about the only thing I have ever eaten which I would swear had a physically stimulating effect on me (outside of the strictly oral pleasure zone) is sea urchins. I'm not saying they made me feel amorous, but after eating about 36 of them (with a friend who was at the time exporting them from Ireland to Paris) I was definitely ready to party.

I have since been told that such an effect may be due to the high concentration of iodine in the roe, which derives from the urchins' diet of kelp and kelp-grazing plankton.

Stimulation aside, sea urchins are one of my favourite seafoods, and a treat I enjoy all too rarely.

Collecting

There are several species of sea urchin found in British waters, and all of the round, spiny varieties are edible (the flat, heart-shaped, sand-burrowing kind are not). The most widespread, and the largest, is the common or 'edible' sea urchin, easily spotted by its attractive pink-purple spines with white tips. Fairly frequent on rocky coasts and kelp beds around Britain, particularly in Scotland, the common sea urchin lives mainly below the low-tide mark, so it is most easily collected by snorkelling or diving, though occasionally they can be gathered in deep rock pools near the low-tide mark.

Less common, but more frequently collected for food (because it is more robust, and occurs so gregariously where it is found), is the smaller, greeny brown (sometimes almost black) *Paracentrotus lividus*, sometimes called the green sea urchin. This latter species occurs in great numbers among the kelp forests on the west coast of Ireland, particularly on the Arran Islands in Galway Bay, and less frequently in Devon, Cornwall and the Hebrides. It is usually gathered by wading and snorkelling just below the low-tide mark. On the lowest tides, the *lividus* may be completely exposed, and can be gathered by walking on the rocks and (treacherously slippery) kelp.

It is, for obvious reasons, essential to wear stout gloves for collecting urchins, whether wading, snorkelling or diving. Place the urchins in a thick sack or canvas duffle bag, and before you leave dip it in the sea. Kept wet (either in the collecting sack or covered in wet seaweed), and in a fridge or cool cellar, urchins will stay alive (and therefore edible) for 2 or 3 days.

Preparation

The entire contents of a sea urchin shell may be consumed, but the delectable morsels are the 5 orange sacs of roe, shaped like little segments from a tangerine. These are sometimes known as 'tongues', perhaps to promote the aphrodisiac image.

To get inside an urchin, turn it 'upside down' (which means mouth side up) and cut an opening in the top of the shell. Aficionados of urchins sometimes have a special tool for this job, called a *coupe-oursin*. I have never been able to find one, but it is also easily done with a pair of kitchen scissors, inserted into the mouth opening and snipped around in a circle. Remove any spiny pieces of shell that fall inside, and serve the opened urchins with a teaspoon for scooping out the tongues.

One day, when I am feeling ludicrously extravagant and have a large amount of urchins on my hands, I am going to make little sea urchin soufflés, baked and served in the shells.

EDIBLE SEAWEEDS
(see page 119 for illustrations)

The *fruits de mer* to be had from the beach are not exclusively for flesh-eaters. Edible marine life on the seashore is also well represented by the plant kingdom.

There are well over 100 species of seaweed to be found around our shores, and according to Sonia Surey Gent, who took me snorkelling for seaweed in the Cornish programme, every single one of them is edible. Not just edible in fact, but highly nutritious, and in some cases with highly potent health-giving properties. Sonia had many health problems as a child, and as a young woman she was told she would not be able to conceive. Just a few years after taking up her interest in seaweed, and incorporating a wide variety in her diet, Sonia found herself pregnant. And she jokingly refers to her son as 'my seaweed baby'.

A general faith in the health-giving properties of seaweed is reflected in the ever-increasing number of commercial seaweed-based 'superfoods' on sale in our chemists and health food shops. These pills and powders may well do you all kinds of good, but they are hardly gourmet fare. How much nicer to pick your own, cook it, and enjoy the unusual flavours and textures that seaweed offers, as well as the benefits. Seaweeds can be prepared in many ways and incorporated into all kinds of dishes, including breads, soups and stews, as well as jellies both sweet and savoury. My own preference is for simple preparations, where the taste and character of the seaweed remains prominent. I particularly enjoy simple salads of raw seaweed, with an oriental dressing, and crispy chips made from frying dried pieces of certain types of kelp (see sweet oatweed below).

I can't yet claim to be a great expert in seaweed cookery, and I must admit that I have never even attempted the elaborate preparations that some species require. But since I met Sonia, I have been inspired to experiment with a few readily available species. The following are my favourites.

CARRAGHEEN OR IRISH MOSS *(Chondrus crispus)*
This is one of the few species of seaweeds that has been widely harvested – for use as a food and as an alternative to gelatine. It is very rich in alginates, which in the past have been extracted on a commercial scale and used to emulsify factory-made ice creams (though this process has been largely discontinued – inevitably in favour of more artificial alternatives). It also has a pleasant, slightly yeasty flavour which will enhance many soups and stocks.

The pale purple branched fronds, turning milky brown at the ends, are up to about 20cm/8 inches long and grow in small clusters. They can be found on rocks all around our coast but are more common in south and west Ireland, Devon and Cornwall. They are often found quite close to the high-tide mark. If you pick half clumps, leaving some fronds still attached to the rock, it will continue to grow.

Preparation and cooking

Carragheen can be used fresh or dry, but should be dried if you are not going to use it straight away. Rinse the carragheen in cold fresh water and pat dry with a cloth. Then either put on a rack in a very cool oven (50-75°/130-160°F/gas mark ¼) for 3 hours, or hang on a string in the airing cupboard (or, on a warm dry day, in the sun). When completely brittle and dry to the touch carragheen can be broken into small pieces and stored in an airtight jar. Dried carragheen can still be bought cheaply in many places in Ireland.

Soups: Carragheen can be used to flavour and thicken soups (it produces a particularly pleasant, velvety texture), and to set mousses and jellies, both sweet and savoury. Dried carragheen should be soaked in cold water for 15 minutes, then rinsed well before using to remove any gritty dust.

Try using it in a simple vegetable soup, made by sweating an onion, a leek, 2 medium carrots and 2 sticks of celery, all finely chopped, with a little butter. Add 1 litre/2 pints good chicken or vegetable stock with 15g/½oz of carragheen, soaked and rinsed. Bring to the boil, and simmer gently for about 25 minutes until all the vegetables are tender and the soup is well thickened. Liquidize, season, and serve.

Mousses and jellies: Carragheen can be used pretty much like gelatine, bearing in mind that 15g/½oz will set about 1 litre/2 pints of liquid. But carragheen will not dissolve, and so must be simmered in the liquid which is to be set for at least 15-20 minutes. When the flavoured liquid has thickened like a custard, it should be strained and poured into a mould to set. You can invent your own jellies and mousses, sweet and savoury. For a good sweet recipe, see page 142.

LAVER (*Porphyra umbilicalis*)

If the Irish have explored the versatility of carragheen, the Welsh must take the credit for the continuing use of laver. Laverbread, the classic Welsh preparation, has become rather popular recently in chic London restaurants.

Collecting

Laver is common on rocky beaches all around our coast, but grows especially on rocks which are settled in, or scattered with, sand. The fronds, which comprise thin, leafy, dark purple-brown sheets, grow in wrinkled layers anchored at one corner to the rock. They look fragile, but can withstand an amazing battering by rough seas. Laver can be collected anywhere between the high- and low-water mark. Avoid very sandy specimens, as its slightly sticky surface can make laver hard to rinse. It can be gathered from March to the end of the year.

Preparation and cooking

To make laverbread: You need a good 1kg/2lb of freshly picked laver. Rinse the laver under a cold tap, tearing up the larger pieces as you do so. Put in a large heavy casserole or stock pot, and pour over enough cold fresh water to cover. Bring to the boil, and simmer gently until the laver has disintegrated to a mush. This may take upwards of 2 hours, and the pot should be checked and stirred regularly to make sure it doesn't stick or boil dry. Alternatively, 25 minutes in a pressure cooker will do the trick.

When the laver is completely soft, any excess liquid should be drained off, and the mush broken to a fairly smooth purée with a wooden spoon. This purée is laverbread, and it can be stored in jars in the fridge for up to a week.

Laverbread is traditionally eaten at breakfast with bacon, either mixed with oatmeal and fried in the bacon fat (a bit like dock pudding – see page 29), or spread on fried bread.

I once made laverbread tartlets – little cases of shortcrust pastry with a small square of fried bacon on the bottom, half-filled with laverbread, then topped with a simple savoury custard (egg yolks mixed with cream and seasoned with salt and pepper). They were very good, and I will make them again.

SEA LETTUCE (*Ulva lactuca*)

The papery fronds of sea lettuce are not unlike a bigger, bright green version of laver, and indeed you can mix the two together if making laverbread (see above).

Collecting

Sea lettuce is very common all around the coast, on rocks and in rock pools – so common that it is worth looking for good specimens, especially if you plan to eat it raw. Favour, therefore, smaller bright green fronds with few holes and whose edges are not too ragged or bleached. You will often find such specimens in pools and wet patches where they are less damaged by the sun, and also if you go snorkelling just below the low-tide mark.

Preparation and cooking

Rinse the leaves well in fresh water and trim, if you think it necessary, the bleached outer edges.

Sea lettuce salad: Slice the sea lettuce into thin 0.5cm/¼ inch strips, put in a bowl, and marinade for ½ an hour in 2 teaspoons of rice wine vinegar. Just before serving, add a teaspoon of light soy sauce and toss well. Use to accompany raw fish.

As a vegetable: Cut into small squares and sweat in a little butter or oil (especially sesame seed oil) for 3-4 minutes until tender. Serve as an unusual accompaniment to fish.

SWEET OARWEED *(Laminaria saccharina)* and other kelps

A very common member of the kelp family, and one of my favourites, sweet oarweed is distinctive for its long, dark brown curly-edged belts, a good 15cm/6 inches wide and sometimes over 2m/6 feet long .

Collecting

Unlike other kelps, oarweed does not tolerate much exposure by the tide. It therefore tends to be found very near or below the low-tide mark, but occasionally further up the beach in permanent and reasonably deep rock pools. Snorkelling over a weedy reef, just below the low-tide mark, is the best method to get really good specimens, which can be seen hanging vertically in the water, swaying in the current.

Preparation and cooking

I always cook oarweed (sometimes called sugar kelp, because of its wonderful sweet flavour) the same way, by making deliciously crispy oarweed chips. It needs to be rinsed in fresh water, then hung up to dry. It need not be completely brittle when you cook it, but should at least be much shrivelled and leathery. Cut cross-ways into 2cm/1 inch strips, and fry in batches in at least 1cm/½ inch of hot oil (ideally sunflower or ground nut). In a matter of seconds the strips will puff up and change colour. Remove with a slotted spoon and drain on kitchen paper.

The most common species of kelp (*Laminaria digitata*), with its fingery fronds branching from a single round stem, can be prepared in exactly the same way, but has a more tannic, salty taste. It is rather strongly flavoured to eat in any quantity on its own, but delicious mixed in with the oarweed chips.

Cornwall: Returning from snorkelling with a good haul of oarweed

Brown Shrimp

Carpet Shell Clam

Carragheen

Common Prawn

Crawfish

Laver

Mackerel

Native Oyster

Razor Clam

Sea Bass

Sea Lettuce

Sea Urchin

Spider Crab

SCALLOPS CHA CHA CHA

I invented the rather silly name for this lovely dish on account of the 3 flavourings in the dressing: chives, chervil and chillies. It is extremely simple, but exquisite. (See illustration on page 90.)

SERVES 2 (3 LARGE SCALLOPS EACH)

small bunch of wild (or cultivated) chives
small bunch of wild chervil (or parsley)
½ teaspoon finely chopped fresh red chilli

a little olive oil
6 large scallops, cleaned, without corals

• Heat a cast-iron skillet, or heavy frying pan, without any oil until very hot.

• Chop the chives and chervil and mix with the chopped chillies and a little olive oil, to get a green and red flecked dressing.

• Lightly brush both sides of each scallop with olive oil, and place quickly on the hot pan. Leave for exactly 1 minute, then carefully turn them over. Cook for another minute, then remove.

• Place 3 scallops each on 2 warmed plates, and trickle them with the cha-cha-cha dressing. Eat at once.

RAPPIE PIE

This recipe is adapted from North Atlantic Seafood, *that great treatise by seafood guru Alan Davidson. His recipe uses soft-shell clams. This version uses the relatively humble (but easier to gather) cockle. The results are excellent, and I see no reason not to experiment further by making the dish with mussels, or even chopped whelks. 'Rappie', by the way, is short for rapture.*

SERVES 6

1.4kg/3lb potatoes,
1kg/2lb cockles
55g/2oz butter

1 large glass white wine (optional)
250g/½lb salt pork or pancetta, diced
freshly ground black pepper to taste

• Peel and grate the potatoes on the coarse side of a cheese grater. Take a cup at a time and place it in a cheesecloth, which then must be twisted so as to wring out as much liquid as possible. (Collect the liquid in a bowl, so that you can measure it; for you will later need the same quantity of clam juices and water.)

• Put the wrung-out potato into a clean bowl.

• Steam the cockles open in butter with a little wine and water. Take the cockle meat out of the shells and set aside. Strain the cooking juices into a measuring jug.

• Fry the the salt pork or pancetta in a heavy frying pan so the fat runs and the meat crisps up a little. Take off the heat, but keep warm.

• Add to the clam juices enough water to bring the volume up to equal that of the liquid extracted from the potatoes. Bring this mixture to the boil, then add the wrung-out potato to it, little by little. The potato will swell up as it absorbs its new liquid.

• When this operation is completed, strain the bacon or pork fat into an ovenproof dish, holding back the meat. Place a layer of potato in the bottom of the oven pan, cover this with a layer of cockles, then another layer of potato and so on – the pie can have 3 layers or 5.

• Season with pepper to taste, and sprinkle the little bits of salt pork or pancetta over the top. Bake in a moderately hot oven (190°C/400°F/gas mark 6) for 20 minutes, then reduce the temperature to moderate (175°C/350°F/gas mark 4) and continue to bake for another hour or so, when the top of the pie will be brown and crusty.

SEAFOOD BEACH BARBECUE

Make a fireplace of large stones and build a wood fire inside it. Keep stoking and burn for at least an hour, then allow to burn down to hot embers. Place a wire rack (or 2) over the embers, and lay an assortment of shellfish on it, to be cooked according to the instructions that follow.

Dublin Bay prawns/Langoustines: Cook, turning occasionally, until the shell is lightly charred and the curved jointed tail has become stiff (about 5-7 minutes).

Velvet crabs: Cook, turning once, until the shell has turned bright orange (about 8-10 minutes).

Squat lobsters: Cook, turning once until orange (3-5 minutes).

Large mussels: Cook until opened and bubbling (2-3 minutes).

Large limpets: Cook upside down, until the meat is bubbling in the shells (3-4 minutes).

Whelks: Cook in the shells, with the opening facing skywards, until bubbling and tender (8-15 minutes, depending on size).

Hermit crabs: Cook in or out of the shells; about 10 minutes if in, nearer 5 if out.

To accompany: (optional) a pan of wild (or tame) garlic butter, made by chopping a small bunch of wild garlic leaves (or crushing a garlic clove), and sautéing it in butter for a few minutes. Do not allow the butter to brown. The various shellfish are dipped into the butter and eaten with the fingers.

The picture overleaf contained all the above items, which were devoured with great relish (and a cold beer) by me and the photographer shortly after the picture was taken.

COCKLE CHOWDER

This is a wonderful recipe from my friend Adam Robinson at the Brackenbury restaurant in Hammersmith — one of the few places where I don't mind paying for food I know I could get for free. Adam cooks it well, and has the decency to charge half sensible prices for it.

SERVES 6

600ml/I pint dry white wine
I large onion, finely chopped
1.4kg/3lb washed cockles
I leek
4 celery sticks
2 large carrots
I fennel bulb
55g/2oz butter

500g/1lb good smoked bacon or pancetta, diced
2 cloves of garlic, crushed
2.5cm/I inch piece ginger root, peeled and grated
600ml/I pint fish stock
2 potatoes, peeled and cut into 1cm/½ inch dice
150ml/5fl oz cream
salt and freshly ground black pepper

• Bring the wine to the boil with half the onion, and add the cockles in batches, removing them with a slotted spoon as soon as they are open (2-3 minutes).

• Strain the liquor through a clean cotton cloth when all the cockles are cooked, and reserve. Shuck (shell) two-thirds of the cockles, leaving the remaining third in their shells.

• Cut the remaining vegetables into 1cm/½ inch dice, and sweat them in the butter, along with the bacon or pancetta, garlic and ginger, in a large saucepan.

• Cook gently without allowing the vegetables to brown, until they are just tender. Add the liquor from the cockles, the extra fish stock, the potatoes, and the cream, and bring to the boil. Simmer gently until the potatoes are tender. Season with salt and pepper if needed.

• Divide the cockles among 8 warmed bowls, so that each has a few with shells, and some without, and ladle the soup over.

MUSSEL AND SEA BEET GRATIN

A simple mixture of creamed sea beet (or spinach) mixed with mussels, and finished with a crispy breadcrumb top.

SERVES 4 AS A STARTER, 2 AS A MAIN COURSE

500g/1lb sea beet (or ordinary fresh leaf spinach)
300ml/½ pint milk
55g/2oz butter
55g/2oz plain flour
pinch of nutmeg
2 tablespoons grated Parmesan cheese

a knob of butter
2 cloves of garlic, crushed
a glass of wine
1kg/2lb fresh mussels
salt and freshly ground black pepper
55g/2oz fresh white breadcrumbs

• Wash and trim the sea beet, then wilt it in a pan with just the water that is clinging to it. When well wilted, drain off excess liquid, and squeeze as dry as possible. Chop finely.

• Heat the milk but do not allow to boil. In another pan, melt the 55g/2oz of butter and add the flour, then cook for a few minutes, gently browning this roux.

• Add the hot milk by degrees, stirring all the time, to get a smooth, thick béchamel sauce. Allow to bubble for just a couple of minutes, then stir in the chopped sea beet, nutmeg, and half the Parmesan.

• In another large pan, melt the knob of butter and fry the garlic for just a minute. Add a splash of wine, and a little water. When this mixture is boiling rapidly, add the mussels, and steam them open (you may have to do this in two or more batches).

• Remove all the mussel meat from the shells, and stir into the creamed sea beet. Thin the mixture just a little with a couple of spoonfuls of the strained mussel cooking liquor. Check seasoning: add black pepper, but salt only if necessary.

• Spread the mixture in an ovenproof dish (ideally a shallow gratin dish). Mix the breadcrumbs with the rest of the Parmesan and sprinkle over the top.

• Bake for just 10 minutes, to heat through and brown the top, in a preheated hot oven at 200°C/400°F/gas mark 6.

CRUSTACEA SOUP

Vying closely with the jugged hare, this is one of my favourite recipes in the book. Indeed, in the world. It was a version of this that I made for Larry McAbe and Sonia Surey Gent on the beach in Cornwall, but the recipe is infinitely variable. You can add fish bones or whole fish to the stock. You can make it with or without prawns, and with just about any species of crab. I like to include velvets, if at all possible, as they have such a wonderful sweet flavour.

The following list of ingredients should be taken merely as a guide.

SERVES 4 AS A STARTER

I very large or 2 medium brown crabs or spider crabs
about 12 velvet crabs and/or large shore crabs
3 or 4 large Dublin Bay prawns, or 225g/½lb
   ordinary prawns, or squat lobsters
2 hermit crabs (optional)
I onion, chopped
I carrot, chopped
I large or 2 small tomatoes, chopped
4 cloves of garlic, crushed

few sprigs of wild fennel (if available)
few sprigs of wild chervil (if available)
parsley stalks (optional)
leek tops (optional)
a whole fresh white fish, such as a plaice or wrasse
   (optional)
pinch of cayenne pepper
salt and fresh ground black pepper

• Boil all the crustacea in fresh seawater for the times specified in the main text.

• When cool enough to handle, discard the dead men's fingers and stomachs of the crabs, and remove as much brown meat as you can from the carapaces and white meat from the larger claws. Peel the prawns (Dublin Bay or otherwise) and set the tail meat aside separately from the crab meat.

• Discard only the main carapace of the brown crabs. All other heads, legs, and shells of the crabs and prawns should be placed in a large bowl or heavy saucepan, and pounded with a hammer or rolling pin.

• In a large clean pan, heat the olive oil and add the onion, carrot, tomato and garlic (also add the wild herbs, and parsley stalks or leek tops if you have any) . Fry gently for a few minutes to soften. Add the hammered shellfish, and the fresh fish if you have one (skinned and gutted, but not filleted), cut into chunks.

• Pour over enough water just to cover everything, and bring to the boil. Simmer gently for just 20 minutes (no more), and remove from the heat.

• This shellfish stock can then be processed in a number of ways. Either strain it through a heavy-duty conical sieve, pressing hard with the back of a ladle to extract as much fishy juice as possible; or put everything in a heavy-duty blender, whizz up, and then pass through the sieve. Or you could attempt, as I did in the programme, to press the stock through a heavy-duty mouli. It's hard work, but it just about works.

• When you have extracted the best from the stock (or excluded the worst of the shells, depending on how you look at it), put it back in a clean pan, over a low heat, and stir in all the white and brown meat you originally saved from the crabs. Season to taste with fresh ground black pepper, cayenne and salt only if it is needed. Heat through, but do not boil. Divide between warm bowls, adding, as a final garnish, the tail meat from the prawns, squat lobsters or, as in the picture opposite, a couple of hermit crabs.

MARINATED MACKEREL

This dish is to be made only with the freshest possible mackerel — ideally fish you have caught yourself, or at least bought on the quayside. It is not as raw as sashimi, *or as harsh as a* ceviche, *but may lead the uninitiated to an appreciation of both these dishes. You can prepare a really fresh herring in the same way.*

SERVES 4 AS A STARTER

plenty of salt (rough crystals or sea salt are best)
500g/1lb fresh mackerel fillets
1 medium onion (ideally red)

4 tablespoons best olive oil
1 tablespoon lemon juice
freshly ground black pepper

• Sprinkle a thin layer of salt over a plate or tray and lay the mackerel fillets on the top of it, skin side down. Sprinkle more salt thickly and evenly over the fillets, and place the dish in the fridge for 2 hours.

• Thinly slice the onion and mix with the oil and lemon juice. Remove the fillets from the fridge after 2 hours and wipe off the salt with a clean damp cloth (rough crystals of sea salt will come off much more easily than fine table salt).

• Peel the skin from the fillets and slice them diagonally into 1cm/½ inch pieces. Toss with the onion, oil and lemon juice, season with black pepper, and return this mixture, covered, to the fridge for at least 4 hours to marinate.

• Provided the fish is entirely covered with the marinade (you can make sure of this by cramming the mixture into a large jar) it will keep for 48 hours, but not longer. I prefer the fish after a light marinade, about 6 hours, when it is not too 'pickled' but still tastes beautifully of the sea.

• Serve with brown bread and butter, to mop up all the marinade, and the little slivers of onion.

CRAB RAMEKINS

You could use bought ready-cooked crabs for this dish, provided you are confident they are quite fresh. Do not fail to include the brown meat from the crab — it has most of the flavour. To get 450g/1lb crab meat, you will need a crab of at least 1kg/2 ¼lb, or 2 crabs weighing 675g/1½lb each.

SERVES 4 AS A STARTER

500g/1lb cooked crab meat (white and brown)
salt and freshly ground black pepper
scant 150ml/5fl oz thick béchamel sauce, made with half milk, half cream
1 teaspoon English mustard
a few sprigs of dill, finely chopped

1 tablespoon dry vermouth (Martini or Noilly Prat)
a squeeze of fresh lemon juice
30g/1oz butter
60g/2oz Gruyère cheese, grated
60g/2oz fresh breadcrumbs

• Pick over the crabs, cracking the claws and legs to extract as much meat as possible (a pair of tweezers is a useful aid). Scrape all the brown meat, including any coral (the red stuff), from inside the main shell. Season to taste with salt and pepper.

• Mix the crab meat with the béchamel sauce, mustard, dill, vermouth and lemon juice. Divide the mixture among 4 ramekins lightly greased with a little of the butter.

• Mix the Gruyère with the breadcrumbs and sprinkle evenly over ramekins. Dot the top of each with small pieces of butter. Bake in a preheated oven (220°C/425°F/gas mark 7) for 8-10 minutes until bubbling hot and crisp on the top.

Variation: For an unusual but delicious Thai-style variation on this dish, substitute coconut milk for the béchamel, and instead of mustard, vermouth and dill, add 2 finely chopped garlic cloves, a small chopped fresh chilli and a walnut-sized piece of fresh ginger root, grated or finely chopped. Omit the Gruyère cheese in the topping.

LATE SUMMER HARVEST

High summer can be a frustrating time for the free food forager: the forests are in full green leaf, the roadside verge is bursting with high grasses and pretty wild flowers, and everywhere seems lush with reproductive profusion. But what are you actually going to eat? The chickweed is straggly, fat hen is going over the top, and the nettles are as tough as hessian. It calls to mind the plight of the ancient mariner:

Water, water, everywhere
Nor any drop to drink,

What a relief then, when some time in early August after a few days of bone-warming mellow sunshine, you stumble on the first half-ripe blackberry. You don't pick it, but take it between finger and thumb, and feel its weight and promise encouragingly. Further down the lane you see a scruffy-barked crab-apple tree. You dig your nail into the tiny, bullet-hard fruit, and touch the juicing scar with your tongue. You screw up a lemon face at the wicked sourness, but it doesn't matter. Summer's hardest work is done, and the fruit is coming on.

If spring is the season for green things, then late summer is definitely the season for sweet things. After all, the sun has spent months doing what it does best: turning starch into sugar. This chapter is therefore devoted largely to the fructal pleasures, unashamedly full of sweet treats for teatime and pudding.

A NOTE ON JAM MAKING

Jams, jellies and 'cheeses' (dense preserves that can be cut almost like fudge) are lovely ways to preserve fruits, both wild and cultivated, so that they can be enjoyed at leisure, long after the trees and bushes that bore them have lost their leaves and reverted to stick status.

But to some people, even keen cooks, the making of such preserves often seems like a scary business, involving the mysterious alchemy of sugar-boiling that maybe only 'old wives' (the kind that tell tales) really understand. There is only one way to rid yourself of such superstition: give jam-making a whirl. The first time you do will convince you that it really isn't that hard, and when you try what you've made you should get all the reinforcement you need to do it again.

Here are a few basic tips to give beginners confidence.

I. Jam or jelly

Jams are made from whole fruits boiled with sugar until they reach a setting point (see below). Jellies are made by simply boiling the extracted juices (no pulp) of fruits with sugar, until they reach a setting point. They are therefore particularly suitable for hard berries without an edible flesh, fruits that do not hold their shape well when boiled, or those which have slightly unpalatable skins and seeds.

Blackberries, blaeberries (if you can get enough), the plum species, and (slightly unripe) gooseberries all make excellent jams, but rowan berries, haw berries, sloes and the like need so much water to extract the flavour that jelly is really the only option. Jellies are traditionally served with meat, but I find they can all be used just like jams, on toast, scones, to fill cakes and (a good one this) with rice pudding.

2. Saucepans
Many recipes call for the use of 'preserving pans' – traditionally made of copper. These are great for jam-making because they conduct heat so well, but it is by no means essential to use one. The important thing is that you should not use flimsy pans, which will buckle and burn on the bottom, or aluminium, which is a poor conductor of heat and may entail some health risk if used for lengthy boiling of sugar. A heavy stainless steel stock pot, or an enamel-coated cast-iron casserole of the Le Creuset type, will do just fine.

3. Sugar
Caster or granulated sugar can be used, but preserving sugar (with a small amount of added pectin) can be useful for 'berry only' jams, as it will help them to set.

4. Water
Sometimes a little water is added to the fruit initially, to help prevent burning and to encourage the juices to run but, as a general principle, the less water you add, the fruitier your jams and jellies.

5. The setting point
Jams and jellies are ready for potting when they reach the setting point. This is 110°C/220°F for jams, and 112°C/225°F for jellies, and can be measured accurately with a good sugar thermometer.

Many cooks prefer to trust their own judgement: the traditional test is to drop ½ a teaspoon of the boiling mixture on to a plate. After a few seconds, when it is cool, prod it with a finger. The top should crinkle, and when divided, the two blobs should not run together. In other words, it is no longer a syrup, but a jam. Test jelly in the same way: it should be just a little more 'set' than jam.

'Cheeses' are made by boiling not just the juice, but the sieved pulp of the fruit, again with added sugar. They are boiled a lot longer (at least an hour), and set firm so they can be cut with a knife. It is hard to give a setting temperature, as this will depend on the fruit, but it is ready when the pulp has thickened considerably, and a little dropped into cold water can be formed into a soft ball.

6. Potting and filling
Jars for jam- and jelly-making should be clean and warm when you fill them. The tradition is to boil them in a large pan of water for a couple of minutes, then put them on a rack, and leave them in a warm oven (75°C/150°F/gas mark 1) until they need to be filled. Handle them carefully with a clean cotton cloth. Jars should be filled to within 1cm/½ inch of the top, but no more. To minimize the chance of mould developing, the jam should be covered, as soon as set, with a neat-fitting circle of waxed paper. It can then be covered with a screw-top lid, or a circle of cellophane sealed firmly with an elastic band. Either way, it must be airtight.

7. Jelly bags
Fine-meshed jelly bags, of either cotton or nylon, are designed to let the juices of cooked fruit drip through, without any pith, pips or pulp. They can be bought in any good kitchen shop, but you can improvise reasonably successfuly with a strong cotton tea-towel or other square of strong cotton. Do not use portions of old bed sheets, as they are not strong enough and let through too much pulp.

Traditionally, the fruit pulp is allowed to drip through a jelly bag overnight, though if you are in a hurry to get on and make your jam you can leave it for just a couple of hours. But do not try and force the juice through the bag or you will press through some of the pulp and your jelly will be cloudy.

For example recipes of the three types of preserves, see bramble jam, rowan jelly and crab-apple cheese (pages 144 and 148 respectively).

FRUITS
(see page 139 for illustrations)

BILBERRY OR BLAEBERRY (*Vaccinium myrtillus*)

Probably the wild ancestor of the cultivated blueberry, the blaeberry (as I prefer to call it) is a delicious little fruit, but laborious in the picking: I defy any individual working alone to pick a pound of blaeberries in less than an hour.

The leafy green bushes cling low to the ground on heaths, moors, and in sparse conifer woods with acid soil. The plants flower from May to June and sometimes bear fruit as early as the beginning of July, particularly in the south, though August and September are the best months.

I have done most of my blaeberry picking in Scotland, and although they are occasionally found on moors in Devon, Dorset and Cornwall they are definitely more common in the north.

Cooking

Blaeberries have a pleasant enough flavour to eat raw, and make a refreshing wayside snack on long highland walks. But they definitely improve with cooking, and it is well worth investing the time to gather enough to take back to the kitchen.

The berries should be lightly rinsed, then put in a heavy pan, still wet, with just a sprinkling of sugar (55g/2oz per 500g/1lb of fruit). Heat gently for just a few minutes, until the juices start to run. Stir very gently to dissolve the sugar without breaking up the fruit. These very lightly stewed berries can then be eaten on their own, with thick yoghurt (for breakfast), cream or ice cream, or incorporated into the wonderful Scottish cranachan (see page 144), or mixed with other fruits for a summer pudding (see page 141).

But whenever I have a decent quantity of blaeberries, the first thing I make is the blaeberry crumble tart on page 146 – perhaps my very favourite of all wild food puddings.

The fresh leaves of a blaeberry bush make a soothing aromatic tea, which is especially good if supplemented by a sprig of fresh mint (see Chapter 6).

Blackberry (*Rubus fruticosus*)

The blackberry is without doubt the best-known fruit of the wild harvest, the one wild food that is known to even the most urbanized cynics, those who actively shun the rustic idyll. If you've never seen a blackberry growing wild, I can only assume you've never set foot in the countryside in the month of September.

Blackberries are abundant and widespread, growing in hedgerows, at forest edges and on wasteland throughout Britain, though they are less common in the highlands of Scotland. One of the curiosities of this easily gathered fruit is the vast number of microspecies (possibly as many as 400), often highly localized and each with subtle differences in size of berry, flavour, and time of fruiting. Sometimes brambles growing within a few yards of each other will produce fruit of noticeably different flavour, and regular pickers will soon make a note of their favourite bushes. On my urban forage in London, the last leg of the first series, countryside guru (and consultant to the series) Richard Mabey took me to some of his favourite brambles, where the plump berries tasted distinctly of grapes. And he made the very sound suggestion that when you find a bush whose fruit you particularly enjoy, you can take a cutting and grow your own at home.

As a general rule, the sweetest, best-flavoured fruits are those that ripen first, usually in August but occasionally as early as the end of July. There is a tradition that blackberries should not be gathered after the end of September, because 'the devil has pissed on them'. (If this was true, you would have thought a *Sun* photographer would have caught the old boy in the act by now.)

Note also the **Dewberry** (*Rubus caesius*), a close relative of the blackberry, with fewer and larger nodules on the cluster and a light, whitish bloom. They have a good flavour, but tend to be delicate when ripe and it can be hard to pick them without squashing them. They can be used like blackberries.

Cooking

In a good year, blackberries can be had in such abundance that it is a pity not to lay down a few good things made from them that can be enjoyed for weeks and months to come. Ice creams and sorbets are two of my favourite ways of doing this, and if you have a soft spot for either (or both), and access to plenty of fruit (both wild and cultivated), you might want to consider buying an ice cream maker.

Blackberry sorbet: Sieve or mouli 1kg/2lb fresh ripe blackberries for their juice, and mix it with the juice of ½ a lemon and a light sugar syrup (made by dissolving 225g/8oz sugar in 300ml/½ pint water, then boiling rapidly for 8 minutes). Pour the mixture into your ice cream machine (you may have to make this quantity in 2 batches) and freeze. Or do it the old-fashioned way, freezing the mixture until half frozen, then whisking it to a slush, refreezing it again, whisking again, etc.

Other 'long-life' blackberry recipes are of course jams and jellies (see page 131), and for drinks made with blackberries, see Chapter 6.

The blackberry crop can be enjoyed more spontaneously in all kinds of pies and tarts, as well as in such dishes as summer pudding (see especially late sumer pudding, page 141), cranachan (page 144) and the blackberry and crab-apple variation of blaeberry crumble tart (page 146). For an unusual and rather greedy blackberry dish of my own devising, try the blackberry and ricotta pudding on page 143.

CRAB-APPLES *(Malus sylvestris)*

The crab-apple is common throughout England, Wales and Ireland, but less so in central and northern Scotland. Its delicate blossom, white with a hint of pink (as a paint company might put it), is a good way to identify a tree in May to which you can return in the autumn in the expectation of fruit.

The true wild crab-apple *(M. sylvestris)* has a small round fruit, rarely much larger than a golf ball, which reaches a golden yellow when ripe (usually late September or early October). But there are other varieties to be found, larger and less perfectly shaped, which are probably the descendants of cultivated apples that have reverted to the wild. The distinction is not that important, as the fruit from any wild apple tree can be put to good use.

Cooking

In most crab-apple recipes the fruit is washed, and quartered or sliced, but not peeled, as there is flavour, colour and (most importantly, for jams and jellies) pectin in the skin.

Pies and tarts: The sour-sharp taste of crab-apples means that they are barely palatable raw, but cooked with added sugar, they reveal a flavour that is both deeply appley, and pleasantly fragrant. They can be added to tarts and pies made from cultivated apples for a tarter flavour, and contribute good texture and essential sharpness to my late summer pudding (see page 141). Like cooking apples, they combine well with blackberries in pies, tarts and crumbles.

Preserves: Crab-apples make one of the best of all wild fruit preserves (see page 148), and their excellent acidity and high level of pectin mean that they combine well with other wild fruits in the making of preserves. Jellies made from blackberries, elderberries, rowan berries and rosehips can all be improved by the addition of crab-apples.

Sorbet: So intense is the appliness of crab-apples that I have been inspired to experiment with them, devising dishes where their fresh, tart taste can be enjoyed in light desserts, not just in 'puddings'. One success has been fresh crab-apple jelly (see page 142). Another has been a refreshing crab-apple sorbet: put 1kg/2lb of washed and quartered crab-apples in a heavy pan, and pour in 150ml/5fl oz of water. Bring to a simmer and cook to a pulp (10-15 minutes), then rub through a sieve. Add a light sugar syrup (made by dissolving 115g/4oz sugar in 150ml/5fl oz water and boiling hard for 5 minutes), then pour into an ice cream machine, or freeze and whisk in the usual way. Interesting variations on this recipe can be made by using a mixture of crab-apples and blackberries, or by adding a few sloes or a fistful of elderberries.

Appleade: If you have a centrifugal juicer, you can make fantastic 'crab-appleade' by juicing the sour apples, adding a light sugar syrup to taste, plenty of ice and enough still or fizzy water to make a long cool drink – and fingers crossed for an Indian summer.

See also crab-apple flowers (page 25), crab-apple wine (page 156) and crab-apple brandy (page 158).

ELDERBERRIES *(Sambucus nigra)*

The elder tree is found all over Britain, in woods and waste places, but especially in roadside hedgerows. If any wild fruit is more prolific than the blackberry, it must be the elderberry: in August and September the heavy sprays of black berries sometimes seem to weigh down the whole hedgerow.

Cooking

It would be a crime to waste such a glut. The bitter taste of raw elderberries is much improved by cooking with added sugar. But even cooked, the elderberry does not (in my opinion) have a good enough flavour to stand up on its own in traditional berry fruit puddings. Better to combine it with other fruits: it can certainly be added to the late summer pudding (see page 141), and works well combined with tart crab-apples or cooking apples in crumbles and pies, as well as jellies and preserves (see page 148). But its real redemption comes in the making of cordials and wines: for more information see Chapter 6.

JUNIPER (*Juniperus communis*)

This short, thorny tree-shrub, with its almost needle-like evergreen leaves, likes chalk downs and limestone hills and appears occasionally on chalky heaths and moors. The berries only ripen towards the end of their second autumn (usually October), so at any one time a tree will bear a mixture of ripe and unripe fruit. In contrast to the bullet-hard green first-year berries, those that are ready for picking will be blue-black, and will give a little when pressed hard.

Cooking

Juniper berries are not expensive, but it is unusually satisfying to gather your own, and it provides a motivation for finding further uses for these powerfully aromatic little fruits. They are used principally as a flavouring — in gin, of course, but also traditionally in sauerkraut, and in stews, particularly of game.

They can also be used to flavour jams and jellies made with other fruits: try adding a handful to a crab-apple jelly, for example (page 142).

Richard Mabey suggests making juniper gin, after the manner of sloe gin, on the sound principle that you can't have too much of a good thing.

MEDLAR (*Mespilus germanica*)

Another Roman introduction, the medlar has, in a modest way, 'gone native', and examples of this slightly delicate shrub crop up occasionally in the hedgerow, particularly in the south.

Its fruits appear to be a curious hybrid of the apple and the rosehip. Like the latter, it should not be picked

until it starts to soften or 'blet'. In late October or November, after the first frosts, the fruit turns from a healthy waxy yellow to a dull russet brown, and the papery skin is soft to the touch. Medlars may be found in such a state both on the tree and as windfalls: in both cases, beware the wasps sure to be taking their last supper on the sweet fermenting nectar.

Cooking

'Bletted' medlars can be baked quickly in the oven, and the mushy flesh spooned out of the skin and eaten with cream. The flavour is somewhere between an apple and a quince, so it's no surprise either that the medlar makes a good jelly, and an even better cheese (see page 148).

ROSEHIPS, from wild rose or dog rose (*Rosa canina*)

The wild rose is common throughout the British Isles in woods and hedgerows, and from late August to November its glossy red ovoid berries can be found in profusion. Rosehips are not edible as a fruit, but they can be used to make a fine syrup (see below) and an interesting country wine.

The timing of the harvest of rosehips is important, since they will produce more flavour, and yield a more vitamin-rich syrup, when they have been softened by the first frost. On the other hand, by early November they are often too withered to be of any use.

Cooking

Making rosehip syrup: Once thought of as a health cordial for sickly children (justifiably, in view of its very high vitamin C content), I prefer to look on home-made rosehip syrup as a greedy treat to pour on pancakes, waffles and ice creams.

It is easily made: bring 2 litres/4 pints of water to the boil, and then roughly chop 1kg/2lb of ripe rosehips. Throw them into the boiling water, bring back to the boil, then remove from the heat, cover, and leave to infuse for ½ an hour. Strain through a jelly bag, then transfer the pulp back to the pan, and add another litre/2 pints of boiling water. Reboil, infuse again, and strain as before. Combine the two liquids in a clean pan, boil, and reduce by half. Off the fire, add 1kg/2lb caster sugar and stir to dissolve. Bring back to the boil, and boil hard for 5 minutes. Pour into warmed sterilized bottles or jars (as for jam), then leave to cool and store in a warm place.

Rosehips make a fine wine (see page 156) and can also be combined with other wild fruits, particularly crab-apples, in the making of cordials and preserves. The leaves are used in tisanes (see Chapter 6).

NOTE: Some garden varieties of rose also produce cookable hips – notably *Rosa rugosa*.

ROWAN or MOUNTAIN ASH (*Sorbus aucuparia*)

This small deciduous tree is common throughout Britain, in hedgerows and scrub land, and often grows on high ground near water (hence mountain ash). Rowan is increasingly popular as a garden tree, and among designers of municipal landscapes, so you may not have to climb a mountain to get your fruit. The waxy red berries appear from August but are best gathered in late September and October when they are ripe but not yet mushy.

Cooking

The berries are not edible in the raw state, and not palatable in the cooked – until they have been strained and made into some kind of preserve. Rowan jelly is a lovely tart preserve, good to serve with venison or duck, or just to have on toast. It can be made either with 100 per cent rowan berries, or by combining the berries with crab-apples or cooking apples (See page 148 for recipe.)

Rowan berries make a good dry wine (see Chapter 6).

WILD CHERRIES (*Prunus avium*, among others)

This deciduous tree is fairly common in woods and hedgerows in England, Wales and Ireland, becoming scarcer further north. Like the crab-apple, many examples may be descended from cultivated trees that have seeded themselves and reverted to the wild. And like the crab-apple, the fruit tends to be smaller and far more sour than the cultivated varieties. Wild cherries usually ripen in July, sometimes early August.

Cooking

They can be used in most recipes that call for cherries, but extra sugar will have to be added to compensate. I like them in a clafoutis (see page 149), where their sharpness contrasts beautifully with the sweet, creamy-bland batter.

Sour cherry soup: A traditional Eastern European recipe, which ends up tasting not unlike bortsch. Put 500g/1lb of stoned, washed cherries (about 750g/1½lb unstoned weight) in a pan with 300ml/½ pint of water, the finely pared zest of ½ a lemon and ½ an orange, and a stick of cinnamon. Bring to the boil and simmer for 10 minutes, until the fruit is a pulp. Remove the cinnamon, pour the soup into a liquidizer with 2 tablespoons of cooked rice (or 2 rice cakes) to thicken, and blend until smooth.

Return to the pan, add a large glass of red wine (elderberry wine is good) and reheat, but do not boil. If the soup is too sour for your taste, add a little sugar, and perhaps take more sugar to the table, to allow for those with a sweeter tooth than yours. Serve hot.

WILD GOOSEBERRIES (*Ribes uva-crispa*)

Near the village where I grew up in Gloucestershire, we used to pick great basketloads of 'goosegogs' from a long line of bushes growing by the side of a leafy lane, and also on the embankment of a disused railway. I have never seen them in such profusion since, though odd bushes and groups of bushes do occur in woods and hedgerows throughout lowland Britain – particularly in Yorkshire and Lancashire. They ripen from July onwards, and are sometimes found as late as September.

I was delighted to find a bush of small but beautifully pink-tinged gooseberries in the New Forest programme, and to be able to collect enough to make one of my favourite ice creams – churned in an antique ice churn by my own fair hand. I took it as a present to the travellers who invited me to supper, and it went down well, and fast. (See below for the recipe).

Cooking

In a very good summer, some plants will occasionally produce fruits sweet enough to eat raw, but the fine flavour of gooseberries is best brought out by gentle cooking. The fruit needs to be 'topped and tailed' and rinsed before cooking.

Stewed gooseberries: To 500g/1lb gooseberries in a pan, add 85g/3oz sugar for starters, and just a tablespoon of water to prevent them sticking. Heat gently until the fruit bursts then simmer gently to get a pulpy purée. Taste for sweetness and add extra sugar if you think it needs it. This purée can be served hot with custard, or cold with cream (or vice versa, come to that). If you don't like the pips and skins, sieve the purée before serving it.

Gooseberry ice cream: Simply add 300ml/½ pint of thick cream to a slightly over-sweetened version of the above purée (sieved), pack your ice cream churn with layers of salt and crushed ice, and churn away until you get a result. (And let me tell you, it takes a while.)

Gooseberries make a good jam, and a fine fool, especially when mixed with elderflowers (see page 145).

Gooseberry sauce: In *Food for Free*, Richard Mabey has an excellent recipe for gooseberry and fennel sauce for mackerel: 'Stew a handful of fruit in a little cider, pulp through a sieve, then mix with chopped fennel and mustard and honey to taste.'

WILD PLUM (also damson, bullace and wild greengage)

Various subspecies of the cultivated plum, *Prunus domesticus*, may be found growing wild. They are primarily garden escapees and their descendants, and can be found in hedgerows and woods, often near orchards and gardens. They can be yellow flushed with red (wild plum or cherry plum), round and green (wild greengage), or small and purple (bullace).

Cooking

The sweetness of such fruits will vary, but some may be palatable (delicious even) raw – particularly wild greengages. Others will need to be cooked with a little sugar to bring out their best, but can then be used to delicious effect in pies, tarts, crumbles and desserts. They will all make fine preserves, and damson or bullace cheese is particularly good (see page 148).

See also damson gin, page 158.

WILD RASPBERRIES (*Rubus idaeus*)

It can be quite a surprise, when gleaning a hedgerow or walking up the edge of a wood, suddenly to find yourself looking at a cluster of bright red raspberries. But the wild form of this much-loved fruit occurs not infrequently in Britain. Most 'wild' raspberries are likely to be descendants of escapees from cultivation, so you often find specimens near human habitation, or near ruined castles and abbeys where there might once have been a fruit garden.

Railway cuttings are another place where wild raspberries seem to occur regularly. I like to imagine that it is because of people throwing British Rail jam sandwiches out of train windows in bygone days, but I don't think this has much credibility as a theory of transmission.

Cooking

Wild raspberries tend to be sparser on the plant than cultivated fruits, but their flavour, though sometimes on the sharp side, is excellent. Do with them whatever you would do with their tame cousins, but do it with that much more satisfaction. The little extra edge of sharpness makes a wild raspberry sorbet particularly special: follow the recipe for blackberry sorbet (page 134), but omit the lemon juice.

WILD STRAWBERRIES (*Fragaria vesca*)

Though theoretically fairly common, a decent crop of wild strawberries is a pretty exciting find. The best place to look in is deciduous woodland and shady scrub on chalky soil. Occasionally small woods will be quite dominated by this perennial herb, but unless such caches remain well-kept secrets, over-picking and the taking of plants for transplanting into gardens can quickly decimate stocks.

Eating

It is very rare to be able to pick more than a small bowlful of wild strawberries. Their subtle and scented flavour doesn't in the least benefit from cooking, and I prefer to eat them on their own, with a light sprinkling of caster sugar and perhaps just a smidgin of cream.

Wild strawberries are far more powerfully scented than the cultivated kind, and one or two can be used to aromatize certain other desserts. I was once taken to lunch at the Connaught, and for pudding I chose an old favourite, crème brûlée. The whole delicious thing was deeply aromatized with the scent of strawberry. At the bottom of my ramekin was a single wild fruit.

NUTS
(see page 139 for illustrations)

As well as being a fruitophile, come autumn I'm also a bit of a nut-case. Of all wild plants, nuts are among the few which provide a good level of carbohydrate, and from a survivalist point of view, anyone living wild would do well to turn squirrel, and stake a claim on a few nut trees.

But wild nuts are also to be treasured from a culinary point of view. Though usually smaller than their cultivated equivalent, they often have a superior taste and, because they can be eaten that much fresher, a higher sugar content. (When nuts are stored for a long time, some of the sugar content reverts to starch.)

The three most worthwhile nut species you will find in the wild are:

HAZEL (*Corylus avellana*)

If you want to find a hazel tree, follow a squirrel. And if you want to get a decent crop of nuts off it, shoot the squirrel (see page 53). One of the problems with wild hazel trees is that the squirrels and birds (particularly jays) often decimate the nut crop before the nuts are really well developed. Luckily, I don't mind my hazelnuts a bit on the green side – even as an accompaniment to fried squirrel.

The hazel is a common tree in woods and hedgerows throughout Britain, and it bears its crop of nuts (also called cobnuts and filberts) from late August, though they are not usually harvestable before mid September.

Cooking

I like to eat my first wild crop of the year *au naturel*, cracking them with my teeth like a squirrel, and munching a decent pile at a sitting. I also like to add shelled raw nuts to a crunchy green salad.

Roasting hazelnuts: When the novelty of new season's cobnuts in the raw state eventually wears off, the oven can be deployed to bring out the deep nutty flavour that lurks within them. Shell a good pile of nuts, and spread the kernels on a baking tray. Place at the top of an oven preheated to 190°C/375°F/gas mark 6, for just 10 minutes, then remove. When cool enough to handle, the papery skin on the nuts can be rubbed off. Roasted cobnuts are delicious as a snack straight from the oven, either just as they are, or tossed in a little salt, or better still, light soy sauce. When cool, they can also be stored in glass jars for a few weeks.

Home roasted cobnuts always seem to have a much better flavour than anything you can buy, and can be used in all kinds of recipes, savoury and sweet. Ground into a powder in a food processor, they are especially good in biscuits, cakes, meringues and crumbles (see page 146). For the best possible flavour, store the nuts whole, re-roast for just a couple of minutes, then process just before including in your recipe.

Hazelnut butters: For a savoury version, process 225g/8oz salted, roasted cobnuts with 85g/3oz of soft butter to a paste, and store in jars in the fridge. Mix with chopped bacon and chives and serve on squares of toast as a drinks snack. For a sweet version, process the same quantity of unsalted roasted cobnuts with the same quantity of butter, and 115g/4oz of finely grated dark sweet chocolate.

SWEET CHESTNUT *(Castanea sativa)*

My parents have two sweet chestnut trees in the hedge at the bottom of their garden, which produce a bumper crop of small but perfectly formed nuts every October. They are a great treat, and though the nuts are on the small side the flavour is superb. Every year we find something new to do with them: a current favourite is sweet chestnut risotto (see page 140).

Probably introduced by the Romans as a crop tree, the sweet chestnut is widespread in woods and parks in England, less common in Scotland. The broad-trunked tree with its spreading branches has pointed dark green leaves and produces its spiny, nut-containing fruit in August. The nuts will not be ready until October, and can be collected as windfalls, among the tree's yellow-brown leaf litter, sometimes until mid November.

Cooking

Most people have enjoyed chestnuts roasted on an open fire, either at home, or from a street vendor in the city, cooking them on an open brazier. There is great comfort and pleasure to be had from this autumnal tradition, but few people in this country realize just how versatile is the chestnut. On the continent, and in Italy in particular, chestnuts are processed and used in all kinds of ways – dried, ground into flour, and tinned both whole and as sweetened purée. They are then used in the making of breads, cakes and biscuits, as well as many savoury dishes. Most of such processes can be executed at home, and if you have access to a large crop of chestnuts it may well be worth your while getting to grips with some of these processes.

Roasting chestnuts: For immediate consumption, there is no finer way to enjoy chestnuts than roasted on an open fire (as Bing Crosby will happily testify, year after year). As with so many wild foods, the pleasure lies as much in the ritual of preparation as in the eating. They should be slit first (or they may explode). I then usually put them on a coal shovel, which I place on top of hot coals scraped to the edge of the fire. Turn occasionally, and they should be ready in 10-15 minutes.

Boiling and parboiling: When chestnuts are required for almost any recipe, sweet or savoury, they must be skinned first. This is most easily done by slitting the skins and covering the chestnuts in boiling water in a pan. Bring back to the boil, simmer for 5 minutes, and take off the heat. Peel, with fingernails (or a sharp knife if you have no fingernails), while still hot but cool enough to handle. You should peel off both the outer and inner skin. They are still crunchy like this, and need further cooking in most recipes.

Blaeberry or Bilberry

Cherry Plum

Gooseberry

Juniper Berries

Medlar

Rowan

Sloes and Dog Rosehips

Wild Cherry

Wild Raspberry

Wild Strawberry

Hazel Nuts

Sweet Chestnuts

Walnuts

Braised chestnuts: Peeled chestnuts can be gently braised in a little stock until tender (20-30 minutes), and served as a side vegetable, particularly with game. They are even better if added, halved or roughly chopped, to braised celery, Savoy cabbage, or creamed Brussels sprouts (great with the Christmas turkey).

Chestnut soup: Sweat a medium onion, a large carrot, 2 sticks of celery (all chopped) and a chopped rasher of bacon (optional) in a little butter to soften them. Add 500g/1lb of peeled chestnuts, and 1 litre/1¾ pints of chicken or vegetable stock. Simmer until the chestnuts are tender (20-40 minutes), then liquidize the soup. Season to taste with salt, nutmeg and cayenne.

Chestnut risotto: Roast and peel 500g/1lb of chestnuts. Make a simple risotto by sweating a finely chopped onion, adding risotto rice, and stirring in hot stock by degrees. Stir in the roasted chestnuts, roughly chopped, at the end. Season well with freshly ground black pepper, stir in a knob of butter and a tablespoon of fresh grated Parmesan, and take more Parmesan to the table. I use roasted chestnuts for the extra flavour, but you can use boiled and skinned nuts: add to the onion before the rice, and they will cook in the stock with the rice.

Sweet chestnut purée: An excellent way to preserve a good quantity of chestnuts for use in desserts and sweet recipes. Dissolve 350g/12oz sugar in 500ml/¾ pint water, and boil hard for 5 minutes to get a light syrup. Add 500g/1lb of chestnuts and simmer until the chestnuts are very tender. Remove them from the syrup and process in a food processor, adding enough of the syrup to get a very thick, but almost pourable consistency. Kept in sealed jars in the fridge, this delicious purée will last for months. Use to fill cakes and meringues, as a sauce for pancakes and ice cream, or like a jam, on toast (with a sprinkling of cinnamon).

WALNUT *(Juglans regia)*

The walnut tree, introduced from Asia about 500 years ago, has not spread well of its own accord, so it is true to say that most specimens have been (more or less) deliberately planted by man. However, they are not uncommon in woods and parkland, and indeed in people's gardens, and it is a shame not to use them when you do find them.

Picking and preparation

Walnuts do not always ripen fully in this climate, and it is best to allow them the benefit of any autumn sunshine – pick them on a dry day in late October or even early November. Ideally the encasing fruit should be split and the shell of the nut showing through. Peel away this fleshy case, and if you are not ready to use the walnuts straight away, or want to keep them for your nut bowl, leave them to dry in an airing cupboard for 24 hours, then transfer to a cool dry place. This should ensure that they don't go mouldy.

Cooking

'Wild' walnuts can be used instead of the imported cultivated kind in any recipe, but because of their particularly strong flavour I prefer to use them in savoury recipes.

Walnut pasta sauce: Shell wild walnuts until you have 175g/6oz of kernels then roughly chop them. Sweat 2 crushed cloves of garlic in 2 tablespoons of good olive oil, then throw in the walnuts and toast for a few more minutes; add a tablespoon of thick double cream, then bubble to reduce, stir in a handful of fresh grated Parmesan, season with freshly ground black pepper, and toss with just-cooked tagliatelle or pasta quills. Take more Parmesan to the table.

Walnuts also make great pesto, used instead of pine nuts.

Walnut soup: Substitute shelled walnuts for peeled chestnuts in the chestnut soup above. Finish with a spoonful of cream, and serve with fresh grated Parmesan.

Pickled walnuts: One thing British walnuts are always good for, when green and unripe, is pickling. Pick young green walnuts in July, wash them well, and prick them all over with a needle. Put them in a bowl and cover with a brine made by dissolving 175g/6oz salt per litre/2 pints of water. Leave the nuts in the brine for 7-10 days, changing the brine every 48 hours. Drain, rinse and dry them and leave them uncovered on a rack to dry for 2-3 days. Then pack in pots and cover with a hot strong pickling vinegar (made by combining 1 litre/2 pints of distilled malt vinegar with a tablespoon each of cloves, allspice berries and white peppercorns, 3 bay leaves and 2 cinnamon sticks, and heating gently for 1 hour without boiling). Seal the jars, and leave in a dark place for at least 1 month, ideally 3.

WILD BERRY LATE SUMMER PUDDING

The important thing about a summer pudding, which some recipes I have tried fail to deliver, is that it should contain enough juice to ensure that the bread becomes completely soaked. For this reason I cook the fruits gently to release the juices, but not so much as to lose the fresh flavours. Elderberries, blaeberries and wild raspberries can also be added to this recipe.

In the last programme of the first series, the bread for this recipe was rescued from a supermarket skip, with a bit of help from members of the Rainbow Centre for the homeless in London's Kentish Town. The rest of the feast I enjoyed with them was made entirely from food discarded by markets and supermarkets — most of which went to great lengths to prevent them from getting it. It's a pretty sad reflection of their cynicism and greed that supermarkets cannot donate their 'leftovers' to a good cause.

SERVES 8

30g/1oz unsalted butter
500g/1lb crab-apples, peeled, cored and
    quartered
170g/6oz caster sugar
1 tablespoon water

750g/1½lb blackberries, or mixed
    blackberries and blaeberries
a small piece of butter for greasing
7-8 slices slightly stale white bread, trimmed
    of crusts

• Melt the butter in a heavy pan, and add the crab-apples, sugar and water. Sweat gently, until the sugar dissolves and the crab-apples are simmering in a light syrup.

• Add the rest of the fruit and heat through, stirring gently, until the juices run. You can allow it to simmer very gently for a minute or two, but do not boil hard. Taste for sweetness, add more sugar if desired, and set the pan aside.

• Lightly butter a small 1 litre/2 pint pudding basin, and line it with the bread slices, cutting wedge shapes to fill any awkward gaps.

• Pour in the fruit to the top of the bread. If it is looking very wet, hold back a little of the juice (you can serve it as a sauce). Cover with the last pieces of bread.

• Cover with a plate that fits neatly inside the bowl, and place a weight on it to encourage the juices to enter the bread. Leave for at least 4 hours in the fridge, or preferably overnight.

• Turn out the pudding on to a plate, and serve with cream or crème fraîche.

CRAB-APPLE JELLY

This is a jelly in the pudding sense of the word, rather than the jam sense of the word. With the addition of a few sloes or blackberries, it comes out a wonderful pale pinky purple colour, and has a refreshingly tart appley taste.

SERVES 6-8

1kg/2lb crab-apples
a handful of blackberries or sloes
125-150g/4-8oz sugar, according to taste
gelatine or dried carragheen (see page 117)

TO SERVE
blackberry syrup (see page 154)
lemon juice

- Wash the crab-apples but do not peel. Quarter them, put them in a pan with the blackberries or sloes, and barely cover with cold water. Add 125g/4oz of the sugar.

- Bring the crab-apples slowly to a simmer, stirring to dissolve the sugar and pulp the fruit.

- When the fruit is soft and pulpy, strain it through a sieve lined with muslin. Extract the maximum amount of juice without too much pulp (though a little won't hurt).

- Taste the liquid for sweetness, and add as much sugar as you think it needs, stirring to dissolve.

- If using gelatine to set: measure the amount of liquid (you will probably have about 1.5 litres/3 pints), dissolve in a small cup of hot water enough leaf or powdered gelatine to set the amount of liquid you have, following the instructions on the packet (1 sachet or 7g/¼oz, usually sets 600ml/1 pint). When the gelatine has completely dissolved, stir into the liquid and pour into rinsed jelly moulds.

- If using carragheen to set: add 15g/½oz dried carragheen for every 1 litre/2 pints of liquid. Cook at a very slow simmer for at least 20 minutes, until the mixture has begun to thicken. Strain out the carragheen, pouring the mixture through a sieve into rinsed jelly moulds.

- Put in the fridge to set for at least 5 hours or overnight.

- To serve, unmould the jelly by dipping the mould briefly in warm water and turning it out on to a plate. Serve with a sauce of blackberry syrup, made tart with a little lemon juice and thinned if necessary with a little water.

BLACKBERRY AND RASPBERRY RICOTTA PUDDING

SERVES 6

350g/12oz each blackberries and raspberries (wild or otherwise)

55g/2oz caster sugar
700g/1½lb very fresh ricotta cheese

- In a large mixing basin, mix together the fruit and the sugar, gently bruising the fruit to release some of its juices, without mushing it to a complete purée.

- Add the ricotta and mix well, but gently: the pudding should contain little curdy pieces of ricotta and pieces of broken fruit.

- Press the mixture into a small (1 litre/2 pint) pudding basin, and chill in the fridge. Turn out on to a plate just before serving.

CRANACHAN

This, the Scottish answer to summer pudding, can be made with all kinds of soft fruit, either a single fruit or a mixture. Try in particular wild strawberries, raspberries, blackberries or blaeberries. Cultivated strawberries, raspberries and redcurrants can also be used.

SERVES 6

750g/1½lb soft fruit (see suggestions above)
600ml/1 pint double cream
4 tablespoons Drambuie or whisky
115g/4oz coarse oatmeal, toasted in the oven
    until crisp

115g/4oz mixed chopped nuts (hazelnuts
    and walnuts, toasted)
115g/4oz dark chocolate, grated

• Pick over and prepare the fruit (blaeberries should be very lightly stewed – see page 133), and divide among 6 large wineglasses (each should be half full of fruit).

• Whip the cream, and stir in the alcohol (sweeten with a little sugar if you use whisky).

• Mix together the oatmeal, nuts and grated chocolate, and sprinkle a layer of this mixture over the fruit. Add a layer of cream, then the oatmeal mixture, then more cream, and a final sprinkling of the oatmeal mixture on top.

• Do not wait long before serving or the oatmeal will lose its crispness.

BRAMBLE JAM

See also the notes on jam-making on page 131. The small amount of apple in this recipe ensures that the jam will have enough pectin to set properly.

MAKES ABOUT 5KG (10LB)

2kg/4lb well-washed blackberries
750g/1½lb crab-apples (or sour cooking
    apples), peeled and diced

300ml/½ pint water
3kg/5½lb sugar
15g/½oz butter

• Place the fruit in a large pan with the water and simmer gently until soft and juicy.

• Add the sugar and stir until it has dissolved, then add the butter and bring to the boil.

• After 10 minutes of rapid boiling, test to see if it has set. When the jam is ready, remove from the heat, and skim off any scum with a slotted spoon.

• Pot and cover in the usual way.

GOOSEBERRY AND ELDERFLOWER FOOL

The marriage of elderflower and gooseberry is sensational, and can be used in all kinds of recipes, including ices, tarts and cordials. You should still be able to find elderflowers when the gooseberries come on in July, but if they are late, you can simply flavour your fool (or sorbet, or ice cream) with a little elderflower cordial (see page 164) and reduce the amount of sugar.

SERVES 6

2-3 elderflower heads
575g/1¼lb gooseberries, topped and tailed
60g/2oz unsalted butter

55-115g/2-4oz caster sugar, to taste
450ml/15fl oz double cream, whipped

- Tie the elderflowers in a little piece of muslin or cotton cloth, and put in a pan with the gooseberries and the butter. Stew gently until the fruit is soft.

- Squeeze the muslin against the side of the pan and remove. Crush the gooseberries with a fork and sweeten to taste with sugar. This gives a rough purée — the gooseberries can be sieved if you prefer.

- Cool in the fridge and mix with the cream. Pile into glasses or custard cups, then chill. Serve garnished with small sprays of elderflowers and accompany with shortbread or almond biscuits.

BLAEBERRY CRUMBLE TART

Made with blaeberries this tart is particularly satisfying, but it can easily be adapted for other fruits —
gooseberries, bullaces, wild cherries (stoned) or a combination of crab-apple and blackberry are all very good.

SERVES 8

FOR THE SWEET SHORTCRUST PASTRY
115g/4oz unsalted butter
200g/7oz plain flour
25g/1oz caster sugar
1 egg yolk
water

FOR THE FILLING
650g/1½lb blaeberries

55g/2oz caster sugar
½ tablespoon lemon juice

FOR THE CRUMBLE
55g/2oz butter
55g/2oz plain flour
55g/2oz ground hazelnuts (or ground
   almonds)
55g/2oz light brown (or caster) sugar

• Rub the butter into the flour (or process in a mixer) and stir in the sugar. Mix in the egg yolk, and add just enough cold water to bring together the pastry. Wrap the pastry in foil or cling film and chill for at least ½ an hour.

• Roll out the pastry to a thickness of about 5mm/¼ inch, and line a 25cm/10 inch tart tin and bake blind (i.e. line the pastry with foil, fill with beans or baking beads, and cook for 12-15 minutes in a hot oven – 200°C/400°F/gas mark 6 – then remove foil and beans and leave for another 2 minutes to dry out the base).

• Meanwhile gently wash the blaeberries and toss with the sugar and lemon juice so the berries are coated.

• To prepare the crumble, rub the butter into the flour until it resembles fine breadcrumbs, then mix in the hazelnuts and sugar.

• Spread the fruit evenly in the cooked pastry case, and sprinkle over the crumble in an even layer.

• Bake in a fairly hot preheated oven (190°C/375°F/gas mark 5) for about 30 minutes, until the crumble top is nicely browned.

• Serve the pie warm, on its own or with cream.

CRAB-APPLE
(and other) CHEESE

This delicious sweetmeat can be served with cheeses or, cut into cubes and rolled in caster sugar, as petit fours with coffee. Damsons and medlars also make a fine cheese, but the best cheese of all is made from quince: not a wild fruit, but one well worth growing in your garden, or scrumping from a neighbour or friend. In all cases, follow the same procedure.

crab-apples (at least 1.5kg/3lb)   sugar
water

• Wash the apples and cut them into quarters, but do not peel or core them.

• Put them in a large heavy pan, and add enough water to come one-third of the way up the fruit. Bring to a simmer, and cook until the fruit is pulpy.

• Rub through a nylon sieve, extracting as much juice and pulp as possible, but leaving behind skin, tough fibres and pips.

• Weigh the pulp, and add an equal weight of sugar. Return to a clean pan, and bring to the boil.

• Boil hard for at least an hour, until the setting point is reached (when a little of the mixture dropped into cold water forms a soft ball when rolled between finger and thumb).

• Spread into a lightly oiled shallow cake tin or Swiss roll tin, and leave in a cool place to set. Then cut into large squares, wrap in waxed paper, and store in a cool place in a tin. Serve on the cheese board.

ROWAN JELLY
(and other wild fruit jellies)

See also the notes on jam-making, page 131.

Great with lamb, venison or game, rowan jelly has a distinctive woody flavour and a beautiful amber colour. It can be on the syrupy side, but is none the worse for that. It will set firmer if combined in a 2:1 ratio with crab-apples.

Follow the same procedure for rosehips and haws, again adding half as many (by weight) crab-apples or cooking apples if you want a jelly that sets well. Jellies made from crab-apples only, or blackberries and elderberries, need much less water (just enough to set the juices running).

rowan berries   water
(at least 1kg/2lb)   sugar

• Remove the berries from their stalks and wash well.

- Place in a large heavy pan with enough water almost to cover. Bring to the boil, and simmer until the berries are very soft and pulpy. Strain through a cotton cloth or jelly bag.

- Measure the juice and transfer to a clean pan with 500g/1lb of sugar for every 600ml/1 pint of juice.

- Stir over a low heat, then boil until you reach the setting point for jelly. Cover and pot in the usual way (see page 132).

WILD CHERRY CLAFOUTIS

The simplest of dishes, a clafoutis is really just 'fruit in the hole'. The classic recipe, from the Limoges region of France, uses a fairly sour cherry — and so should you if you buy the fruit for this recipe. It works well with wild cherries, as well as other kinds of wild fruit — try blaeberries in a layer 2 berries deep in the tin, or bullaces, damsons or wild greengages. Blackberries mixed with crab-apples (peeled, cored and quartered, then tossed in sugar) are also very good.

SERVES 8

butter for greasing	a pinch of salt
500g/1lb wild cherries (or sour variety)	3 eggs, lightly beaten
85g/3oz caster sugar	300ml/10fl oz milk
125g/4½oz plain flour	30g/1oz icing sugar

- Lightly grease a 25cm/10 inch round, or a 25 x 20cm/10 x 8 inch ceramic or tin baking dish.

- Rinse and de-stalk the cherries but do not stone them. Toss with 30g/1oz of the sugar. Spread the cherries in the bottom of the dish.

- Sieve the flour, the salt and the remaining sugar into a mixing bowl. Make a well in the middle and pour in the eggs. Mix well, drawing in the flour from the sides. Beat in the milk, a little at a time, until you have a smooth batter. (This can all be done in a food processor.)

- Pour the batter over the cherries, and bake in a preheated oven at 180°C/350°F/gas mark 4 for about 35 minutes, until lightly browned and puffed up like a Yorkshire pudding.

- Clafoutis should be eaten lukewarm. Dust with the icing sugar just before serving, and serve plain or with cream.

A
TOAST TO THE WILD

As I hope you are beginning to discover, there are infinite ways to enjoy the fruits of forest and field. As far as the timing of the consumption of your harvest is concerned, however, I like to think in terms of three. First, there is instant gratification, or what countryside guru Richard Mabey calls, rather charmingly, 'ambulant consumption'. This is when the leaf, nut, berry, mushroom or other edible item you have happened upon (I must confess I have done it with raw prawns) goes not into the collecting basket but, with just the briefest flick or blow to remove any debris or untargeted wildlife, straight into your mouth. This can be great fun, and I always think it is a particularly good game to see how many different species I can sample on a country walk, depending on the time of year.

Secondly, there is the more dedicated procedure of setting out in pursuit of a known quarry, either animal or vegetable, and collecting or killing enough to make a dish or a meal – for 1, 2 or 20 – that requires some preparation back in your own kitchen (mobile or otherwise). It is of course this kind of latter-day hunter-gathering, in which the whole countryside is your greengrocer (not to mention your butcher and fishmonger), that features principally in the television series, and to which most of the chapters and recipes in this book are intended to be a guide.

But there is a third and, I think, particularly fine and convivial way to enjoy consuming the fruits of your foraging (*particularly* the fruits, as it happens) – one that can prolong the life of your wild harvest, and the pleasure of sampling it, for months, years or even decades. I am talking not of deep-freezing a glut (ten years would be pushing it) or of making biltong out of your wild meat (now there's an idea...), but of the very civilized art of brewing and wine-making. If you've never experienced the viticulturist's pride in popping the cork on the first bottle of a new vintage, or the brewer's magnanimous pleasure in watching friends get merry on a beverage of his own making, then the time to start is now – or at least soon. If there are two words guaranteed to bring a smile to the lips of just about anybody, they must be 'free drink'. And if you can lay down a few dozen bottles of the stuff every year, you'll be laughing all the way to the cellar.

The pleasures of country wines are much misunderstood in some quarters. And if you think, as many professed oenophiles apparently do, that all country wines and home brews are at best 'drinkable plonk' and at worst downright disgusting, then all I can say is either you've been drinking the wrong bottles, or missing the whole point about country wines – probably a bit of both. The best wild brews, or at least the ones I like to make and drink, are not intended, as some seem to think they should be, to be imitations of grape-based wines or hops-and-barley beers. On the contrary, the idea is to introduce a range of tastes, bouquets and flavour notes into your drinking life that you will never encounter in the alcoholic drinks you buy in shops. You may not like them all, but you will, I pledge, find a few firm favourites – the ones you will want to make and lay down year after year.

Another myth to scotch about home-brewing is that it is both difficult and very time-consuming. In most cases the only thing that takes much time is the gathering of the fruit or other flavouring agent – and all that usually takes is a pleasant few hours in the countryside. It is true that things can go wrong during fermentation, and occasionally after bottling – but the reasons why they do are rarely mysterious. Follow a few simple rules and you have every chance of first-time success – which is usually all you need to become a regular convert to home-brewing, who can toast the wild all the year round.

THE RANGE OF COUNTRY DRINKS

This chapter is not, however, devoted solely to the pursuit of fermenting alcohol. There are many ways of deriving liquid refreshment from wild ingredients, and not all of them are intoxicating. Tisanes are an instantaneous way of enjoying the aromas and essential oils of leaves, flowers and fruits. Syrups and cordials make refeshing drinks that do not need time to mature. Children love them as well as adults, and they can be used as sauces and flavourings for ices and other puddings, as well as to make drinks.

According to my informal system of categorization, there are about five types of home-made drink with which to 'toast the wild'. I describe them for you below, in ascending order of potency. And after outlining a basic procedure for each, which is adaptable for many different primary flavourings, I offer you a selection of tried and trusted recipes to get you started.

TISANES

Infusions made from fresh or dried leaves and flowers of wild plants and herbs have been used for centuries, both medicinally and as a simple refreshment. There is a great deal of folklore, and a certain amount of supporting science, governing the medicinal use of herbs in infusions. If you are interested in knowing more about the subject, invest in a good guide to herbalism, such as *Culpeper's Complete Herbal*. In the meantime I will not dwell at any length on the possible tonic effects of herbal infusions, save to mention, in italics after the name of the plant, some of the more well-known properties associated with certain tisanes in the list below.

The following leaves, flowers and berries can all be used to make tisanes. Note that not all of them are mentioned in the main text in Chapter I, and I have included a few garden herbs and flowers as well.

angelica leaves		marjoram leaves	
bilberry (blaeberry) leaves		meadowsweet flowers and leaves	*analgesic*
borage leaves	*soothing*	mint leaves	*digestive*
camomile flowers	*sedative*	nettle leaves	*invigorating*
cowslip leaves (garden-grown only)		pine needles	
dandelion leaves	*purgative, diuretic*	rosehips	
elder leaves and flowers		salad burnet leaves	
ground elder leaves		thyme leaves	
hop leaves		valerian leaves	*sedative*
juniper berries	*diuretic*	violet leaves	
lime flowers	*invigorating*	yarrow leaves	*soothing*
marigold flowers	*soothing*		

Leaves and flowers for infusions can be combined to balance flavours and effects. Here are a few suggested 'cocktails' (you can of course invent your own):

camomile and mint	*sedative, digestive*	rosehip and blackberry	*fruity, aromatic*
lime flower and elder	*invigorating*	meadowsweet and juniper	*diuretic, analgesic*
nettle and pine needles	*invigorating*		(hangover cure)

DRYING LEAVES AND FLOWERS

You can make tisanes using fresh or dried leaves and flowers: fresh have the edge for flavour, but drying leaves for tisanes is very practical as they can be kept for a few months, either individually or in special mixes (for the morning, bedtime, after a meal, etc.). Dried leaves will not keep their flavour for ever. Replace them at least once a year.

Drying leaves is easy: simply hang up small bunches with string or cotton, in a warm place such as an airing cupboard, or above an Aga or radiator. When they are completely desiccated (brittle to the touch), transfer to airtight jars or tins and keep in a dry place. (It may save space, but I prefer not to break up dried leaves for storage: more of the essential oils are released if you break them up just before infusion.)

THE PERFECT CUPPA

You can make a tisane in either a pot (for several servings) or an individual cup. In either case, you want the brew as hot as possible for maximum infusion. So rinse out the pot, or cup, with hot water, then add the leaves, and pour over just-boiled water.

Exact quantities of a herb or flowers required for a good tisane vary from species to species, but as an initial guideline (which you can vary with experience), use a tablespoon of fresh leaves per cup (or per person in a teapot), and half that amount of dried leaves. Most wild leaves need rather longer than ordinary tea for infusion: 5-7 minutes usually does the trick. I don't mind leaves floating in my tisanes, but if you are going to strain your cup, do so into another warmed cup so as not to lose heat.

You can buy special tisane mugs (especially from oriental kitchen shops). These are slightly larger than an ordinary coffee mug, and come with their own lid, so the water retains its heat for longer, to get maximum flavour from the infusion. You can get exactly the same effect, of course, by putting a small saucer over a coffee mug. Be aware that an infusion made in a warmed cup with a lid on it is liable to be hotter than your average cup of tea – take care not to burn your mouth with the first sip.

Tisanes can be sweetened to taste with honey or sugar.

CORDIALS AND SYRUPS

Be honest, who doesn't love a glass of Ribena now and then? And your kids? Ever thought of making your own? And what about wild ribena? Mmmmm...

It's easier than you think. And if you doubt it is worth the trouble, then perhaps I can tempt you with the thought that there are more interesting ways of diluting your finished syrup than with water. Chilled white wine added to a little trickle of a syrup made from wild fruits gives you deeply satisfying variations on the kir theme.

The process of converting soft fruits (wild or cultivated) into syrups is very similar to making jellies (see page 131), except that none of the hard boiling and testing for setting is required.

The basic procedure outlined below is for blackberries, but it can be used to make a syrup from elderberries, blackberries, raspberries, gooseberries, redcurrants – and even blaeberries, if you can get enough of them, for a superb *crème de mures*. With the more acidic fruits, such as blackberries and gooseberries, there is no need to add the lemon juice.

BASIC RECIPE FOR (BLACKBERRY) SYRUP

about 2.5kg/5lb ripe blackberries
juice of a lemon
600ml/1 pint of water

1 egg white
caster or preserving sugar
a little brandy

- Rinse the berries well in cold water, and add to a large pan with the lemon juice and water. Cook gently over a very low heat, without allowing it to simmer more than a tremor, until the fruit is soft and pulpy.

- Strain the juice through a cotton cloth or jelly bag. Measure it, and then measure out (but do not yet add) 650g of sugar to every 1 litre of juice (12oz per pint).

- Put the sugar in a warm place, and put the juice into a pan with the lightly whisked egg white . Bring the juice to the boil, whisking occasionally. A frothy scum will arise as it comes to the boil. Skim this off.

- Add the sugar and stir to dissolve. Bring to the boil, skimming off any further froth that rises to the top. Simmer the syrup for just 5 minutes. Test the thickness of the syrup by cooling a small quantity in the bowl of a large metal spoon. If you think it should be more 'syrupy', simmer for a little longer.

- Remove from the heat, and pour into clean, warm bottles, through a plastic funnel, to within about 1cm/½ inch of the top. Pour a teaspoon of brandy into each bottle and seal with a screw top or cork.

- The syrup can be kept in corked bottles or jars for a few weeks, in a cool cellar or fridge. But if you want to keep it for any longer, you will need to sterilize the bottles. For this process, bottles are required that will not throw their corks under pressure from the high heat of the sterilization process. They can be bought from home-brew shops – or you can recycle Grolsch-style beer bottles with a self-sealing rubber stopper.

- The filled bottles should be stood upright, not touching each other, in a baking tray filled with at least 2.5cm/1 inch of hot water. Place in a preheated oven at 120°C/250°F/gas mark 1, and leave for 2 hours. Remove from the oven and leave to cool down at room temperature. Sterilized bottles of syrup will keep indefinitely.

The recipe for the very excellent elderflower cordial (which is slightly different) appears on page 164.

COUNTRY WINES AND BEERS

When it comes to brewing alcoholic drinks from wild fruits and plants, the distinction between wine and beer is of no great consequence: the use of one term rather than the other refers simply to drinking style, alcohol content, and the length of time it takes before the brew is ready to drink – it is on that basis alone, for example, that the nettle beverage described on page 163 goes by the name of beer.

True beers are made with malted barley, and other flavourings such as hops. The only real ale you will learn how to make in this chapter is the heather ale described on page 162 – and a very fine brew it is too.

This section is really concerned with wine-making – using fruits and flowers, and occasionally other things, as flavouring. The first priority is to get to grips with the basic procedure for country wine-making. It is really only quantities and timings that vary from recipe to recipe.

With this in mind, what follows are two detailed procedures for each of the two most common types of country wines: those flavoured by fruit (and including the juice of the fruit in their bulk) and those flavoured by flowers. If you follow these instructions closely you have every chance of producing a good clear wine which will age well. The recipes for various wines at the end of this chapter are abbreviated, in that they assume knowledge of the steps outlined below.

There is no doubt that some people seem to have a knack for wine-making, and everything always goes right for them. If you're not one of the lucky ones, don't despair – neither am I. But I still manage to make plenty of bottles that don't explode, and taste great.

As a general 'bible' for wine-making I recommend a clear and friendly volume, *First Steps in Winemaking* by Cyril Berry. It gives chapter and verse on each step of the process, plus some good recipes for wild and cultivated ingredients found throughout the year.

But before the procedures, a list of essential, and useful, wine-making equipment:

Airlock Clear plastic or glass device, generally with a U-bend with 2 bubbles on either side. Fill the U-bend with a clear sterile solution of water and part of a Campden tablet or just with plain water (and put some cotton wool in the open end of the airlock). This allows the carbon dioxide from the fermenting wine to escape but does not allow in oxygen and wine-spoiling organisms. Cup-type airlocks are also available.

Bucket A white 'brew-bin' for the initial soaking and mashing of your raw material. A robust synthetic material such as polypropylene is ideal. Do not use metal containers, as they can affect the end product.

Bung An airtight method of stoppering a demijohn. Made of rubber with a hole in the centre for an airlock.

Citric Acid Aids fermentation with non-acidic fruit and other wines.

Corks or Stoppers Do not use old corks as they can affect the wine. Corking machines are available from home-brew shops or you can use plastic stoppers, which are re-usable.

Corking Gun Used to put corks right down into bottles.

Campden Tablets A convenient form of sulphur dioxide for sterilizing equipment. Also sold as crystals. Crush and mix with water to sterilize equipment. Avoid inhaling the fumes. A less-concentrated solution can also be used to kill any wild yeasts on fruit and to stabilize the end wine.

Fermentation Jar A 1-gallon glass jar with 2 small handles at the neck. Also called a demijohn.

Funnel To get the liquid into bottles or a demijohn.

Pectinol An enzyme which helps break down the fruit and stops the wine from being cloudy. It can be added to help clear the wine, either initially or at the first racking stage.

Saucepan It is best to have a large stainless steel saucepan, such as a preserving pan, with a capacity of at least 4-6 litres/1-1½ gallons – the minimum amount of wine you are likely to make.

Siphon Tube A metre or so of narrow PVC tubing to 'rack' the wine (i.e. move it from one demijohn to another). You can also use a smaller piece of stiff tubing, perhaps with a J-bend at the end, stuck into the end of the siphon tube.

Strainer A nylon jelly bag or muslin cloth for straining off liquid from solids.

Tannin Improves the ageing quality and flavour of many wines. Many raw ingredients (e.g. plums, apples, grapes and oak leaves) are already rich in tannins and need no additional tannin, but some wines, particularly flower wines, will be the better for it. A rough-and-ready method is to add cold tea to the wine with the yeast.

Yeast Multiplies rapidly, given the right food and temperature, converting the sugar present to alcohol and carbon dioxide. Yeast works best at warm temperatures, between 16-21°C/60-69°F, but is killed by too much heat (above 38°C/100°F). Either baker's or brewer's yeast can be used. In specialist home-brew shops you can find many different kinds of wine yeasts designed specifically for different wines, and some may give better results than ordinary baker's yeast – talk to an expert in the shop. Dried baker's yeast must be 'started' first by mixing the yeast with some warm water and sugar and leaving it for an hour in a warm place. Most varieties of brewer's yeast can be added directly to the must without being started first.

Yeast Nutrients Compounds which help the yeast to multiply. Can be useful if wine-making on a large scale.

BASIC RECIPE FOR FRUIT WINES

• Start with a rough minimum of 2 kilos/5lb of fruit. Chop up any large pieces of fruit and take out any stones and blemished bits. Put the fruit in a polythene bucket which has been sterilized with a solution of 1 Campden tablet dissolved in 300ml/½ pint water and 1 teaspoon of lemon juice. (This solution can be kept in a bottle and re-used.)

• Pour about 2 litres/4 pints of boiling water over the fruit, just to cover it. Leave for 24 hours, covered, stirring it around occasionally with a sterilized bottle.

• Mix half the sugar in the recipe (a 1kg/2lb bag per 4 litres/8 pints of water/juice is a rough guide) in a saucepan with 2 litres/4 pints of water. Heat gently until the sugar has dissolved. Leave until it is lukewarm (approx 21°C/69°F). Add the yeast (baker's yeast, and some brewing yeasts, should be started first – see **Yeast** in list above), the juice and rind of an orange or lemon or some citric acid (up to 3 level teaspoons, according to the acidity of the fruit). Pour this mixture over the fruit and water in the bin.

• Leave this mixture (called the 'must') to ferment for up to a week, covered with several layers of cloth or a polythene sheet, secured around the bucket with string. Stir it up with a sterilized bottle at least once a day.

• Strain the liquid into a sterilized fermentation jar, or demijohn, so it comes just up to the shoulders. Add the rest of the sugar.

• Stop up the jar with a bung and an airlock (which needs some water or sterile solution in the U-bend). Shake the jar a bit to help dissolve the sugar.

• Put the jar in a warm place, anywhere in a centrally heated house, particularly the kitchen, but not too near an oven which could overheat the jar and kill the yeast.

• After a week or so, when the initial fermentation has quietened down, top up the demijohn with boiled and cooled water or a light sugar syrup.

• Fermentation can take 3-6 months. You know when fermentation has stopped and the yeast has turned as much sugar as possible to alcohol when there are no more bubbles in the airlock.

• Siphon off the wine from any gunk at the bottom of the demijohn (a process called 'racking'). Put one end of a plastic tube in the liquid, above any sediment at the bottom. Put the other end below the fermentation jar and suck to get the liquid flowing. Put the end into another sterile demijohn and fill it up with the liquid.

• Put an airlock in the new demijohn, and leave for another couple of months. You may have to rack 2 or 3 times to clear the wine. (Some people are prepared to take a more hit-and-miss approach to wine making, which means the process of racking several times to clear the wine is reduced to a single operation, after which the wine is immediately bottled. This is fine, so long as you are prepared to sacrifice the odd bottle which may explode if secondary fermentation occurs. Once in a while, a whole batch may be lost.)

• Put the wine into sterilized bottles or leave in the demijohn with a safety bung, in case it starts fermenting again. Store in a cool place. Some wines can be drunk straight away and others improve greatly by being left for 6 months to a couple of years. Only time will tell...

BASIC RECIPE FOR FLOWER WINES

Flower wines lack the body that comes naturally from pulpy fruits and is necessary for the formation of a good must. The must is therefore created using raisins.

Never put your flowers into boiling water: excessive heat will scald the scent- producing parts of the flower and stop their essential oils flavouring the wine.

The procedure below suggests quantities of sugar and water for a medium dry wine — which is a good balance for a highly scented flower wine. If you like something drier, or sweeter, add less or more sugar.

• In a sterilized bucket or bowl, make a must by mixing 225g/8oz of sultanas or raisins, 500g/1lb 2oz of sugar, 1 litre/2 pints boiling water and the juice of 2 lemons. When it has cooled down to blood temperature and the sugar has dissolved, add some yeast (which can be started first in some warm water and sugar).

• Cover the bucket or bowl and leave to ferment for a week, stirring at least twice a day with a sterilized bottle.

• Put about 2 litres/4 pints of your chosen flowers in a bowl and crush them lightly. Pour over 500ml/ 1 pint of warm (but not boiling) water, and stir well, breaking up the flowers a little more as you do so. Add this flowery mulch to the must in the bucket.

• Leave to ferment for 5 more days. Strain off the flowers and dried fruit and pour the liquid into a fermentation jar.

• Dissolve the rest of the sugar (usually another 500g/1lb) in 2 litres/4 pints of hot water. Cool to blood temperature and top up the fermentation jar to the shoulders. Add the rest later, when the fermentation has quietened down.

• Leave until fermentation is finished, then rack and finish as for fruit wines above.

Most flower wines are quite drinkable after just a couple of months in the bottle, though they may benefit from a year or two ageing.

SPIRITS OF THE WILD

You need a licence (and rather an expensive one) to distill spirits. There are, however, some very fine tipples to be made using wild ingredients, combining them with commercially made spirits (usually gin or vodka), and perhaps some sugar.

The best known of these wild fruit liqueurs is sloe gin, but there are many other possibilities, using other fruits (as well as vegetables, and even mushrooms) and other spirits. This is an area ripe for experimentation: my own current experiments include crab-apple brandy and tomato vodka (using sweet yellow cherry tomatoes). Both tasted very promising at the bottling stage – shortly after the picture on page 130 was taken. I'm trying to resist the temptation to sample them for a few months yet.

Here is the recipe for sloe gin (or sloe vodka, which I slightly prefer). The same procedure can be followed for gins or vodkas of damson or bullace, wild cherry, gooseberry – and no doubt for numerous other combinations that the wild imagination can come up with.

SLOE GIN

The idea is to have enough fruit to half fill 2 bottles, so that when you pour in the vodka or gin you get 2 full bottles. When you come to strain off the sloes, you're back to your original bottle – with a bit left over to sample the progress of the vintage.

750ml/1¼ pint sloes
I bottle gin or vodka

55g/2oz sugar
a few drops almond essence

- Sloes don't usually need to be washed. Simply prick each one several times with a needle or pin and put them into bottles or jars.

- Add all the other ingredients. Screw on the lids. Leave for 3 or 4 months, shaking gently at least once a week.

- Strain off the sloes, and filter the liqueur back into a bottle through a funnel lined with a cloth or coffee filter paper. Keep for at least 6 months – a year is even better.

BEN LAW'S BIRCH SAP WINE

*I made birch sap wine — or rather watched coppicer and all round woodsman Ben Law make it —
on a chilly March day at the beginning of the second series. We went on to taste the previous year's vintage,
along with a selection of Ben's other country wines. All were interesting, and some were excellent,
but the birch sap was the best of the lot.*

4 litres/just under 1 gallon of birch sap   yeast
150ml /¼ pint water   the juice of 1 lemon
3 tablespoons runny honey

• The best time to collect the sap is usually during the middle 2 weeks of March, but it can be later if spring is a slow starter. You need a plastic tube (the kind used for racking your wine is perfect) and a large container (such as a demijohn). Bore a hole (the width of your tube) into the bark of the tree, about 45-60cm/18 inches-2 feet off the ground, at a slight upwards angle. It need be no deeper than a centimetre or two/½-1 inch, and the sap should start coming out immediately. If it doesn't, or if it is very slow, try again a few days later.

• Insert the tube so that the sap trickles out, and place the other end into a demijohn. Seal the neck around the tube with a wad of cotton wool, to keep out insects. If the sap is flowing well, 2 trees, tapped overnight, or one, left for 2 or 3 days, should give you the 4 litres/ 1 gallon or so you need. After collecting the sap, plug the hole with a bit of mud, clay or soft wax, and the tree will make a full recovery.

• Heat a little water with 3 tablespoons of honey so it dissolves. Let it cool down to blood temperature. Add some yeast and leave to start. Add to the birch sap with the lemon juice.

• Put in a bung and an airlock and leave to ferment. Complete as for fruit wines above (page 156). If it seems very dry on bottling, you can add a little light sugar syrup.

BLACKBERRY AND ELDERBERRY WINE

A reliable red wine which can, with a bit of luck and in a good year, be excellent. (See illustration on page 150.)

1kg/2lb each elderberries and blackberries	1 orange
	1 lemon
4.5 litres/1 gallon water	2 teaspoons dried baker's yeast
1kg/2lb caster sugar	2 teaspoons sugar

• Tidy up the fruit but do not wash it. Put it in a sterilized bucket.

• Bring 2 litres/4 pints of water to the boil.

• Pour the water over the fruit. Mash it up roughly to help release the juice from the fruit. Leave to stand for a couple of days, stirring daily.

• Strain the liquid through a jelly bag, squeezing the pulp to get out as much juice as possible.

• Put 2.5 litres/5 pints of water in a pan. Add the sugar and heat gently to dissolve. Grate the orange and lemon and squeeze out the juice. Add to the wine. Leave to cool.

• Mix the yeast with a little warm water and sugar and leave in a warm place until it starts fermenting. Add to the wine. Pour into a demijohn with an airlock.

• Leave until it stops fermenting before racking it off into another demijohn. Leave to mature for at least 6 months before bottling. This wine may benefit considerably from ageing.

BLACKBERRY WHISKY

Another fruit-flavoured spirit in the sloe gin mould – and one of the very best. This recipe comes from that doyenne of the farmhouse kitchen, Prue Coates.

2kg /4lbs blackberries	1 bottle whisky
225g /8oz sugar (or less according to taste)	

• Place the fruit, sugar and whisky in a large screw top or kilner style jar. Shake every few days until the sugar has dissolved.

• Place in a dark cupboard for three months, turning slowly to mix once every two weeks or so.

• Strain and bottle. The whisky will have turned a deep, dark purple. It can be drunk straight away, but the flavour will continue to improve for up to 2 years.

CHANTERELLE VODKA

This recipe comes from The Times *cook Hattie Ellis, whose assistance on this project has been invaluable, to put it mildly. You can also use schnapps or cachaca (sugar cane spirit) for this. It should be served ice cold, like an aquavit, with caviare, pickled fish and other salty foods.*

a dozen very fresh chanterelles
I small dried red chilli

a bottle of vodka

- Clean the chanterelles scrupulously and cut them into pieces which will fit through the bottle's neck.

- Put the chanterelles and chilli into the vodka.

- Leave for a few months for the flavour to develop. The orange colour of the mushrooms will fade but their flavour and colour will go into the vodka, which takes on a pale amber hue.

DANDELION AND BURDOCK BEER

2 large burdock roots
2 dandelion roots
4.5 litres/I gallon water
500g/Ilb caster sugar

2 tablespoons black treacle
juice of I lemon
yeast

- Wipe the roots clean and cut off their leaves. Cut the roots up into small pieces.

- Put the chopped roots into a pan with 2.2 litres/4 pints of water. Boil for 30 minutes.

- Add the sugar, treacle and lemon juice to the rest of the water in a large pan. Simmer, stirring, until the sugar has dissolved.

- Strain off the roots and leave to cool.

- Meanwhile, mix the yeast with some warm water so it starts fermenting.

- When the root liquid is tepid, add the yeast. Leave it to ferment in the bucket for 3-4 days.

- Put into bottles, and drink after a week

WILD HEATHER ALE

Bruce Williamson makes this excellent beer commercially — and so passionately that he now has his own heather ale web site on the internet: http://dialspace.dial.tippex.com/heather.ale

The version we brewed up together on the Gastrowagon did not like being driven up and down Scottish country roads and, I'm sorry to say, never made it to bottling! The picture below was taken on the day we brewed.

MAKES ABOUT 15 LITRES/10 PINTS

2.5kg/5lbs milled pale malted barley	8 large handfuls heather flowers
250g/8oz milled crystal malt	2 handfuls bog myrtle leaves
cold water	2 teaspoons baker's yeast or beer yeast
small pieces of fat (animal or vegetable)	1 level teaspoon sugar or honey per bottle

- Put the milled pale malted barley and crystal malt into a 3 gallon jam or jelly pan.

- Mix with cold water, then add more water to cover the grain and stir into a slack, sloppy mixture.

• Heat very slowly, over 3 hours, keeping it warm, but do not allow the temperature to go over 70°C/158°F. Use a thermometer or the following old fashioned method: put a small piece of solid fat (animal or vegetable) in the beer. When it is solid the temperature is cool, when it is runny it is the right temperature, but when the fat breaks up into small beads, the mixture is too hot. If the liquid gets too hot, remove from the heat, remove the fat and mix until cooler. Mix every half hour, removing the fat with a spoon each time while mixing.

• Peg a coarse dishcloth over a second pan or bucket and strain out the liquor. Rinse the grains with several kettles of hot water and leave to drain over the bucket. Boil the strained liquid for 1 hour with 5 large handfuls of heather flowers and 1 handful of bog myrtle leaves.

• Rinse the dishcloth and peg over the fermentation bucket. Place 3 handfuls of heather and 1 of bog myrtle in the cloth and then pour the hot liquor over this into the bucket. Make up the bucket to about 15 litres/30 pints with cold water and leave to cool to body temperature.

• Add 2 teaspoons of baker's yeast started in a little warm water, or a sachet of beer yeast, and leave for 6-8 days to ferment. (Adding more wild heather flowers will ferment the ale, instead of the yeast, but the flavour will be more sour and wine-like.)

• Once the ale has stopped fizzing, pour it into returnable strong screw-top lemonade or beer bottles. Add one level teaspoon of sugar or honey to each bottle, replace the top and store in a cool place until clear.

NETTLE BEER

This simple and refreshing brew has the great advantage of being ready to drink within a week of being made.

12 litres/2½ gallons water	1.5kg/3lb sugar
1 carrier-bagful of young nettle tops	55g/2oz cream of tartar
juice of 1 lemon and 1 orange	yeast

• Bring the water to the boil, and pour over the nettles. Mix well, then leave to infuse for at least an hour, until cooled down to blood temperature.

• Strain into a pan. Add the lemon and orange juice, the sugar and the cream of tartar. Heat gently, stirring, until the sugar has dissolved.

• Leave the mixture until it is tepid and stir in the yeast (started in a little warm water and sugar). Cover and leave for 2-3 days.

• Remove any scum which has risen to the top in fermentation. Decant, or rack as for wine, to get the liquid off the sediment. Put into beer bottles, and leave for just 2 more days (but up to a month, if you have the patience).

• Drink cold with a sprig of mint.

ELDERFLOWER CORDIAL

1 litre/2 pints elderflowers   granulated sugar
water   lemons

• Gather enough elderflower blossoms to fill a 1 litre/2 pint measure when lightly packed.

• Cover the elderflowers with water. Simmer for 30 minutes. Top up the pan if necessary, to keep the liquid covering the flowers.

• Strain the flowery liquid through muslin or a jelly bag, gently squeezing it to extract all the juice. Measure the amount of juice.

• Add 350g/12oz granulated sugar, and the juice of ½ a lemon, to each 500ml/1 pint of liquid. Heat gently to dissolve the sugar. Bring to a gentle simmer and skim off any scum. Let the cordial cool.

• Pour the liquid through a funnel into clean bottles, up to about 1cm/1 inch below the top. Seal the bottles with screw tops or a cork.

• Thus bottled, the cordial will keep for several weeks in the fridge, but if you wish to keep the cordial for much longer, you will need to sterilize the bottles to ensure that there are no yeasts or bacteria present which could cause fermentation: follow the procedure as described for blackberry syrup on page 154.

OAK-LEAF WINE

I was treated to a demonstration of how to make this wonderfully drinkable wine by white witch Ros Foskett, in the first ever episode of A Cook on the Wild Side. She gave me half a dozen bottles of the previous year's vintage, so that I might be fortified by the strength of the oak throughout my journey. But I'm sorry to say I'd finished the lot within a week. I was on a steep learning curve...

5 litres/10 pints oak leaves   1kg/2lb sugar
4.5 litres/1 gallon water   yeast
2 lemons

• Pick young, fresh oak leaves at the beginning of the summer.

• Bring the water to the boil and pour over the oak leaves. Mix well, squashing the leaves slightly, and leave the mixture overnight in a fairly warm place.

• Strain the liquid from the leaves into a large pan, bring to the boil, and simmer for 15 minutes.

- Finely grate the lemon rind and squeeze out the juice; add with the sugar to the simmering liquid, and stir until the sugar has dissolved. Cool to blood temperature.

- Add the yeast, and leave in a covered bucket for 5 days.

- Funnel into a demijohn. Put in an airlock and leave in a warm place until it has stopped fermenting.

- Rack off the wine and bottle as usual. If it is not clear, you can add pectinol after the first racking and leave for a few more weeks. Bottle, and leave for a couple of months, but drink within a year.

BERNARD'S PARSNIP WINE

This wine was coracler Bernard Thomas's contribution to the meal I cooked for him, of deep-fried minnows and hogweed shoots. Some might say that I got a better deal than he did.

It's not a wild brew, but something of a classic country wine nonetheless.

1.5kg/3lb parsnips	yeast
5 litres/10 pints water	juice and rind of 1 lemon
1.2kg/2½lb caster sugar	

- Cut the parsnips into small cubes. Bring the water to the boil and then simmer the parsnips for about 10 minutes.

- Strain the liquid off the vegetables into another pan. Stir in the caster sugar and simmer until it has dissolved.

- When the liquid is at blood temperature, add the yeast and the lemon juice and rind. Leave to ferment for 5 days, covered.

- Pour into a demijohn, so it comes up to the shoulders of the jar. You can top it up when fermentation has quietened down with the same concentration sugar syrup.

- Keep in a warm place until fermentation has stopped. This can take many weeks, and the wine can end up being on the strong side – though it's none the worse for that. Rack off, bottle and store in the usual way.

Slainte!

THE MAGIC OF
MUSHROOMS

Not so long ago we were, as a nation, largely ignorant as to the edibility of our native fungi. We knew what a field mushroom was, and if we lived in the country we may even have had the confidence to pick and eat it. But just about everything else was a toadstool, pregnant with the risks that this ancient pejorative implies.

That's all changed now. As a nation, we have latterly become food-wise. And one of the foods we are proudest to be wise about is wild mushrooms. 'Are the ceps fresh?' you will hear besuited yuppies loudly asking the waiters in expensive London restaurants from September onwards. And down in the country at weekends, people are opening the boots of their mud-spattered Range Rovers to take out not a labrador and a shotgun, but a wicker basket and a field guide to fungi. Look in the small ads of the leisure pages in the Saturday papers, and you will see dozens of mycophiles offering their services as trail guides, in pursuit of the edible fruit bodies of the mysterious underground mycelium (for that is the fungus proper).

To mix culinary metaphors, we seem to have gone nuts about mushrooms. And I have spent not a few idle moments wondering how this has come about. I am certain it is not simply a function of food fashion, though this has clearly played a part. There are other, deeper reasons why the mushroom's time has come. As I said at the beginning of the book, the feeling of a sincere and honest communion with nature is one of the many satisfactions offered by the gathering of all wild foods. With wild mushrooms, it seems to me, you get this in spades. Relative to green leaves, or even ripe fruits, mushrooms seem to have character, maybe even soul. And this feeling is not just a modern fancy: mushrooms have a long association with pagan religions and country lore. In the time of the druids it was considered a taboo for anyone outside the priesthood to handle mushrooms. And the hallucinogenic properties of certain species (which in past times often had a religious application) are very well known. I suspect the fact that wild mushrooms (and the pursuit of them) have become popular alongside the burgeoning interest in New Age spiritualism may not be entirely coincidental, even if the overlap between enthusiasts of the two interests is not that great.

What this all adds up to is that there is something rather intense about mushroom collecting. It is less casual, and more committed, than other forms of food foraging. It often seems to me more like hunting than gathering: in fact it may well be the perfect way to satisfy the sublimated blood-lust of those reluctant to kill for food.

For all these reasons, I feel somewhat strange as I embark on the writing of this chapter. On the one hand mushrooms are one of the aspects of the the wild larder I enjoy the most, both in the gathering and in the cooking. And, as with other wild foods, it's a joy I'm keen to spread. On the other hand, I can't but hesitate in inviting you to share with me the bosky, spooky charms of the autumnal forest floor. It seems there are plenty of you at it already.

Perhaps this is one of the reasons, besides approximate seasonal order, that I have decided this chapter should be the last in the book. And if you happen to have turned to it first, may I politely suggest that you go back to the beginning, and read about hedgerow plants. My grandmother was always very strict about this: you can't have your pudding treat until you've finished your greens.

Now, on with the practicalities...

SAFETY

There are some 3,000 species of large-bodied fungi growing in this country, of which most are quite harmless, about 100 are both edible and worthwhile, and about twenty may be seriously harmful, even fatal. The priority of all mushroom gatherers must be to home in on the happy hundred, and avoid at all costs the terrible twenty.

The first thing to say on that score is that nothing on the pages that follow, neither the text nor the pictures, is intended to be a foolproof guide to the identification, and therefore absolute safety, of edible mushrooms. I have perforce been selective in the mushrooms I am writing about, and selectivity always rules out absolute certainty. At the end of the day, it is more important to be able to identify a poisonous mushroom than an edible one, and as you will see, there are no poisonous mushrooms illustrated in this book.

The only foolproof field guide, therefore, is a fully illustrated and comprehensive one, as it allows you to make direct comparisons between the edible target mushrooms, and similar-looking fungi which may be inedible or poisonous. If you are serious about mushroom collecting, you should certainly get one. My own favourite manual is Roger Phillips's awesomely thorough *Mushrooms and other Fungi*, published by Pan, with excellent colour photographs for identification.

Having said that, I am also of the opinion that it may be a mistake to dash into a wood armed with a field guide, attempt to identify every fungus you see, and pick all the edible ones you can lay your hands on. Better to start with a few species and slowly build up a repertoire as you gain confidence and expertise. One good strategy is to carry two containers: one basket for collecting the edible species whose identification you are certain of, and another container (maybe a plastic box) for a few individual specimens you are not quite sure about. Do not overfill the latter, but restrict yourself to a manageable number (half a dozen or less) to identify at home.

NEVER MIX mushrooms whose identity you are uncertain about with those you are planning to eat.

GENERAL COLLECTING RULES

For safety, efficiency, and environmental friendliness, it pays to observe the following guidelines.

1. Place your collected mushrooms in an open, well-ventilated container, such as a wicker or wire basket. This helps preserve the condition of the mushrooms you have picked, and may also have the added benefit of scattering the spores of mature specimens. Plastic bags or pockets will just do in an emergency, but take the mushrooms out at the earliest opportunity. They can start to sweat, and you will have a slimy soup even before you get back to the kitchen.

2. You will save a lot of aggravation back in the kitchen if you give each mushroom an initial clean in the field. Otherwise once you start piling mushrooms into your basket, grit from the stems of the ones on top can end up in the gills of the ones underneath. And that can be very boring when you get your harvests back to the kitchen. So cut away the base of the stem if it is very muddy, flicking away any

loose dirt or leaf matter. A stiff pastry brush is a good tool for this job. You can actually buy a mushroom collector's pocket knife, with a special brush blade.

3. If in doubt about identification, always pick the whole mushroom: the shape of the stipe (the base where the mushroom enters the ground) may be a salient factor.

4. Mushrooms are vulnerable to infestation from insect larvae and other parasites, and it is the recurring tragedy of the mushroom collector to happen on a fine specimen, only to find the maggots have already begun the feast without you. I prefer to endure this tragedy in the field, rather than in the kitchen: provided I only put sound mushrooms in my basket, I know what I've got. The process of discarding fully three-quarters of your harvest after you get back home is particularly demoralizing.

So cut the end off the stalk: if it is riddled with holes, discard it. But check the base of the cap: it may still be clean. In a large specimen, partially infested, you may be able to salvage a few decent slices from the edge of the cap, as the maggots seem to start in the middle and work outwards. I don't usually worry about a minor infestation: a few little holes, and even the odd fungus-fattened maggot, will not hurt.

5. As a general rule, do not pick mushrooms on a wet day. They can soak up a lot of water, and lose condition quickly after you pick them. (I often disregard this rule when picking ceps in Scotland, since it is always raining, but I make a point of dealing with my mushrooms as soon as I get home to minimize problems.)

6. Don't bother with really tiny specimens. A little chanterelle, for example, may be no more than a pea-size button of orange. Why bother? In a few days' time, it will offer some other hungry being (human or otherwise) a substantial morsel. Also, mature specimens are more likely to be already shedding spores, which you may spread as you swing your basket.

7. Confirm your identification of each specimen back at home, in good light, before cooking. If in doubt, chuck it out. And if you suspect that a seriously poisonous mushroom may have found its way into your basket, then I'm afraid you will have to chuck the whole lot out.

Inevitably, a good collecting trip furnishes the collector with a number of mushrooms, varying in quality and often in species. An initial grading is therefore in order. The first priority, for me, is to identify the prime specimens, the ones I want to feature in a dedicated mushroom dish, such as a crostini, a risotto, or a lasagne. If I have done well, there will be enough left over for a good soup pile. Into this go waterlogged, bruised or otherwise out of condition specimens, whose texture might leave something to be desired, but whose flavour and bulk can fill out a liquidized soup.

When I have scored a bumper crop, I may want to dry some specimens, to extend their possible use.

DRYING MUSHROOMS

Drying mushrooms is not difficult, and although you can buy special mushroom-drying equipment, I have never felt the want of it in my own improvised kitchen method.

Perhaps the most important thing is the selection of mushrooms: you need prime specimens, with a minimum of bruising or damage, which are already reasonably dry (waterlogged specimens are liable to rot before they have desiccated).

Larger specimens (most boletus, for example) will need to be sliced fairly fine. Smaller ones (and in some species, such as blewits, just the caps) may be dried whole.

Place the slices, caps or whole mushrooms on a clean wire rack in such a way that they do not overlap. Place the rack in a reliably warm and dry place, for example on top of an Aga, in an airing cupboard, or in a very low oven. Leave until they are completely dry and brittle to the touch (sacrifice a piece to make absolutely sure).

An alternative method, which works very well with whole morels and the caps of other species, is to thread the mushrooms on a string and hang it above an Aga, a boiler, or in an airing cupboard. Mushrooms dried in either way should be stored in airtight jars.

Reconstituting dried mushrooms: Place the mushrooms in a bowl or cup and pour over enough boiling water to cover them. Leave to soak, stirring once or twice, until the water is cool. Strain off the soaking liquid, but don't discard it as it is full of flavour. Pass it through a cloth or coffee filter to dispose of any fine grit, and use it in the dish you are cooking. The reconstituted mushrooms should be rinsed in a sieve to wash away any grit, then sweated in a little butter, with a few spoonfuls of their soaking juice, before being incorporated into a recipe.

FUNGI FIELD GUIDE
(see page 175 for illustrations)

As I have said, the guide that follows is not exhaustive. I have simply selected 15 or so of my favourite wild mushrooms, on the basis of distribution, ease of identification, and above all taste. I hope you enjoy them as much as I do.

Please note that the cooking suggestions for each species are often little more than conceits (as opposed to receipts). All are subject to variation according to your personal whim, and many (most, probably) may be appropriate for species other than those for which they are specified.

FIELD MUSHROOM (*Agaricus campestris* and others)

The term 'field mushroom' is a loose one, used to refer to several members of the *Agaricus* family. Perhaps the defining characteristics of the fungi that go by that name are that they grow mainly on pasture and grassland, and look much like the 'ordinary' cultivated mushrooms that you see in the shops.

They are among the most common wild mushrooms, and among the easiest to find, since they grow on pastureland and are about as well camouflaged as a golf ball on a well-watered fairway in May. (Talking of which, golf courses can be happy hunting grounds for mushrooms.) The colour of the cap is generally white, or off-white, sometimes buff or grey-brown. The gills can be pale pink when the mushroom is young and fresh, changing to pale brown as it first opens, and darkening almost to black when the mushroom has opened right out and been standing for a few days.

Besides the *campestris*, other common species of *Agaricus* are the (sometimes saucer-sized) **horse mushroom** (*Agaricus arvensis*), with its buff-coloured cap and aniseedy smell, and *Agaricus bisporus*, father of the cultivated mushroom, with its slightly flaking cap, beloved of compost and broken waste ground (I have even found it pushing through cracked tarmac in a London car park).

It is sometimes hard to be sure exactly which species of *Agaricus* one has encountered, but there is only one that will do you any harm: the aptly named yellow stainer, which superficially resembles the ordinary field mushroom but whose cap has yellow streaks, deepening when handled or bruised. When cut, it smells distinctly of carbolic acid. It is not lethal, but could cause a stomach upset.

The gathering of field mushrooms is widely thought of as an autumnal pursuit, but they can occur as early as July, if the right combination of damp weather followed by sunshine occurs. While mowing and grazing seem to encourage the growth of mushrooms, the greatest enemy of all field mushrooms is chemical farming. You are far more likely to find a good crop on organic pastureland and untreated hay meadows – sadly fewer than they once were.

Preparation and cooking

Like all mushrooms, field mushrooms should be checked for maggots and other parasites. Field mushrooms rarely need washing or peeling: simply wipe off any dirt, grit, or leaf matter with a cloth.

Freshly gathered field mushrooms can be used in any recipe that calls for cultivated mushrooms – to which they will always be superior. Although field mushrooms complement many other ingredients, especially shellfish, generally speaking I like those I have gathered simply cooked, and simply served, so that they taste as much as possible of themselves. Here are a few suggestions, all of which are easily adapted for many other species of wild mushroom.

Raw: When still 'buttoned-up' and squeaky fresh, or just opening and pink-gilled, field mushrooms are delicious raw. But I think it is a waste to mix them up with a lot of salad leaves: serve them sliced, on their own, in a dish rubbed with garlic. Trickle a few drops of best olive oil over them, and garnish, perhaps, with a sprinkling of wood sorrel or chopped chives.

Sautéd: This is the way I most frequently cook field mushrooms. Cut any small button mushrooms in half, and slice the larger ones into 0.5cm/¼ inch slices. Heat a tablespoon of olive oil and a generous knob of butter in a large frying pan. Add the mushrooms, and throw in a little salt at once (it encourages them to sweat). Sauté the mushrooms, turning or tossing frequently, and evaporating the water they release. Add a crushed clove of garlic and a sprig of thyme. Keep cooking until they are dark, rich, and much reduced. Check for seasoning, add a little more butter if you feel buttery, and perhaps a squeeze of lemon if that appeals.

Mushrooms cooked like this can be served all kinds of ways: on toast (which is hard to beat), with wet polenta (and plenty of Parmesan), inside an omelette, on the side of simply grilled kidneys and bacon, or with buttered smoked haddock and mashed potato.

This basic recipe can then be adapted or added to, to create other mushroom dishes:

Mushroom sauce: Stir in a little cream, bubble until it thickens, and you have a creamy mushroom sauce to mask simply grilled pork or veal, white fish, or chicken.

Mushroom soup: Add chicken, beef or vegetable stock, liquidize, stir in cream or crème fraîche, and you have a delectable cream of mushroom soup. Serve with fried bread croûtons. You can hold back some of the sautéd mushrooms then stir them into the creamy soup, for a little texture and bite.

Mushroom tart: Spread the sautéd mushrooms in the base of a blind-baked savoury shortcrust tart case, and sprinkle over grated Gruyère and Parmesan (or good Cheddar). Pour over a savoury custard of egg yolks whisked with double cream (3 large egg yolks per 300ml/½ pint of double cream). Bake in a fairly hot oven (180°C/375°F/gas mark 5) for about 30 minutes, until puffed and golden.

Baked mushrooms: This dish is one exception to my 'keep it simple' rule for mushrooms – not that it's that elaborate. When I've picked field mushrooms of all shapes and sizes, I like to stuff the larger ones with a 'duxelle' made from the smaller ones, and bake them. Choose one good-sized open cup mushroom per person, remove the stalks and sweat those selected gently in a little butter, to soften. Then set aside. Chop all the other mushrooms, and cook with a little chopped shallot and crushed garlic, in a mixture of olive oil and butter, until all their water has been released and cooked out. Stir in a little chopped parsley, and spread this duxelle over the large mushrooms. Top with breadcrumbs and a little Parmesan, and dot with butter. Bake for 10 minutes in a hot oven (450°C/220°F/gas mark 7) until crispy on top.

Drying: Field mushrooms are not suitable for drying.

CEP *(Boletus edulis)* and other boletus
The French call it cep, the Italians call it porcini (little pig), and we used to call it (most charmingly of all, I think) penny bun. Nowadays we refer more often to boletus or cep, but whatever you call it this is the mushroom that is widely considered the greatest culinary prize of the fungus hunter.

Here in Britain, we've cottoned on to it rather late. It seems that until about twenty years ago we hardly knew that we played host to these fat-capped delicacies. But the wet autumn that came at the end of the long hot summer of 1976 produced one of the biggest crops of boletus in living memory. Professionals from the continent came to gather our mushrooms and alerted a few of our own chefs, and amateurs, to the harvest.

The recent excitement in this country about wild mushrooms, and the rapid self-education undertaken by those who share it, began with, and remains largely focused on, the cep and other edible members of the boletus family. So much so, that known cep habitats to which the public have access (such as the New Forest) are literally becoming overrun by mushroom collectors, both amateur and professional. The result is that in some places you'd have to get up a lot earlier than I for one would be prepared to, just to stand a chance of finding a cep.

I don't, however, condemn those who pick mushrooms and sell them on commercially. They have as much right to profit from their own special expertise as a scallop-diver or lobster-potter. But I don't like to compete with them either, as it's a competition I (and other amateurs) can hardly win. Luckily, for the time being at least, I have a few stamping grounds for boletus, which are not yet main roads on the mushroom map. I wish you luck in finding the same.

The whole boletus family is distinguished by their round-capped, classic toadstool shape, but more precisely by the lack of gills of the kind that field mushrooms have. Instead, you will find under the cap a mass of tiny tubes which make the underside look like a fine sponge. In the case of the cep, the cap is dark brown (very much like a well baked bun, as the old English name suggests) and the pores are creamy white, turning yellowish in older specimens. They grow near trees, often in grassy clearings and along the edges of woods. They can be huge – sometimes as much as 20cm/ 8 inches across, and weighing almost half a kilo/1lb.

Other species of boletus are just as worthwhile: the **summer cep** (*Boletus aereus*), with its toast-brown stem, which is found near beech and oak; the **bay boletus** (*Boletus badius*) which has a thinner stem and a chestnut-brown cap; and the **orange birch boletus** (*Leccinum versipelle*), which is found near birch and has an unusually long stem. All are good eating, and make a worthwhile contribution to a mixed bag of boletus.

Note also another common member of the tribe, **slippery jack** (*Suillus luteus*). This grows near conifers and pine, and looks much like a penny bun except that the cap is covered with glutinous slime (especially after rain). It has an excellent flavour, but if added in any quantity to a soup or ragout of other boletus, it will impart an irredeemably slimy texture to the dish which many will find unpalatable. The solution is to peel the caps and then dry them (see page 169 above). When reconstituted, all the sliminess is gone.

There are many other types of boletus, some good to eat, some indifferent, and one or two poisonous. The only really nasty member of the tribe is the devil's bolete (*Boletus satanus*), distinctive for its white-grey cap with red-orange pores underneath, and flush of red veining on the stem. It is not thought to be deadly, but can certainly cause severe gastric upsets. If in any doubt, you should (as with all mushrooms) consult a comprehensive field guide.

Where possible, pick boletus mushrooms on a dry day, as once picked, wet mushrooms lose condition rapidly.

Preparation and cooking

The boletus family, and particularly the penny bun, are sadly prone to larval infestation. Check using the procedure described above (page 169).

If you come back with a good harvest, and a variety of boletus species, a quick grading may be in order. Just how you do this depends on what recipes you have in mind for your harvest. I like to choose the freshest, firmest specimens for immediate consumption, in a dish where their texture will be retained, such as the boletus crostini (see below), a risotto (page 183), or the excellent porcini lasagne (page 179). Mushrooms in less good condition I tend to put in a soup pile (see fresh cep soup, page 180). (The spongy pores of specimens that are in very poor condition may have to be discarded, but the firmer flesh of the cap can often be salvaged even when the pores are practically a mush.) Finally, if I have a lot of slippery jacks, or a surplus of other boletus that I will not consume within a day or two, I set them aside for drying.

Cleaning: How much you need to do will depend on how thoroughly you cleaned them in the field. Each mushroom should be inspected carefully, and any dirt or debris removed with a brush or the tip of a knife, or simply wiped off with a cloth. The stems of some specimens should be trimmed and peeled, to remove the tough, flaky surface. For most recipes, your ceps should then be sliced – not too finely, in my view: about 0.5cm/¼ inch is about right.

Fried ceps: This is my favourite preparation for ceps and other boletus, which can then be used in a number of ways. Heat a generous tablespoon of olive oil in a large frying pan, and throw in a crushed clove (or 2) of garlic. Add the sliced ceps before the garlic takes colour, and a light sprinkling of salt to help release the juices. Cook fairly gently, tossing and turning the mushrooms until the water they release has evaporated (if there is a lot of it, which there will be if the mushrooms were very wet, turn up the heat to boil it off, then turn it down again). Cook until the mushrooms are tender and tasty, and any liquid left in the pan is sufficiently reduced to be a sauce rather than a nuisance. Season to taste with salt and freshly ground black pepper, and stir in a knob of butter. Boletus cooked like this can be served on toast or, better still, on a mound of creamy mashed potato. Or try one of the following.

Crostini di porcini: This is just glorified mushrooms on toast. And very glorious it is. Fry some penny buns or other boletus as described above. Grill or toast some good country bread, rub it with a clove of garlic, and trickle over a little olive oil. Pile the fried mushrooms on to the toast, and sprinkle over a little finely chopped wild chervil or parsley. Serve hot. A sprinkling of Parmesan is optional.

Polenta con porcini: Make a batch of polenta while your mushrooms are frying, and stir the cooked porcini into the wet polenta, with a very large knob of butter, and plenty of fresh grated Parmesan.

Cep soufflé omelette: This sensational dish is actually quite simple to prepare. Fry some ceps as described above, then finely chop them, with a mezzaluna or in a food processor, until you have a thick coarse purée (it must still have some texture in it). For each omelette mix 2 tablespoons of the mushroom purée with 2 egg yolks and a generous teaspoon of double cream. Add a little extra seasoning. Whisk the 2 egg whites saved from the eggs until stiff, and fold carefully, and not too thoroughly, into the mushroom mixture. Pour this mixture into a small heated frying pan with a little butter melted in it, and fry gently. (If you only have a large pan, you can double the quantities and divide the omelette in two when you serve it.) After a couple of minutes, the base of the omelette should be set and very lightly browned, allowing you to flip one half of the omelette over on to the other. The omelette should already be nicely puffy. Place the pan in the centre of a fairly hot oven (190°C/375°F/gas mark 5) for 6-7 minutes, and it will rise even further.

Timing and a little practice should result in a beautifully puffed-up soufflé omelette with a creamy middle. After a while you should be able to do 2 at a time, in separate pans. Even if you do not get the physics right first time, it is sure to taste great anyway.

See also fresh cep soup (page 180) – my favourite mushroom soup recipe, wild mushroom risotto (page 183), and porcini lasagne (possibly the best mushroom dish of all, page 179).

BEEFSTEAK FUNGUS *(Fistulina hepatica)*
One of the two most worthwhile bracket fungus (the other being chicken in the woods - see below), the beefsteak looks like a large slab of liver (hence *hepatica*) growing out of the side of old chestnut and oak trees. It is often found close to the ground, in the damp or shady forks of roots, from late summer until the first frosts.

It is one of the fattest and most succulent of all edible fungi, and tasty too: quite worthy of being served in meaty slices, as the main event on the plate.

Preparation and cooking
Check that your beefsteak is fresh and firm, not dried out or woody. Borderline specimens can sometimes be salvaged by ruthless trimming: the bit which joins the fungus on to the tree is anyway usually too fibrous to eat.

To serve 'veal marsala style': Wipe the fungus clean, trim off any woody bits, and carefully slice into 1cm/½ inch slices. Gently sweat a little chopped onion or shallot and a crushed clove of garlic in a large knob of butter until softened. Add the beefsteak slices and continue to cook for a few minutes, turning occasionally, until the juices start to run. Pour over a ladle of stock or water, just to cover the fungus, and bring to a simmer. Cover the pan loosely with a lid or foil, and simmer the fungus for 10 minutes until tender. Remove the fungus and put in a warm dish, then boil the remaining liquid to reduce to just a couple of tablespoons of sauce. Add a dollop of double cream, boil to thicken, and season well with salt, black pepper, nutmeg and cayenne. Pour the sauce over the beefsteak, and serve with creamy mashed potato and braised leeks or celery.

Stews: The fungus is also good added in large cubes to meaty stews of beef and lamb (especially beef cooked in Guinness). Sweat the cubes lightly for a few minutes in a little oil or butter, to encourage the juices to run. Then add, along with any juice from the pan, to your stew, for just the last 20 minutes of cooking time.

Drying: Thin slivers of beefsteak fungus can be dried in the usual way and used to flavour soups and stews, or added to a medley of mushrooms.

CHANTERELLE *(girolle* Fr. or *Cantharellus cibarius)*
Chanterelles are one of the prettiest and best-flavoured of all wild mushrooms and happening on a patch is a joyous affair. They are to be found in all kinds of woodland, but are especially associated with pine, beech and birch.

I have had my best successes in Scotland and Ireland, where chanterelles can be locally prolific in the mossy banks and grassy patches of damp woods. They can be found as early as July, in wet summers, and as late as December in mild winters.

The egg-yellow, trumpet-shaped mushrooms have forked veins that are almost continuous with the stem. The caps of larger and older specimens can be ragged at the edges. They are widely, and rightly, said to smell of apricots – appropriate enough, given the colour.

Preparation and cooking
Chanterelles are firm-fleshed and robust – one of the few mushrooms that can stand washing (not that they need it, if picked carefully). I rarely combine them

with other ingredients in composite dishes, preferring to prepare them to their own greater glory, and enjoy them on their own. They are good simply sautéd in butter with a little garlic and chopped wild chervil (or parsley), but my favourite preparation is to cook them in milk (see page 180).

CHICKEN IN THE WOODS or
SULPHUR POLYPORE (*Laetiporus sulphureus*)

This is the other particularly worthwhile bracket fungus – not as common as the beefsteak fungus, but often even larger. When you do find one, its many layers of sulphur-yellow meat may sometimes provide you with well over 1kg/2lb of excellent fungal flesh.

I had my first introduction to the chicken courtesy of mycophile Clive Houlder, in a wonderful Norfolk oak forest. I had to shin up an old oak to get it, but it was worth the trouble, as it added wonderful flavour and texture to my up a tree pie (see page 60).

Chickens grow on old trees, favouring oak and yew, though they are occasionally found on willow and sweet chestnut. They may appear any time from the onset of mild weather in April until the first frosts of late autumn. Only fresh young specimens are really good for the pot: the yellower, the better. Older, woody specimens fade to dull pale yellow and eventually to white.

Preparation and cooking

Wipe the fungus clean and cut into slices or cubes (according to your recipe), trimming away any damaged, tough or woody pieces as you go.

Chicken in the woods really can be treated pretty much like meat. Why not chicken? Slices or chunks can be blanched in boiling water for a couple of minutes, then rolled in seasoned flour, dipped in beaten egg, tossed in breadcrumbs, and deep fried – better than any chicken nugget you'll get in a takeaway, with or without a 'Mc'.

They also complement real chicken (the feathered kind) as well as pork and beef, and can be added in cubes or thick slices to stews and casseroles made from any of these meats. Always add to a simmering pot just about ½ an hour before serving.

GIANT PUFFBALL (*Langermannia gigantea*)

A good-sized giant puffball in decent condition is one of the great fungal finds – all the better, because it usually comes as a surprise. Although giant puffballs are not uncommon in grassy fields, hedgerows and wood edges, the effort of looking for them is rarely rewarded. They are more likely to be encountered while searching for other species, and most likely of all on a long autumn walk when fungi are far from the mind.

Puffballs have been found well over a metre/3 feet in circumference, but the more usual size is somewhere between your fist and your head. To be worthwhile, a specimen must be a clean, milky white and largely unblemished, both on the outside and throughout. Older specimens will start to wrinkle and darken, until they are a grey-brown dried-out shadow of their former selves, puffing out their spores (some 7 billion of them) into the autumn winds.

All the smaller species of puffball are also edible, provided they are young, fresh, and the flesh is creamy white throughout. However, a similar and related species, the common earthball, can cause gastric upset and should be avoided. It is shaped like a small puffball, but is identified by its hard, scaly brown surface. If in doubt, consult a comprehensive field guide.

Preparation and cooking

In a good fresh specimen, little cleaning is needed. Simply wipe the puffball clean, and cut a thickish slice off the base end to check the inside is white right through.

The texture and flavour of the giant puffball is like that of a firm young field mushroom, with no gills. Thin slices of puffball can be used like sliced field mushrooms, sautéd and served on toast, or made into risottos, sauces and soups. They are also good cooked in milk (like chanterelles – see page 180). But the great joy of the giant puffball is its very size, and I prefer to serve it in ways that preserve the spectacle.

Puffball breakfast: Fry some good bacon as you like it, then set aside and keep warm. Cut large steaks, 2cm/¾ inch thick, from your puffball and fry in the bacon fat for about 5 minutes each side. Serve each steak with a fried egg (single or double) on top, and the bacon on the side. There can be no better cooked breakfast. A more sophisticated version of the puffball/egg/bacon partnership appears on page 181.

Stuffed puffball 'turkey style': This is based on a spectacular suggestion from our series consultant, Richard Mabey. Hollow out a large puffball, to a shell about 2.5cm/1 inch thick. Chop the insides of the puffball, and fry up with a chopped onion and some minced beef. Mix

Cep or Penny Bun

Chanterelle

Chicken in the Woods

Field Mushroom

Giant Puffball

Horse Mushroom

Morel

Ox-tongue Fungus

Oyster Mushrooms

Parasol Mushroom

St George's Mushroom

Shaggy Inkcap

Wood Blewit

this with breadcrumbs or cooked rice, season very well, and stuff back into the puffball. Cover the puffball with rashers of streaky bacon, and wrap in foil. Bake for about 1 hour in a preheated, moderately hot oven (180°C/375°F/gas mark 5). Remove the foil and turn up the oven to 210°C/425°F/gas mark 7, and cook for a further 15 minutes to crisp up the bacon.

MOREL (Morchella esculenta)

Morels are among the most sought-after, and therefore expensive, of all wild mushrooms. I suspect that this is due rather more to rarity, and their very distinctive shape, which looks so good on a plate (chefs in expensive restaurants love to use them as a garnish) than to their taste. Not that they don't have a good flavour: they are pleasantly musty and distinctive. But £15 an ounce? Do me a favour. On the other hand, if you can get them for free...

I certainly found the process of stalking wild morels, with ace mushroom hunter Peter Jordan, distinctly exciting. I thought we'd be lucky to find one or two, but in the end we found a couple of dozen, thanks to Peter's finely honed technique of following the wind line. Knowing the common wind line in a wood is useful in collecting many kinds of mushroom, but particularly morels, as they start to release spores almost as soon as they emerge from the ground. Mark the first morel you find with a stick, and walk away from it in the direction of the usually prevailing wind. If you don't know the wind line, you can walk around the stick in an ever-increasing spiral. When you find a second mushroom, mark that too, and walk in the line indicated by joining the two sticks.

Morels are distinctive in a number of ways, besides their price. They are strictly a spring mushroom, occurring from March to May in open woodland and other shady places, mainly on chalky and sandy soil. They are sometimes found on sand dunes, and burnt ground is also thought to encourage them (though attempts to cultivate the morel on this kind of ground have been entirely unsuccessful). The cap is wrinkled and pitted like a sea sponge, between 2.5 and 7.5cm/1 and 3 inches across, and the stem white, and hollow inside.

There are 2 other kinds of morel and both are very similar (almost indistinguishable) to the *esculenta*: both the larger, yellow-brown *Morcella rotunda*, and the smaller, more pointy *Morcella vulgaris* are edible, so there is no great anxiety about identification. The only problem on this score is the superficially similar false morel.

Of similar size and colouring, close examination reveals that instead of pitted sponge, the cap comprises tubular lobes, like a brain.

Preparation and cooking

The base of the stem will usually be earthy and should be cut off and discarded. The deep pits in the cap of the morel are a favourite hiding place for tiny insects, and the priority of preparation is to remove them. A good flick and shake will get rid of some of them, but there may be persistent lurkers. Morels can therefore be dropped into well-salted water, and left until the insects crawl out. They are then usually cut in half – the cap and stem are both hollow, and bisection exposes the final hiding place for debris, be it animal, vegetable or mineral.

The spongy cap of the morel makes it a good absorber of sauces – another reason why these mushrooms are often used to garnish expensive dishes in top restaurants. Meat and game are served with an intense reduction of juices which the spongy morel can nicely soak up.

One upmarket morel dish which particularly appealed to me comes from top London restaurant Les Saveurs, where chef Joël Antuñes combines the mushrooms with another wild freebie: garden snails. My version of this imaginative and outrageously good recipe appears on page 182.

If you haven't paid a fortune for your morels, you can feel liberated to use them in ways, and quantities, that a Michelin-starred chef would consider criminally extravagant. In the second series, I made 2 dishes with my morels. One was distinctly experimental: I included some roughly chopped sautéed morels in my improvised woodland fritters. The other principal ingredient was woodlice. The recipe appears on page 184, and the woodlice are optional.

Morel tart: Vegetarians, or those unenthusiastic about woodlice for other reasons, might like to try a morel and wild garlic tart. This was the back-up dish I brought to Bibi Laher's picnic, and it went down very well. Make it as for a field mushroom tart (page 171), substituting quartered morels for sliced field mushrooms. Throw in 2 tablespoons of shredded wild garlic leaves just before you pour over the egg and cream custard. Omit the cheese.

Otherwise, morels are best deployed in recipes where their distinctive texture and appearance can best be appreciated. They make a particularly beautiful risotto.

Drying: Morels dry well, whole and threaded on a string.

OYSTER MUSHROOM (*pleurottes* Fr. or *Pleurotus ostreatus*)
A good find of oyster mushrooms can be spectacular, but you are unlikely to make one unless you remember to look up, as well as down, when you are tramping the woods.

Oyster mushrooms are found on the trunks or branches of dead or dying deciduous wood, especially beech: they grow in layered shelves, rather like a bracket fungus, but they have the veins to indicate that they are a true mushroom. The colour varies from silvery grey ('the colour of a Weimeraner dog', as a friend of mine once observed) to a fawny beige.

Oyster mushrooms are now being cultivated on a large scale, and can be bought relatively cheaply in the supermarket. But the cultivated variety do not have the strength of flavour of the truly wild mushroom.

Preparation and cooking
Since they grow off ground, oyster mushrooms are usually very clean, needing barely a wipe.

Even in the wild oyster mushroom, the flavour is not strong, though it is pleasant enough, and the texture is good. I like to fry them up whole, or in large slices, in olive oil with plenty of garlic.

Clear soups: Oyster mushrooms are also particularly good in oriental-style clear soups, where the distinctive texture contrasts nicely with the softness of noodles and the crunch of spring onions. A good clear stock, of beef or chicken, should be boiled with crushed garlic and grated ginger and well flavoured with soy sauce. Strain, add Chinese-style noodles, and simmer until the noodles are cooked. Stir-fry slices of oyster mushroom with short lengths of spring onion, and add to the soup. Add a dash of chilli oil if you like it hot.

PARASOL (*Lepiota procera*)

and SHAGGY PARASOL (*Lepiota rhacodes*)
Not uncommon on wood edges, grassy clearings, and road verges, as well as open fields, the parasol is an impressive mushroom, tall (sometimes almost 30cm/ I foot tall), with a wide cap (up to 20cm/8 inches across) with a raised nipple in the centre. Both stem and cap are slightly scaly, and there is a distinctive ring on the stem where the cap was attached before the mushroom opened.

They are excellent eating, if you get to them in time: either just before, or just after, the cap has opened away from the stem. Once they have been fully open for a while they have a tendency to dryness, and are rather less palatable.

The shaggy parasol is similar in appearance, except that the scales on the cap are rougher, and pale brown, and the stem is somewhat smoother. They prefer shadier ground than the common parasol, but can be prepared in the same way.

Preparation and cooking
Unopened specimens, with a fully domed cap, can be used entire, once the muddy base of the stem has been removed. On fully opened specimens, however, the stem, which is hollow, will usually be too dry and should be discarded.

Young fresh specimens (unopened) have a firm texture and can be used, sliced, like field mushrooms, or fried up as part of a wild mushroom medley.

Fritters: The open caps, before they become too dry, make perfect fritters. Use smaller caps whole, but cut the large saucer-sized ones into quarters. Dip in batter (for example, the flower fritter batter on page 32) and deep fry until crispy and golden. Serve well seasoned with flaky salt and freshly ground black pepper.

SHAGGY INKCAP (*Coprinus comatus*)
This worthwhile mushroom has a liking for land cultivated or mown by man, and is not uncommon in gardens, on road verges and near compost. It sometimes appears as early as June, but is more common in late summer and autumn.

The shaggy inkcap is not dissimilar to the parasol, with its scaly white cap. However, the cap never opens to the full horizontal canopy of the parasol, but rather flares at the base, darkening to black (the ink of its name) around its scraggy edges. By the time it reaches this stage, it is no longer good eating.

Shaggy inkcaps should therefore be picked before the cap opens, ideally when it is still a tight (and distinctly phallic-shaped) bud around the stem.

Preparation and cooking
Inkcaps have a tendency to disintegrate somewhat during cooking. This can be overcome if tightly budded young specimens are left whole and deep-fried in batter (or beaten egg and breadcrumbs). Borderline specimens should be sliced and combined with other wild mushrooms for soup, pasta sauce, etc.

ST GEORGE'S MUSHROOM (*Tricholoma gambosum*)

The St George's mushroom is supposed to appear every year on the day of its eponymous saint (23 April). In reality it will usually be early May before the first specimens appear, but it's none the less welcome for that, being one of the very few worthwhile fungi (others would be the Jew's ear, morel and chicken in the woods) which can be found before high summer.

It likes pastures, meadows, grassy wood edges and road verges, and is usually found in small clusters or rings. The creamy-white-brown colour of the cap makes the unpicked mushroom look like an unfeasible premature field mushroom, but the colour of the gills (the same creamy white) makes identification at this time of the year fairly foolproof.

Preparation and cooking

St George's mushrooms are usually very clean, and barely need a wipe. Smaller ones can be kept whole, and used as buttons. Larger ones should be sliced. Generally speaking, they can be prepared like field mushrooms (though they are less palatable raw). They have a particularly good texture, so I never liquidize them into a soup, though I sometimes add them, lightly sautéed, to a creamy soup made from cultivated mushrooms.

Pasta sauce: Sauté St George's mushrooms the same way as field mushrooms (page 171), add a dollop of double cream or crème fraîche, then boil to thicken. Serve with tagliatelle. You can also add chopped ham or pieces of crispy fried bacon to this lovely sauce.

WOOD BLEWIT (*Lepista nuda*)
and FIELD BLEWIT (*Lepista saeva*)

Both species of blewit seem to relish the harsh damp conditions of late autumn, and they are worth looking for in November and even December when many other species have succumbed to the frosts.

Field blewits are distinctive for the blue-violet flush on their stem from which they take their name. The cap is slightly jellyish in texture, pale brown to grey in colour, occasionally with a hint of the bluish flush in the legs. Once very popular in England, they were sold in markets alongside field mushrooms.

Wood blewits are common, and in some seasons highly prolific, in beech woods, where they grow in or near the late autumn leaf litter. Young specimens are bluish or violet all over, making them unmistakable, but as they open and mature they turn to grey-brown, with just a faint violet flush on the stem. They tend to be taller and thinner-stemmed than the field blewit. They have a strong and pleasant smell, slightly farmyardy, almost like a good red burgundy.

Preparation and cooking

Both species of blewit are excellent all-rounders, and can be used, like field mushrooms, in all kinds of ways (although some people react badly to wood blewits eaten raw). I like to sauté them with a little finely chopped onion, rather than garlic, and serve them on toast, or in an omelette. Masked with a little cream, sautéd blewits make a delicious accompaniment to a piece of grilled chicken.

They are very good cooked in milk, the same way as chanterelles (see page 180).

PORCINI (CEP) LASAGNE

This recipe comes from my friend Mauro Bregoli, chef at the excellent Old Manor House restaurant in Romsey, Hampshire. Mauro cooked this dish for a bunch of hungry fishermen after a great day's trout fishing on the River Test in October. It is quite the best mushroom/pasta combination I have ever had. Mauro is reluctant to give quantities: 'Make sure you have plenty of everything, and then there will be enough' is his sound philosophy.

I have inserted some quantities of my own, but they are no more than a rough guide. The dish can be made with reconstituted dried porcini, but it will not be quite as good. (See illustration on page 166.)

SERVES 6 AS A STARTER, 4 AS A MAIN COURSE

at least 250g/8oz fresh Parmesan

at least 500g/1lb fresh porcini, or other boletus (ideally twice that quantity)

white lasagne sheets: ideally fresh, but dried can be used (enough to make at least 3 layers in an 20x25cm/8x10 inch baking tray)

about 175g/6oz Parma ham, sliced very fine

truffle oil (optional)

butter

FOR THE BECHAMEL

55g/2oz plain flour

55g/2oz butter

600ml/1 pint hot milk

a pinch of nutmeg

salt and freshly ground black pepper

• Make the béchamel sauce in the usual way: mix the flour with the melted butter in the pan and cook it for a few minutes. Add the hot milk by degrees, and stir to thicken. Bring to the boil and allow to simmer for just a minute. Season with nutmeg, salt and pepper.

• Grate half the Parmesan and stir into the béchamel. The finished béchamel should be a thick pouring consistency. Add a little more hot milk if necessary.

• Prepare the rest of the ingredients: slice whole mushrooms into large but very thin slices. If you are using dried lasagne of the kind that requires pre-cooking, cook according to the packet instructions. Scrape the rest of the Parmesan into shavings, using a large knife blade or a potato peeler.

• Pour a small amount of béchamel on to the bottom of an ovenproof dish. Put a layer of white lasagne on top, followed by a layer of thinly sliced raw ceps, a layer of Parma ham and a layer of Parmesan. Season with a few drops of truffle oil.

• Then pour over a layer of béchamel and repeat the layers. You can make as many layers as you have ingredients, or space for, but finish with a layer of béchamel, some grated Parmesan and a few knobs of butter.

• Bake for around 20-30 minutes in a fairly hot oven (190°C/375°F/gas mark 5) until nicely browned on top.

FRESH CEP SOUP
(Crème de bolets)

An excellent soup, and a particularly good way to use ceps (and other boletus), that are waterlogged or slightly bashed up. Other wild mushrooms, spare stalks, etc. can all be added to this mix.

at least 500g/1lb ceps or other boletus
1 large onion, finely chopped
2 cloves of garlic, crushed
1 medium carrot, finely chopped
60g/2oz butter
1 tablespoon olive oil

1 tablespoon plain flour
1 litre/1¾ pints good chicken or vegetable
  stock
3-4 tablespoons thick cream
small bunch of wild chervil or parsley, finely
  chopped

• Clean the mushrooms, slice the caps and chop the stalks.

• Sweat the onion, garlic and carrot in the butter and oil until softened. Add the ceps, and cook gently for a further 10 minutes.

• Stir in the flour, cook for another couple of minutes, then add the hot stock by degrees. Bring to a simmer, and cook until the mushrooms are completely tender. Liquidize the soup in a blender. (You can keep back a few of the mushrooms and add them to the soup, as they are or roughly chopped, for extra texture.)

• Reheat, without boiling, check the seasoning, stir in the cream, sprinkle with the chervil, and serve.

CHANTERELLES COOKED IN MILK WITH WOOD SORREL

This is an elegant way to serve chanterelles that brings out the very best of their subtle flavour. (See illustration on frontispiece.)

chanterelles (or blewits or St George's
  mushrooms)
butter
full cream milk

salt and freshly ground black pepper
nutmeg
wood sorrel, sorrel, or tarragon

• Leave the smaller mushrooms whole. Cut the larger ones in half, and any real monsters into quarters.

• Heat a knob of butter in a frying pan and add the chanterelles. Sweat gently for a few minutes, then pour over enough milk almost to cover them.

- Boil, stirring frequently, until the milk has greatly reduced, then top up with enough milk almost to cover again. Boil to reduce the milk to a thick, creamy sauce. By now the chanterelles should be nice and tender. If not, you can add a little more milk, and boil that down too.

- Season to taste with salt, pepper and a pinch of nutmeg, and garnish with a sprinkling of wood sorrel leaves, or chopped sorrel, or fresh tarragon. Serve at once with good bread to mop up the milky sauce.

PUFFBALL FRITTERS

This is a particularly nice way of presenting puffballs — maybe as a dinner party starter.

SERVES 2

4 slices pancetta or streaky bacon
olive oil for frying
2 cloves of garlic finely chopped
4 whole eggs
4 large slices from a puffball, about
   1 cm/½ inch thick

2 eggs, beaten
salt and freshly ground black pepper
125g/4oz white breadcrumbs (from a day-
   old loaf)
a few salad leaves, lightly dressed

- Chop the bacon or pancetta into thick matchsticks, and fry in a little olive oil until crispy. Throw in the chopped garlic, and fry until it starts to take colour. Remove the garlicky pancetta and put on kitchen paper.

- Bring the 4 whole eggs to the boil in a small pan of cold water, and boil them for just 4 minutes.

- Dip the puffball slices in the beaten egg which has been seasoned, and coat well in the breadcrumbs. Fry in the same oil left from frying the pancetta (with perhaps a little extra added), turning once, until crispy and golden brown.

- Drain each puffball slice quickly on kitchen paper and then place them on warmed plates. Peel the soft-boiled eggs carefully and cut them in half. Place 2 halves, yolk upwards, on each fritter, and season well with salt and freshly ground black pepper. Sprinkle over the garlicky bits of pancetta.

- Serve with a few dressed salad leaves on the side.

MORELS WITH SNAILS AND PAIN PERDU

I first had this dish at Les Saveurs restaurant in London, and I thought it an excellent demonstration of what dizzy gastronomic heights can be achieved using wild ingredients. I particularly liked the touch of serving the snails and morels on slices of pain perdu — better known to you and me as 'eggy bread'.

I don't know exactly how chef Joël Antuñes makes his, but this improvised version works very well.

SERVES 2

24 garden snails (*Helix aspersa*), purged (see page 57)
12 large morels, fresh or dried
500ml/18fl oz good beef stock, strained and skimmed of fat
150ml/¼ pint red wine
100g/4oz soft butter
small sprig of thyme
small sprig of rosemary
2 eggs
1 tablespoon double cream
salt and freshly ground black pepper
2 slices slightly stale white bread, crusts removed

• Prepare the snails 'French style', as described on page 57, and remove from the shells.

- Reconstitute the morels, if dried, in boiling water. Reserve the liquid, and strain through fine muslin or a coffee filter. Slice the morels (reconstituted, or fresh) in half, and rinse well.

- Put all but 2 tablespoons of the beef stock into a pan with the wine, and any strained liquid from reconstituting the dried mushrooms. Boil hard to reduce to an intense, dark sauce, and whisk in one-third of the butter, in small pieces, to thicken. Keep warm.

- Melt another third of the butter in another pan, and add the snails, mushrooms and herbs. Sauté gently together for a few minutes, then add 2 tablespoons of the beef stock. Bring to the boil, and cook until the liquid has almost completely boiled away. Keep warm.

- Beat the eggs with the cream and season well with salt and pepper. Dip the bread slices in the egg until well soaked and coated. Fry the slices in the remaining butter, until lightly browned on each side. Drain briefly on kitchen paper, and transfer at once to 2 warmed plates.

- Mix the snails and morels with half of the reduced sauce to coat well. Divide between the 2 slices of eggy bread, piling up in a mound. Pour the remaining sauce over the snails and mushrooms, and around the edge of the plates. Serve at once.

WILD MUSHROOM RISOTTO

You can also make this risotto with reconstituted dried wild mushrooms — in which case be sure to add the liquid from soaking them, strained through muslin or a coffee filter, to the stock. It is full of flavour.

I litre/1¾ pints good stock
125g /4oz butter
I medium onion, finely chopped
350-500g/¾-1lb porcini/ceps (or other
    fresh wild mushrooms), cleaned and sliced

350g/12oz Arborio rice
salt and freshly ground black pepper
I tablespoon best olive oil
at least 125g/4oz fresh Parmesan

- In a large pan, bring the stock almost to the boil and keep hot on a very low flame.

- In another pan, melt the butter and sweat the onion until softened, but not brown. Add the sliced mushrooms and cook for a few more minutes.

- Add the rice, stir well, and cook until well coated and slightly translucent.

- Add a ladle of hot stock and let it simmer gently until absorbed by the rice. Add another, and so on, until the rice is cooked (15-20 minutes). As a general rule for risottos, you need 4 times as much stock as rice, by volume. And the rice is done when tender, but still just a tiny bit chalky in the middle.

- Check the seasoning and stir in the olive oil, remaining butter, and a couple of spoonfuls of grated Parmesan.

- Serve at once, with the rest of the Parmesan on the table.

FRITTERS OF MORELS AND 'WOOD SHRIMPS'

This is the experimental recipe I prepared for the Laher family barge picnic after enlisting the kids to help me collect woodlice. Bibi Laher and her husband, Sahid, whose barge picnic I gatecrashed, were not convinced. But the kids admitted (off-camera, as luck would have it) that they were really rather good. I thought the woodlice gave a nice crunch, and a pleasant slightly bosky shrimp flavour that married very well with the morels. If you're not convinced, you could always leave out the crustaceans.

For those interested in further investigating the possibilities of entymological cuisine, I can highly recommend the charming little volume Why Not Eat Insects? *It's on sale in the gift shop of the Natural History Museum, among other places.*

MAKES A DOZEN FRITTERS

1 small onion, finely chopped
1 small carrot, finely chopped
2 tablespoons olive oil
125g/4oz split red lentils
300ml/½ pint water or stock
10-12 large morels, fresh or dried
2 tablespoons woodlice

1 egg
1-2 tablespoons plain flour
oil for frying (i.e. sunflower)

FOR THE DIPPING SAUCE (optional)
chives, chervil, and a small chilli, chopped fine
and mixed with olive oil and a pinch of sugar

• Sweat the onion and carrot in 1 tablespoon of the olive oil until softened, then add the lentils. Stir for just a minute, then pour over the water or stock, and bring to the boil.

• Simmer until the lentils are completely soft and have absorbed all the water. Season well, and beat to a purée with a wooden spoon. Set aside.

• Reconstitute the morels, if dried. Clean well, if fresh. Cut into quarters, rinse throughly, and sauté in a pan with the rest of the olive oil. Set aside.

• 'Riddle' the live woodlice in a sieve, removing bits of debris and leaf litter. Rinse briefly in cold water, then toss into boiling salted water. Boil for just 2 minutes.

• Mix the morels and woodlice into the lentil purée, along with the egg, and enough flour to bind the paste. It doesn't need to be stiff, but should hold together on a spoon.

• Heat 0.5cm/a good ¼ inch of oil in a large pan, and fry dessertspoonfuls of the mixture, turning when nicely browned. Fry in batches, piling the fritters up on kitchen paper, and keeping them warm until all are done.

• Serve plain, or with the dipping sauce.

FURTHER READING

This selective bibliography is really just an extension of my acknowledgements, since the books I include are, for the most part, ones I know intimately. Some have been long-time companions over the years, and the extent to which they have informed my text could hardly be measured. Others are, among the many books scattered around my desk during the writing of this book, the ones whose depth of knowledge has proved most valuable in my research. They are not all books specialising in wild ingredients, but they will all make a great contribution to the range and repertoire of the wild food enthusiast.

A particular thanks is due to Richard Mabey, our series consultant, and author of two of the books mentioned below.

Mrs Beeton's Book of Household Management, Cape, 1968.

Cyril Berry, *First Steps in Winemaking*, Nexus Special Interests, 1996.

Prue Coates, *The Poacher's Cookbook*, White Lion, 1993.

Nicholas Culpeper's Complete Herbal, Wordsworth Editions, 1995

Alan Davidson, *North Atlantic Seafood*, Penguin, 1991.

Francis Dipper and Ann Powell, *Field Guide to Water Life of Britain*, Readers Digest, 1984.

Euell Gibbons, *Stalking the Wild Asparagus*, Hood.

Jane Grigson, *The Mushroom Feast*, Penguin, 1987.

Holt & Vincent, *Why Not Eat Insects?*, Pryor Publications.

Trevor Houseby, *Shore Fishing*, Angler's Library, 1974.

George Lassalle, *George Lassalle's Book of Middle Eastern Food*, Kyle Cathie, 1993.

A.D. Livingstone and Helen Livingstone, *Edible Plants and Animals*, Facts on File, 1994.

Richard Mabey, *Food For Free*, Harper Collins, 1989.

Richard Mabey, *Flora Britannica*, Sinclair Stevenson, 1996.

Chris Maynard and Bill Scheller, *Manifold Destiny*, Villard Books.

Roger Phillips, *Mushrooms and Other Fungi*, Pan, 1983.

Roger Phillips, *Wild Food*, Pan, 1983.

Rosamund Richardson, *Hedgerow Cookery*, Penguin, 1987.

Constance Spry and Rosemary Hume, *The Constance Spry Cookery Book*, Pan, 1979.

Rick Stein, *English Seafood Cookery*, Penguin 1988.

John Wilson, *John Wilson's Fishing Encyclopaedia*, Boxtree, 1995.

PICTURE ACKNOWLEDGEMENTS

All food cooked, styled (and eaten) by the author.
The publisher wishes to thank the following: **Copyright © Andrew Palmer 1997** – pictures on *frontispiece*, and pages 10, 35, 39, 42, 59, 66, 82, 84, 86, 90, 99, 110, 122, 123, 127, 130, 142, 143, 147, 150, 166, 182. **Channel 4/ Stuart Sadd** – p 2 Bain Marie; **Channel 4/Patrick Sutherland** – p 6 Gastrowagon; **Channel 4/Chris Chapman** – p 118 Gathering Seaweed; **Channel 4/Charlie Crawford** – p 162 Gathering Heather; **John Wilson** for pictures on p 79 Bleak, Brown Trout, Carp, Dace, Eels, Minnows, Pike, Salmon, Sea Trout, Zander; p 119 Sea Bass; **Hugh Fearnley-Whittingstall** for pictures on p 23 Wild Chervil; p 139 Medlar; **A-Z Botanical Collection Ltd** for pictures on pp 22,23 Anthony Cooper – Fennel; W. Broadhurst - Hogweed; Anthony Cooper – Dandelion; G.W. Miller – Bistort; Geoff Kid – Alexander; Roger Standen – Watercress; G.A. Matthews – Wintercress; David Hughes – Meadow Sweet; p 119 Maurice Nimo – Laver; p 139 Maurice Nimmo – Wild Cherry; D.W. Bevan – Wild Raspberry; Maurice Nimmo – Juniper Berries; p 175 Iris Lane – St George's Mushroom; S. Taylor – Chicken of the Woods, Morel; W Broadhurst – Field Mushroom; **Holt Studios International** for pictures on pp 22,23 Nigel Cattlin – Chickweed, Common Mallow, Fat Hen, Hairy Bittercress, Sow Thistle, Wall Pennywort; Bob Gibbons – Wild Garlic, Corn Salad, Lime Leaves; p 26 Nigel Cattlin -Primrose, Sweet Violet, Elder, Broom, Hawthorn, Lesser Celandine, Lime Tree; Primrose Peacock: Red Clover; Bob Gibbons – False Acacia; p 79 Primrose Peacock: Fishing for Elvers; p 119 Dick Roberts – Sea Lettuce; p 139 Primrose Peacock: Chestnut, Cherry Plum; Inga Spence – Walnut; Bob Gibbons – Gooseberry; Willem Harinck – Hazel Nuts; p 175 Primrose Peacock: Parasol Mushroom; Nigel Cattlin – Horse Mushroom; **Nature Photographers Ltd** for pictures on p 23 Paul Sterry – Sea Beet; p 119 Andrew Cleave – Carragheen; Paul Knight – Mackerel; **NHPA** for a picture on p 22 Jim Bain – Common Sorrel; **Planet Earth Pictures Limited** for pictures on pp 22,23 Peter Gasson – Hedge Garlic; John Lythgoe – Rock Samphire, Marsh Samphire; Thomas Broad – Wood Sorrel; p 26 Martin King – Crab Apple; Allan Parker – Dog Rose; p 79 John Lythgoe – Elvers; p 119 Jim Greenfield -Crawfish, Razor Shell Clam; David George – Native Oyster, Spider Crab; Linda Pitkin – Sea Urchin; Chris McTernan – Common Prawn; p 139 Steve Nicholls – Bilberry; Frank Blackburn – Dog Rosehips; Nigel Downer – Wild Strawberry; Jan Tove Johansson – Rowan; p 175 Georgette Douwma – Giant Puffball, Oyster Mushrooms; Robert Franz -Shaggy Inkcap; M. King – Ox-Tongue Fungus; Allan Parker – Wood Blewitt, Cep; Nigel Downer – Chanterelle; **Oxford Scientific Films** for a picture on p 23 Ian West – Sea Kale; **Woodfall Wild Images** for pictures on p 23 Bob Gibbons – Horseradish; p 119 Paul Kay: Brown Shrimp; Sue Scott – Carpet Shell Clam.

INDEX